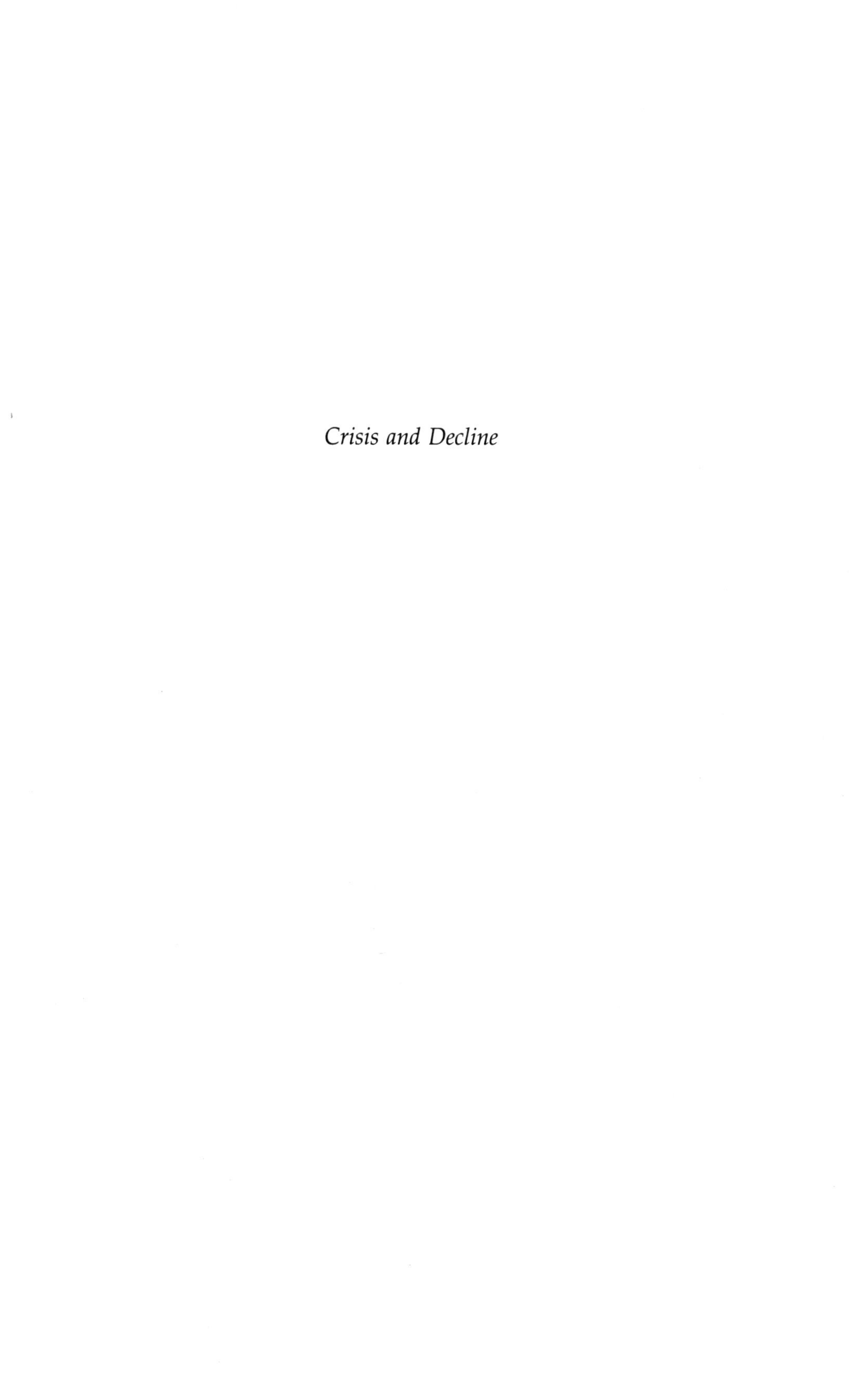

Crisis and Decline

Crisis and Decline

The Viceroyalty of Peru in the Seventeenth Century

Kenneth J. Andrien

University of New Mexico Press
Albuquerque

Library of Congress Cataloging in Publication Data

Andrien, Kenneth J.
Crisis and decline.

Bibliography: p.
Includes index.
1. Finance, Public—Peru—History—17th century.
2. Finance, Public—Spain—Colonies—History—17th century. 3. Spain—Colonies—America—Economic policy.
I. Title.
HJ971.A53 1985 336.85 84-23436
ISBN 0-8263-0791-4

An earlier version of chapter 5 appeared as "The Sale of Fiscal Offices and the Decline of Royal Authority in the Viceroyalty of Peru, 1633–1700," by Kenneth J. Andrien in *Hispanic American Historical Review* 62:1 (February 1982), pp. 49–71.
Manufactured in the United States of America.
First Edition

To my family

Contents

Illustrations

Tables

Acknowledgments

I have received generous support from various sources during the preparation of this study. Financial assistance from the Graduate School of Duke University, the Tinker Foundation, the National Endowment for the Humanities, and the Fulbright-Hays Foundation paid for my archival research in Spain and South America. Since coming to the Ohio State University in 1978, the History Department and the College of Humanities have provided an ample computer budget, manuscript typing assistance, and released time during the spring quarter of 1981 to prepare the study for publication. The staffs of the Archivo General de Indias in Seville, the Biblioteca del Palacio Real in Madrid, the Archivo General de Simancas in Simancas; the Archivo General de la Nación, the Biblioteca Nacional, and the Biblioteca Municipal in Lima; the Archivo Departamental in Cuzco, the Archivo General de la Nación in Buenos Aires, and the Archivo Nacional in Santiago de Chile were always courteous and helpful. Dr. José Antonio Calderón Quijano of the Escuela de Estudios Hispano-Americanos in Seville also extended his support and hospitality during my stay in that city between 1975 and 1976.

I have benefited greatly from the advice and assistance of my colleagues and teachers. Jacques A. Barbier, Mansel G. Blackford, Mark A. Burkholder, Donald B. Cooper, J. H. Elliott, and John J. TePaske all read the manuscript and offered helpful comments and criticisms. I also profited from conversations with Peter J. Bakewell, Kendall W. Brown, Brian R. Hamnett, and Miles L. Wortman. Special thanks, of course, are reserved for Professor John J. TePaske, who directed this project from its inception as a doctoral dissertation and has proven an unfailing source of encouragement, guidance, support, and friendship. Any errors of fact or interpretation which remain, however, are my responsibility.

Finally, I would like to dedicate this book to my family. In this project, as in all other things, I owe them a great debt. Their advice, generosity, confidence, and love helped me to overcome the many problems that inevitably arise in preparing a doctoral dissertation and finishing a monograph. Deserving of special mention is my wife Anne, who endured the difficult moments and whose presence enriched the happier times. My only regret is that my father, Maurice P. Andrien, did not live to see the completion of this project. I can acknowledge and hope to repay my debts to others; this last and deeply personal one, I can not.

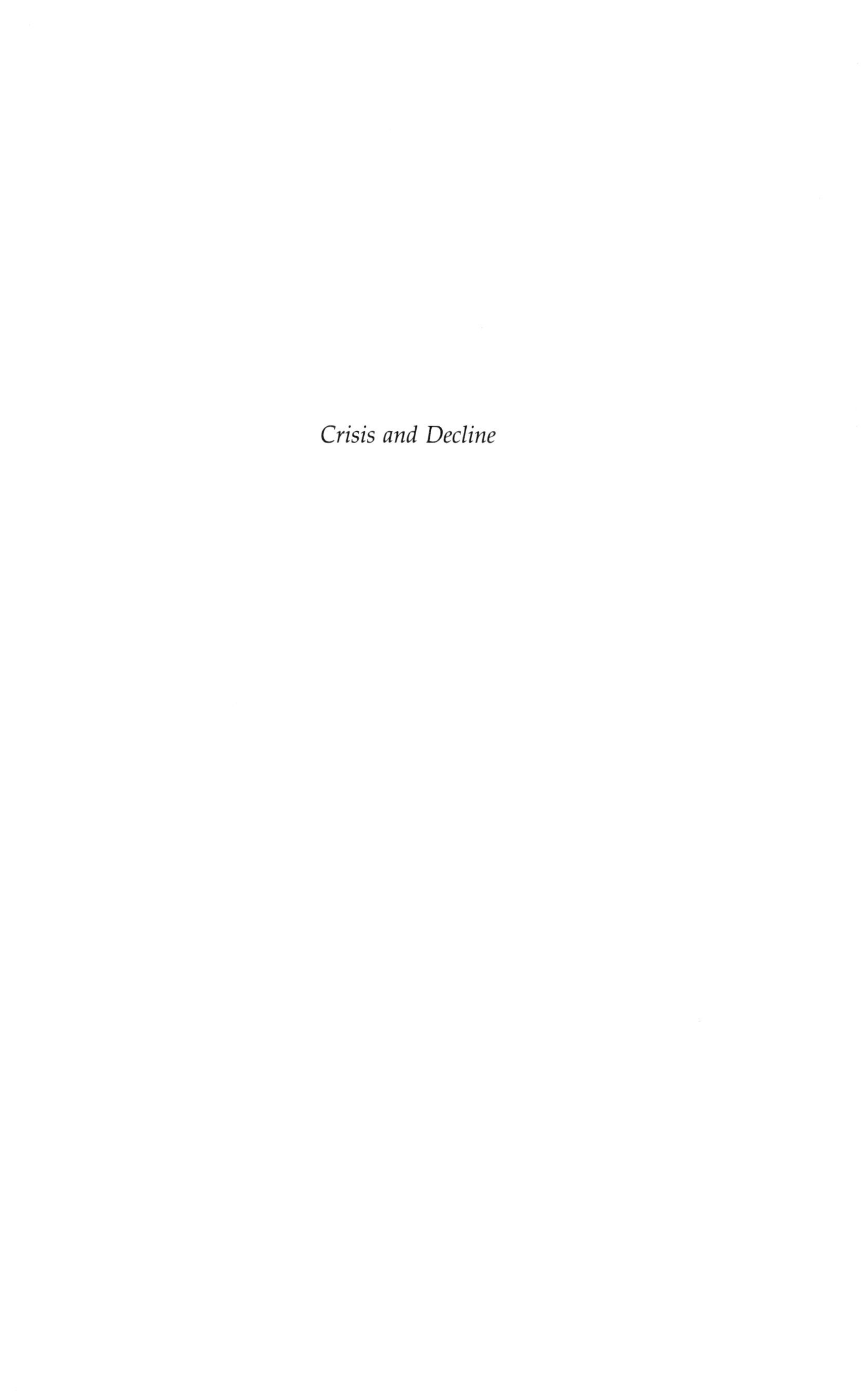

Crisis and Decline

1 *Introduction*

After thirty years of debate, historians still disagree about whether a political, social, and economic crisis gripped Europe and Spanish America during the seventeenth century. The aim of this study is to shed some new light on this historiographical controversy by examining the impact of certain key political and economic changes during the seventeenth century in the rich Spanish possessions in the Viceroyalty of Peru. Specifically I argue that escalating fiscal demands by the Spanish crown coincided with a period of economic readjustment and diversification in the viceroyalty and led to political turmoil and the onset of a serious fiscal crisis by the 1660s. During these years of turbulence colonial treasury officers played a decisive role: mediators between the financial demands of the crown and the resistance of local elites to any new taxes. Prompted by events in Europe and local economic changes in the viceroyalty, this fiscal crisis strained the political relationship between Peru and Spain and ultimately undermined the imperial system in South America. In short, this study is an examination of Spanish imperialism and its decline in the Americas.

The historiographical debate over the seventeenth-century crisis in Spanish America began in 1951, with the publication of Woodrow Borah's controversial essay, *New Spain's Century of Depression*. Extrapolating from his exhaustive demographic studies, Borah proposed that a declining Amerindian population led to severe labor shortages in New Spain and ultimately precipitated an overall depression during the century.[1] The results of later studies gave support to Borah's initial findings. Along with the shrinking Amerindian labor force, they found that the rise of self-sufficient large estates (Chevalier), a recession in the Atlantic trade between Spain and the Indies (Chaunu), and declining prices for certain commodities like cattle, indigo, and cacao (MacLeod) each contributed to a general economic malaise, or depression, lasting for most of the seventeenth century in the Spanish Indies.[2] This depression thesis still finds strong adherents in the field. In his more recent studies of Mexico, for example, Jonathan Israel argues that an economic depression, along with fiscal pressure from Spain to increase tax contributions and a movement of "nondoctrinal puritanism" to eliminate corruption and waste, led to prolonged political conflict in the colony.[3]

This dismal picture of an unstable declining empire has been challenged during the last ten years by a number of historians. These revisionists have argued that Spanish decline led to greater self-sufficiency in the Indies, as local producers provided more of the goods needed by colonials (Frank), and greater amounts of wealth were retained within the empire for local defense and administration (Lynch and Clayton).[4] There was no sustained depression during the century, not even in key industries like silver mining and shipbuilding (Bakewell and Clayton).[5] John Lynch has even argued that the seventeenth century was a time when a "fundamental shift" within the Hispanic world took place, and Spanish America began to replace the metropolis as the senior partner in the empire.[6] In short, these historians view the century as an era of prosperity, when the colonies developed more independently of the constraints of colonialism.

More recent revisionist scholarship has begun to move away from this "depression-prosperity dichotomy," to focus instead on the century as a period of transformation and change in the Spanish Indies.[7] The problems that arose from periodic labor shortages or the decline of metropolitan Spain varied in each area of the empire and even affected social classes differently. These studies stress the diversity of the Indies and try to put aside the broad generalizations associated with the depression thesis or its early critics.[8] In a recent article in *Past and Present,* for example, John J. TePaske and Herbert S. Klein contend that the results of their exhaustive study of the Mexican treasury accounts (*cuentas*) for the century show a stability in mining tax revenues, which clearly contradicts the depression thesis. At the same time, the high level of bullion exports to Manila and Spain indicate that royal funds were not retained in the Indies, as Lynch proposed, to promote local economic development.[9] The authors conclude that "some prevailing interpretations have either been revised or discarded."[10] Other studies of Mexico, Peru, and Central America have also emphasized the development of more diverse and stable regional economies (Super, Taylor, Boyer, Wortman, and Assadourián), the gradual integration of the Spanish and Amerindian economies (Wortman, Stern, and Spalding), and the adjustments made by European elites to maintain their power and status (Hoberman, Wortman, Cushner, and Andrien).[11] The picture that emerges from these studies is of a century characterized by cycles of prosperity and recession, with some regions or groups indeed experiencing bad times, while others rose to greater economic well-being.

Like much of the recent scholarship on seventeenth-century Spanish America, my own work on the Viceroyalty of Peru does not attempt to attack or defend the depression thesis or its early critics. Neither of these broad, general theories has proven particularly useful in attempting to explain the onset of the fiscal crisis in the viceroyalty during the seventeenth century. Instead, I have traced the political and economic causes of this crisis and evaluated its impact on the imperial system in Spanish South America. In this way I hope to add to our knowledge of colonial Peruvian history and also contribute to the ongoing debate over the so-called crisis of the seventeenth century.

The origins of the fiscal crisis may be found in both Spain and the Viceroyalty of Peru. In Europe the militant foreign policy of Philip IV led to the outbreak of a series of wars, which placed a heavy burden on the depressed Castilian economy and the overextended resources of the Spanish treasuries. To help defray the cost of the war effort, the crown initiated a tax reform program between 1625 and 1643, aimed at raising additional revenues, particularly in the more lightly taxed, non-Castilian provinces of the empire. In the Viceroyalty of Peru, however, a series of economic changes led local taxpayers to oppose these efforts to increase their tax burden. The decline of the dominant silver-mining industry and the trade with Spain by the 1620s encouraged greater economic diversification as agriculture, intercolonial trade networks, and local industry absorbed more of the investment capital in the viceroyalty. In this period of transition from mining to a more diversified base, colonial elites were unwilling for higher taxes to drain investment capital from these lucrative new enterprises. In short, the fiscal policies of the crown were diametrically opposed to the needs of colonial taxpayers. Both sides in this conflict looked to a powerful group within the viceroyalty to protect their interests—the officials attached to the royal treasury, centered in Lima. These bureaucrats had direct responsibility for implementing the controversial tax levies demanded by Madrid, and their loyalty and obedience was vital to the success of the royal program.

The lack of scholarly interest in the officers of the imperial treasury is surprising, considering their overall importance within the empire. Fernando de Armas, José María Ots Capdequi, Clarence Haring, and Ismael Sánchez Bella have all written groundbreaking studies; but they deal with broad institutional questions that concerned all areas of the empire.[12] Much more scholarly attention has been given to the more visible members of the audiencia, especially for the seventeenth century (Phelan, Burkholder and Chandler).[13] In addition, a group of scholars including John J. TePaske, Herbert S. Klein, Miles Wortman, and María Encarnación Rodríguez Vicente have all compiled long time series of the accounts of the treasury offices of the Spanish American Empire, in order to outline the major economic and political trends.[14] Still, detailed information on the activities of the officials serving in the tribunals of accounts and the treasury offices of the Indies is meager. As Mario Góngora wrote in 1975, "the social and political position of the Treasurers, *Contadores*, *Factores*, and *Veedores* of the royal treasury have not been, as far as we know, the subject of detailed research."[15] Since the Viceroyalty of Peru experienced a fiscal crisis, rather than a demographic or subsistence crisis, such an examination of the financial activities of the treasury officers is vital.

As a result, this study will not provide a detailed examination of viceregal society or regional economic growth. These topics will only be discussed when they pertain to those financial and political issues that comprised the so-called crisis of the seventeenth-century Viceroyalty of Peru. Instead, this book will focus on (1) how the activities of the Peruvian treasury officials during this period of stress led to the onset of a serious fiscal crisis, and (2) how the crisis undermined the imperial system in the viceroyalty by the end of the century. My aim is to provide new information on the evolution of the seventeenth-century imperial crisis and also to fill a gap in the historiography of the Spanish colonial administration.

Since so few works deal with either the seventeenth-century crisis or the treasury in the Viceroyalty of Peru, the foundations of this work rest on materials found in extensive archival research conducted at the Archivo General de Indias in Seville, the Archivo General de Simancas in Simancas, the Biblioteca del Palacio Real in Madrid, and the Archivo General de la Nación, the Biblioteca Nacional, and the Biblioteca Municipal in Lima. Shorter research trips to the Archivo Departamental in Cuzco, the Archivo Nacional in Santiago de Chile, and the Archivo General de la Nación in Buenos Aires also yielded useful information. The most important of these archival sources proved to be the accounts of the royal treasury. It is my contention that these treasury records reveal the financial parameters of the viceregal government and provide insights into the strengths and weaknesses of the colonial system over time. When related to a variety of other more traditional materials, such as government correspondence, workbooks, trade records, policy proposals, judicial documents, and reports from royal inspection tours, the accounts can help to identify some of the basic continuities and changes in the political and financial life of the viceroyalty.

In addition to these archival sources, I consulted laws, legal commentaries, letters, diaries, genealogical studies, and secondary works in the Perkins Library of Duke University and the William Oxley Thompson Library of the Ohio State University. The study begins in 1607 because in that year the tribunal of accounts began operating, and the institutions of the viceregal treasury system remained unchanged for the rest of the century. It ends in 1700 because that year marks the end of the Habsburg era. In addition, by 1700 the salient issues of the seventeenth-century crisis in the Viceroyalty of Peru had been resolved.

The work itself is divided into three interconnected parts, which cover the key components of the seventeenth-century fiscal crisis—economic and financial trends, institutional changes in the treasury system, and political struggles over taxation policy. The two chapters in part one examine how economic changes in the viceroyalty led to a fiscal crisis during the seventeenth century. Chapter one examines how the transition from an export-oriented economy based on silver mining to a more diverse series of regional economies led local elites to oppose any royal efforts to raise taxes. The impact of this opposition on viceregal finances is examined in chapter two. A detailed quantitative analysis of the Lima treasury accounts reveals that colonial bureaucrats failed to impose new taxes capable of expanding the tax base of the realm and counterbalancing the drop in mining levies. The net result was a serious fiscal crisis and a cutback in the amounts of money sent to Spain by the 1660s.

The chapters in part two examine how the structure of governmental institutions and the sale of treasury offices hindered efforts to deal with the fiscal crisis. Chapter three demonstrates how the institutional weaknesses in the decentralized, patrimonial viceregal bureaucracy led to jurisdictional conflicts, inefficiency, and corruption; and handicapped efforts to impose unpopular tax levies. Chapter four examines how the sale of fiscal offices in 1633 accentuated these structural weaknesses by allowing corrupt, inexperienced, and inept officials with strong local connections to dominate the treasury in this period of crisis.

The chapters in part three explore the political struggles over tax reform in Peru. Chapter five deals with the failure of Peruvian officials between 1625 and 1643 to impose permanent tax levies capable of meeting the needs of the crown and averting the fiscal crisis. Chapter six traces the efforts of royal inspections in 1664, 1669, and 1677 to enforce the tax levies demanded by the crown during the reform period and their ultimate defeat by the combined opposition of local elites and their allies among venal officeholders in Lima. Finally the conclusion explains how the whole century-long process of economic change, fiscal crisis, and political turbulence undermined the imperial system in Peru and weakened the crown in its struggles in Europe.

PART ONE
Economy and Finance

2 *The Viceregal Economy in Transition*

The seventeenth century was a period of transition and readjustment for the economy in the Viceroyalty of Peru. More than three generations had passed since the turbulent years of the conquest. By 1600 the Spaniards had subjugated the Amerindian population, ended the disruptive civil wars among the initial conquerors, and imposed an extensive imperial bureaucracy to insure their dominance. During these formative years an essentially complete Spanish society had been transplanted to the viceroyalty, and this diverse group of colonizers had laid the foundations of a prosperous market economy, tied to Europe. Rich silver deposits in the highlands of Peru and Upper Peru provided the basis for this colonial economy and furnished the capital necessary to finance support sectors like agriculture, grazing, and manufacturing. As the productivity of the silver lodes declined and commercial ties with Spain weakened, investment capital flowed to these other productive enterprises. Mining still dominated the colonial economy, but the more extensive development of wine, textile, and artisan industries, along with the production of cotton, olives, grains, sugar, grapes, and cacao gave the viceroyalty a more diversified economic base. At the same time trade links in both legal and contraband goods evolved along the Pacific coast of South America and beyond to Central America, Mexico, and even the Far East. The seventeenth century was a period of evolutionary change, from a pillaging, conquest economy based on mining to a more stable, self-sufficient, and mature economic order.

A wide range of factors combined to stimulate aggregate demand and promote economic change in the Viceroyalty of Peru. The growth of urban centers and the Amerindians' more active participation in the colonial market economy led to a rise in consumer demand for locally produced goods. Moreover, clerical organizations played an important role by investing in land and extending credit to local producers and the government. The viceregal government also provided a stimulus to the restructuring of the economy by withholding tax income normally sent to the metropolis and spending it within the colony. At the same time, shortages and high prices caused by the recession in the Atlantic trade encouraged merchants to invest in local enterprises, engage in contraband trade with Europe, or turn to commerce in the Pacific. The economic changes which resulted from these forces prompted neither a prolonged depression nor sustained prosperity. Indeed, the vigor of these economic trends undoubtedly varied over time in each area of the viceroyalty and even affected colonial social groups differently.[1] Regions within the viceroyalty experienced cycles of hard times and prosperity throughout the century. The dominance of some regions involved in the mining industry, for example, clearly faded with the silver lodes, while other areas rose to greater prominence. On the whole, the internal economic changes during the seventeenth century provided a new range of opportunities and pitfalls for colonial elites.

Economic changes also brought political difficulties. During much of the century, the Habsburg monarchy attempted to surmount a sustained financial crisis, and officials in Madrid began demanding larger contributions from the viceregal government to avert the economic and military decline of the crown in Europe. At the same time, elites in the viceroyalty vigorously opposed heavier taxes that threatened to drain important investment capital needed during this transitional period from an economy dominated by mining to a more diversified base. These economic changes in the Viceroyalty of Peru and the financial problems of the crown in Europe led to a political struggle between the Madrid government and colonial magnates. Its outcome would have a decisive impact on the political and economic relationship between Spain and the Viceroyalty of Peru during the seventeenth century.

The Silver Metropolis

At the outset of the seventeenth century the economy and society of the viceroyalty revolved around the mines of Peru and Upper Peru and the transatlantic trade network, centered in Lima. These economic core regions, however, were supported by a host of agricultural, grazing, and manufacturing enterprises in surrounding provinces, as well as in more distant areas like Quito, Chile, Paraguay, Tucumán, and the Río de la Plata. The key links in this integrated colonial economy of Spanish Peru were the Lima merchants.[2] These enterprising traders facilitated the exchange of silver and other colonial goods for European products, supplied most of the markets of the interior, and in general controlled much of the commercial life of Spanish Peru.

By 1600 the driving force of the colonial economy remained silver mining. Gold mines at Carabaya, Cotabambas, and Condesuyos produced at high levels, but they never compared with the output from the key silver lodes at Castrovirreyna, Cailloma, Chachapoyas, Bombón, Pasco, San Antonio de Esquilache, Carangas, Laicocota, Oruro, and of course, Potosí. The mines at Potosí alone produced nearly 50,000,000 marks of silver during the seventeenth century, and in its peak years the single mine of La Fragua in San Antonio de Esquilache yielded silver deposits worth over 1,400 pesos daily.[3] The mines of Spanish Peru produced at levels far in excess of their counterparts in New Spain, until late in the seventeenth century, when silver yields from the northern viceroyalty finally began to overtake Peru as a source of bullion.[4]

The high productivity of the silver industry in the sixteenth and early seventeenth centuries gave way to a gradual period of decline by 1650. Some of the reasons for this decline may be traced to inevitable structural difficulties of the industry, such as flooding in the mineshafts, increased cost of the mercury used in the refining of the silver ore, and a decline in the quality of the ore itself. In addition to these problems, mismanagement of the mercury supply led to shortages, high taxes sapped profits, and shortages of Amerindian forced laborers (*mitayos*) all contributed to rising costs and falling outputs. At Potosí, for example, many miners (*azogueros*) began accepting cash payments from *indios de faltriquera*, mitayos who bought their way out of the mita by paying the equivalent of the wage of one free wage laborer (*minga*). In some years as much as half of the delivery of cheap *mita* labor was made in such cash payments. The *azoqueros* were supposed to use these payments in silver to hire substitute laborers to work the mines, but in practice they seldom did so. As a result these cash subsidies to the miners led to production cuts, as *azogueros* left their increasingly unproductive mines unworked and lived off the cash provided by the *indios de faltriquera*.[5] Another evitable cause of the industry's decline was frequent unrest and lawlessness at the isolated mining towns, which plagued administrators and upset the normal operation of the mines. Regardless of the cause, however, silver production declined, the industry became less profitable, and debts for mercury and imported merchandise grew. In the largest mining center at Potosí, production fell in value from 7,129,719 pesos in 1600 to 4,428,594 pesos in 1650, and finally to only 1,979,128 pesos by 1700.[6] Although this decline in silver production was particularly severe at Potosí, it was characteristic of most of the major mining centers of the viceroyalty during the century. Productive new strikes, such as Laicocota in the Puno area in 1657, temporarily worked to offset the falling productivity of the industry, but as the seventeenth century progressed, the decreasing output of the older and larger mining centers like Potosí led to an overall decline.[7]

The productivity of the silver industry was closely related to the supply of mercury extracted from the mines of Huancavelica. Silver miners employed the patio, or amalgamation, process, which used mercury to separate the silver ore from the rock during the refining process. Indeed, the system allowed miners to extract silver from previously unrefinable ore (*des-*

montes), contributing to the great mining boom of the late sixteenth century.[8] At its peak Huancavelica supplied miners at Potosí alone with 5,000 *quintales* (hundredweights) of mercury each year.[9] The crown recognized the crucial importance of the Huancavelica mines, and from 1582 mercury production was a crown monopoly. The government retained legal ownership of the mines, only leasing the right to operate them to the local miners' guild (*gremio*). The terms of the agreements between the guild and the crown varied over the century, but generally the government agreed to fix the price of mercury, pay a yearly subsidy to the guild, and insure that local magistrates provided an adequate supply of mitayos from the surrounding provinces. In exchange the miners promised to produce a preestablished amount of mercury each year.[10]

The system worked well and kept the silver miners supplied with mercury until early in the seventeenth century. Up to the 1590s the principal layer of ore, *la descubridora,* was worked using the relatively inexpensive open-cast technique. After that time the miners had to sink subterranean shafts to reach the ore, which proved expensive and dangerous in the soft sandstone of the region. In addition, without adequate supervision the shafts became hopelessly labyrinthine. Extraction problems were more difficult in the deep mineshafts, and poor ventilation exposed the Amerindian laborers to the toxic mercury fumes. These technological problems at Huancavelica were compounded by the tardiness of the silver miners and the crown in meeting their obligations. By 1657 the crown alone owed nearly 1,000,000 pesos to the miners at Huancavelica, leaving them to depend on merchants, called *aviadores,* to supply the necessary capital.[11] The unpaid debts of the crown and the silver miners, the increasing cost of production at the mineheads, and the indebtedness of the mercury miners to the aviadores all contributed to the decline of registered mercury at Huancavelica from a high of 13,611 quintales in 1582 to a low of 2,015 quintales in 1689.[12] This fall in output during the century led the mercury miners to sell contraband quicksilver to the aviadores in order to meet their debts. The traffic in illicit mercury in turn intensified the flow of contraband silver, contributing to the decline in taxes from the mining industry.

During the heyday of the silver industry, Lima and its port city of Callao were the commercial hub of Spanish Peru. Spanish law required that all imported European merchandise be channeled through Callao, where the traffic could be more easily supervised and taxed. From there all of the other mining, agricultural, manufacturing, and administrative centers of Spanish Peru depended on the Lima merchants to sell their goods and supply them with merchandise from Europe, Asia, and the Americas. The key element in this trade was the exchange of silver from the mines of Peru and Upper Peru for these imported goods, at the trade fair at Portobelo in Tierrafirme. Silver from most of the mines in Spanish Peru was usually shipped overland to the Pacific port of Arica. From Arica merchants put the specie on ships for the ten-day voyage to Callao. In late May Lima merchants loaded the gold and silver on the ships of the Pacific Fleet, which began the month-long trip to Tierrafirme. The armada usually contained only two or three warships and a similar number of merchant vessels. They disembarked at the port of Panama and made the overland trip to Portobelo, to meet the Atlantic fleet. Here merchants from Lima and Europe held a trade fair in late July or August, where specie was traded for European products needed in the viceroyalty. The merchants then returned to Lima with the newly acquired merchandise by late November or early December.[13] The whole time-consuming process could prove immensely profitable for the Lima traders, who maintained high prices by controlling the supply of the highly desirable imports.

The commercial stranglehold of the Lima merchant community eventually declined, along with the mining industry. Profits became more difficult to maintain as the productivity of the silver mines declined. The dangers from pirates in the Pacific also increased. In addition, imports of bullion from the Indies had contributed to a price revolution in Spain, which further drove up the prices of European goods for the Lima merchants. One of the ironies of the mining boom was that it contributed to inflation in Europe and diminished the value of silver at precisely the time that yields at the mineheads began to fall.[14] Another factor that cut into profits from the Atlantic trade was the decline of Castilian industry. Goods sold at the Portobelo fairs were often obtained originally from producers in France, Britain, and the Netherlands.[15] Since middlemen in Seville marked up the price of these foreign goods to make a profit on the transaction, the overall price of European imports rose even higher, further curtailing the profits of the Lima merchants. Added to all of these difficulties were the normal hazards, inconveniences, and costs of the trek to disease-infested Portobelo. Even when they arrived at the fairs, the Lima merchants were often at a disadvantage. Spanish merchants could always threaten the limeños with selling their goods in Veracruz or even taking them directly to Lima itself, if they did not receive a suitable price for the merchandise. To overcome all of these disadvantages, Lima merchants began trying to restrict the supply of European goods, in order to keep prices high and their profits at an acceptable level. As a result, the number of sailings from Callao to Panama fell from twenty-nine in the first half of the century to only nineteen between 1650 and 1700.[16]

The decline of the economic and commercial base of Spanish Peru during the first three decades of the seventeenth century provided a powerful impetus for economic diversification. Merchants, miners, and other magnates undoubtedly saw the need to invest in other lucrative ventures in the viceroyalty. By the time seventeenth century ended the viceregal economy provided a wide variety of such investment opportunities, apart from mining and the transatlantic trade.

The Diversified Economy

The Viceroyalty of Peru was rich in natural resources, which Spanish and creole entrepreneurs exploited to service the burgeoning urban centers in the coastal and highland provinces. The early Spanish settlements along the coast and in the mountain valleys formed the nucleus of an ever-widening group of regional economies. As investment opportunities in mining and the transatlantic trade dwindled, capital flowed to these more vibrant regional centers. Provincial economies in Saña, Cuzco, or Cochabamba in Peru and Upper Peru, and in more peripheral regions such as Chile and Quito, acquired a buoyancy of their own and produced a wide variety of agricultural and manufactured goods. According to one observer, Spanish Peru had achieved near self-sufficiency by 1600: "all Peru lacks is silk and linens, for they have a surplus of everything else, and do not have the need to beg nor wait for any other kingdom or province in the world."[17] This trend toward greater self-sufficiency and economic diversification continued throughout the seventeenth century.

A major stimulus to economic growth in Spanish Peru continued to be silver mining. Although mercury and silver production clearly declined, the industry as a whole never shrank to insignificance. New strikes kept productivity levels high, and older centers like Potosí continued to surmount the challenges of high taxes, rising costs, and declining yields to remain major silver producers. Even in its worst years of the seventeenth century, Potosí produced over 225,000 marks of silver, which compares favorably with the highest yields recorded at Zacatecas, the largest mining complex in New Spain.[18] On the other hand, mining no longer served as the financier of other economic sectors of Spanish Peru, and it also failed to attract so much of the investment capital during the century. In many cases investments in enterprises like farming or manufacturing proved more stable than money spent on the less dynamic silver industry.

While mining declined overall during the seventeenth century, the rural economy of Spanish Peru flourished. As the Amerindian population fell victim to disease or migrated to Spanish population centers, fertile land became vacant along the coast and in the highland valleys, particularly in coastal Peru, where the Amerindian population fell from 900,000 in 1530 to under 75,000 in 1630.[19] These vacant lands served as a powerful magnet, drawing settlers and investment capital to the rural economy. In addition, Spaniards and creoles often used their considerable political and economic power to buy or even usurp good farm and pasture land from the Amerindians.

The growing demand for foodstuffs, the widespread network of markets established by the Europeans in the highlands and along the coast, the availability of good land, and the eagerness of Spaniards to gain the wealth and prestige that landholding promised, all led to the growth of the rural economy. These profitable agricultural and pastural enterprises made a vital contribution to the prosperity and self-sufficiency of the viceregal economy.

Throughout the seventeenth century the fertile valleys of the Peruvian coast produced a wide variety of agricultural products. Sugar was cultivated in the north-coast region from Piura to Lima, with the most productive estates located in Lambayeque. Farmers also cultivated cotton in the north, particularly in the provinces of Lambayeque, Trujillo, Jaen, and Santa. The southern coast usually specialized in growing grapes, olives, and even sugar in Nazca. The central coast, particularly in the Chancay, Cañete, Lurin, and Rimac valleys, provided most of the wheat and other grains needed in the coastal cities. In addition, farmers in all of the coastal valleys raised other crops such as fruit and vegetables, while the scattered oases (*llomas*) along the arid coastal region proved well suited for livestock raising.

Spanish and Amerindian farmers in the highlands of Peru and Upper Peru also raised a wide variety of agricultural crops and stock animals. The most fertile of the highland valleys were in Cajamarca, Jauja, Azángaro, Andahuailas, Yucay, Cochabamba, Tarija, Cuzco, Chuquiabo, and Chuquisaca. The moderate climate in these regions allowed the cultivation of most of the commodities found along the coast. Farmers grew grapes, sugar, cereals, olives, and peppers (*ají*) with particular success in the Arequipa region, while cotton estates were centered in Huánuco, Cajamarca, and Chachapoyas. Potatoes and cereals were grown in virtually all of the fertile mountain valleys, and tobacco production was most successful in Saña and Cuzco. Sugar cultivation was common in Cuzco, while indigenous crops like coca flourished in Huánuco, Huamanga, Vilcabamba, Cuzco, La Plata, and La Paz. In the deeper mountain valleys in Vilcas, Abancay, and Apurimac, the intense summer heat and a constant shortage of water created an inhospitable environment for many farming and ranching enterprises. The most productive of these lowland regions was Santa Cruz de la Sierra, where farmers raised some cereal crops, cotton, and stock animals. While the high plains regions, such as Collao, were usually too dry for farming, they served as excellent pasture for stock animals. All of these productive centers supplied the steady demand for agricultural and livestock products in the mining centers and other urban concentrations in the highlands.

Areas more peripheral to the rural economy of Peru and Upper Peru, such as Chile, the Río de la Plata, Tucumán, and Quito also produced a variety of commodities for local consumption and export. Chile, for example, yielded a surplus of olives, grapes, cereals, and stock animals, particularly after the Araucanian Wars subsided, later in the century. In the Río de la Plata and Tucumán, wheat, corn, and barley were cultivated. In addition, the cultivation of grapes in Mendoza formed the basis of a productive wine industry. *Yerba mate,* a kind of strong tea, was the chief contribution of isolated Paraguay, and ranches throughout the Río de la Plata provided meat, skins, wool, and pack animals for export to Upper Peru, Brazil, and Europe. At the same time, the more developed economy of Quito produced cereals, coca, potatoes, cotton, sugar, wool, and stock animals. The lowlands around Guayaquil yielded some cochineal and large quantities of cacao.[20]

Throughout Spanish Peru no single pattern of land tenure predominated. Amerindian farmers, clustered in the highlands and a few coastal valleys, usually engaged in farming and livestock raising on communal holdings, while the Europeans more commonly favored privately owned commercial farms. In each province the particular type of landholding depended on a number of factors, including the crops or animals raised, the demands of consumers, the distance and strength of the markets supplied, the availability of investment capital, and good land, and the climate of the region.[21]

In areas where the market for agricultural produce was good and prices remained high, small estates, or *chacras,* developed. Chacras throughout Spanish Peru supplied a variety of crops for strong regional and local markets. Small holdings in the Cochabamba Valley concentrated on growing wheat sold in the marketplaces of Potosí, while those in the highlands of Upper Peru often grew coca. Chacras on the rich coastal soil of southern Peru specialized in producing grapes for the local wine industry.[22]

Although the wine industry experienced steady growth for most of the seventeenth century, coastal and highland chacras producing grapes were subject to regional economic fluctuations. In the Arequipa region, for example, chacras produced grapes in Condesuyos, Vitor, Mages, Moquequa, Siguas, and Locumba in the sixteenth and early seventeenth centuries.[23] These small estates took part in a profitable trade in wine and brandy to Cuzco, the silver mines in Cailloma and Upper Peru, and Lima. Arequipa's strong rural economy fell into decline by 1650, however, when estates in Ica, Nazca, and Pisco took over the wine and brandy market in Lima, and made serious inroads into the trade with Upper Peru.[24] Chacras in these coastal valleys took advantage of the excellent soil and close proximity to the Lima market to outdistance their competitors in Arequipa; they remained the center of the Peruvian wine industry for the rest of the century.

Larger estates, or *haciendas*, developed where variable market conditions made chacras unprofitable. In the wheat-producing regions surrounding Lima, such as Lurín, Cañete, Carabaillo, and La Barranca, few chacras remained by 1650.[25] The *cabildo* (city council) and the merchant community of Lima controlled the price of wheat, flour, and bread during the century, which limited the profitability of farming in the area to larger estates capable of controlling sufficient labor and water to restrict supply when prices were low.[26] These haciendas in the central region of the coast also produced commodities other than wheat and livestock, but they were primarily commercial farms that supplied grain to the Lima market.

Like the chacras of Arequipa, the haciendas around Lima experienced distinct cycles of prosperity and decline. Early in the century these haciendas, called *estancias de pan llevar* by the local residents, supplied over 150,000 bushels of wheat each year to feed the residents of Lima.[27] The *cabildo's* price regulations began having a detrimental effect, however, on the profitability of these estates by the 1630's. After a bad harvest, the prices set by the cabildo, which ranged between two and four pesos per bushel, were insufficient for the farmers (*hacendados*) to make a profit. As a consequence, the hacendados then curtailed production or even refused to market their wheat until prices recovered. In 1635, 1642, and 1651 these tactics created artificial grain shortages in the city, and the cabildo sent soldiers to force the farmers to harvest their wheat and sell it in Lima at the established prices.[28] By 1650 these price controls contributed to a gradual decline in the haciendas of the central coast, particularly in the Chancay and Cañete valleys. Jamaican wheat began to supplant the Peruvian product in the markets of Panama, and for the first time Chilean producers began to make inroads into the Lima grain market.[29]

Another type of large estate, called the manorial hacienda, specialized in farming and grazing in the Andean regions of Spanish Peru. These estates usually relied on a large Amerindian labor force and produced for smaller and often unreliable markets. To turn a profit the hacendados usually tried to control the supply of goods and the market price by continually producing below capacity. In times of economic stress, they could simply become self-sufficient until the recession ended. The owners of these marginal enterprises usually acquired the estates to gain the indirect social and economic benefits derived from controlling the land and labor of the region.[30]

Manorial haciendas were commonly located in areas surrounding the mining zones of the Andes and prospered or declined along with the mines. In all likelihood the estate owners were usually associated with the mines and used the farms to supply food and labor for the nearby towns. In some cases they may even have owned and operated the mines themselves. In the Huancavelica region, for example, the nearest estates occupied only moderately fertile farmland and failed to supply enough foodstuffs to meet the seasonal needs of the mining town. In addition, manorial haciendas in regions like Huancavelica changed ownership frequently, as the mines declined and the owners went bankrupt and left the area.[31]

The most capital-intensive landed estates in Spanish Peru were the plantations. Most were large or medium-sized holdings, located on the north coast of Peru. These estates commonly relied on Amerindian migrant laborers and African slaves to produce tropical goods such as cotton, sugar, and cacao. Among the most profitable of these enterprises were the sugar plantations of Lambayeque. The rural economy of the region developed around the city of Trujillo in the sixteenth century, producing wheat, corn, beans, rye, grapes, olives, and fruits. With the introduction of sugar cultivation, however, the city of Saña rose to preeminence, and the province achieved great prosperity between 1650 and 1720. Unlike the Brazilian estates of the same period, the sugar plantations of Lambayeque were smaller enterprises of one hundred to two hundred acres and employed under fifty slave or migrant Amerindian laborers. In addition the Lambayeque estates supplied regional markets rather than the far-away European consumers.[32] High prices and stable markets in Lima, the availability of relatively inexpensive slave labor, and access to investment capital all contributed to the prosperity of the region after 1650.[33] Indeed, the northern region of the coast had the largest number of sugar plantations in the Americas, outside of Brazil and the Caribbean islands.

Ranching was another profitable activity in Spanish Peru during the seventeenth century. Estates of all sizes raised stock on uncultivated agricultural lands as a secondary source of income, and many enterprises specialized in ranching on more marginal farmland. In the Andes ranchers usually raised goats, sheep, llamas, and alpacas, while along the coast cattle, pigs, sheep, and goats were more common. Ranching did not require a large labor force nor substantial capital outlays to feed, transport, and supervise the herds.[34] As long as markets in the coastal urban centers and the highland mining towns kept demand high, local ranching remained profitable.

Spanish Peru never became as self-sufficient in manufactured goods as it did in agricultural produce. Nevertheless, a vigorous textile industry developed to meet the regional need for cotton and woolen clothing. This was particularly true after the recession in the Atlantic trade from the 1620s, which restricted the supply of European textiles. The textile mills (*obrajes*) produced coarse sackcloth, various qualities of woolen and cotton cloth, blankets, hats, sandals, and ship rigging. The largest and most productive of these obrajes were in the northern provinces of Quito, Conchucos, Huaylas, Cajamarca, and (by 1650) Cuzco.[35] Local sheep raisers, for example, sent over 350,000 head of stock to provide wool for the obrajes of Cajamarca.[36] In the Audiencia of Quito, mill owners (*obrajeros*) frequently owned estates that provided the cotton and wool for their own enterprises.[37] Obrajes could be small enterprises or very large operations. Near the town of Piscobamba in Conchucos, for example, a single obraje employed over four hundred laborers.[38] Obrajes also prospered, although on a smaller scale, in provinces such as Santa, Chachapoyas, Huánuco, Huamalíes, Canta, Chancay, Cajatambo, Jauja, Lima, Huamanga, Tarma, Arequipa, Abancay, and Puno.[39]

The seventeenth century was a time of expansion and prosperity for many of the Andean obrajes, particularly those in Quito. Unlike much of Peru and Upper Peru, the Amerindian population in Quito grew during the century, which kept labor costs low.[40] In addition the crown provided mill owners with levies of cheap mita laborers from the surrounding provinces.[41] Should the regional supply of mitayos prove inadequate, mill owners could still hire wage laborers for salaries of only ten to thirty pesos per year.[42] The Quito obrajes were founded in the sixteenth century by local *encomenderos,* but when the grants fell vacant, they reverted to the crown. These public sector enterprises ultimately proved less profitable than privately owned mills, and by the middle of the seventeenth century the private sector accounted for most of the output of the region's famous cloth (*paño azul*).[43] During most of the century, over 10,000 laborers toiled in obrajes within the Audiencia of Quito and produced an average of 100,000 *varas* (yards) of paño azul, worth between one and two million pesos in the marketplaces of Lima and New Granada.[44] The low operating costs of the mills, the need for cheap, low-quality cloth, and the inability of the decadent Spanish textile industry to supply the merchandise, all combined to insure the growth of the industry.[45] In the case of Quito, the obrajes remained prosperous until the 1690s, when a series of epidemics decimated the Amerindian population at precisely the time when the demand for paño azul in Lima began to decline.[46]

Wine production also enjoyed some prosperity during the century. Estates in Arequipa and later Ica, Nazca, Pisco, Chile, and Mendoza provided grapes which were turned into high-quality wine and brandy. The crown discouraged the industry from the reign of Phillip II (1556–98), because it feared that local Peruvian producers would undercut the more expensive Spanish wines.[47] By the next century, however, it became apparent that viticulture would not be suppressed, particularly as Spanish imports declined. As a result the crown simply gave in and taxed the produce of the industry.[48] Peruvian producers supplied wine to the mining towns and coastal urban centers, and also exported considerable amounts of their produce to Mexico and Central America.

A growing shipbuilding industry also contributed to economic diversification in Spanish Peru. Isolated from European shipyards and the large works in Havana, Pacific traders had to depend on local builders. From the sixteenth century, shipbuilding installations flourished in Panama and Realejo, in Nicaragua, but the largest Pacific yards were located on the Guayas River, near Guayaquil.[49] The need for ships to defend the silver fleets moving from Callao to Portobelo and the expanding intercolonial commerce in the Pacific both stimulated this independent industry. The Guayaquil yards received most of their wood from nearby forests, cloth for sails from the highland obrajes, rope and fittings from Chile, and pitch and tar from Piura and Nicaragua.[50] This ability to minimize the use of imported goods from Europe allowed shipbuilders to keep the prices for their ships low and still turn out three or four ships each year for the viceregal navy and local merchants.[51] The growing economic diversity and self-reliance of the viceregal economy supplied the resources and capital necessary to launch and maintain this important local industry.

A frequently overlooked sector of the viceregal economy during the seventeenth century is that of artisan, or craft, industries. These small-scale operations flourished, particularly in the urban areas, to replace the uneven flow of merchandise from the metropolis after the recession in the Atlantic trade. Spanish cities, agricultural estates, and the development of other industries created the need for a wide variety of locally produced goods. Spanish, Amerindian, and black craftsmen all worked to meet the demand for leather goods, glass, arms, furniture, wood products, and work tools. European craftsmen still continued to supply many of the higher-quality finished goods, but local artisans made much of the lower-cost merchandise.

Throughout a large part of the seventeenth century, Lima remained the commercial and economic hub of Spanish Peru. Apart from its dominance of the Atlantic trade, the Lima merchant community also had the capital to invest in the lucrative Pacific trade. Quito obrajeros, for example, took the initiative in shipping their paño azul to Lima, but Lima merchants actually marketed the cloth in the viceroyalty.[52] This commercial activity yielded large profits to limeños, and early in the century over sixty merchants had assets over 100,000 pesos; and some could even muster capital of from 500,000 to 1,000,000 pesos.[53] They reinforced this economic power with the judicial and political privileges of the merchant's guild (*consulado*), the only organization of its kind in Spanish Peru. By the end of the century Lima merchants were complaining of competitors in Buenos Aires and Santiago, but they still retained an important economic role in Spanish Peru.

The role of the Lima merchant community in the economic diversification of Spanish Peru received a devastating blow in 1687, when a major earthquake hit the central coast of Peru. Serious damage occurred in the city itself. On October 20 and again on December 2, 1687, these severe quakes damaged scores of buildings and left thousands injured and homeless.[54] Damage in the countryside also impeded the flow of food to the city and caused prices to soar. According to the viceroy, the conde de Monclova (1689–1705), the government was forced to control the sale and distribution of bread to prevent hoarding and even starvation.[55] Outbreaks of disease followed the food shortages, and within five years the city's population had fallen from nearly 80,000 to under 40,000, as Amerindians in particular fled to the countryside.[56]

Even more destructive than the damage to the city of Lima was the harm done to the agricultural valleys of the central coast. The irrigation system in the semiarid coastal region was nearly destroyed in some areas, and erosion, drought, and an early frost combined to cause a drastic drop in crop yields.[57] Food imports from the highlands proved inadequate to feed the coastal population, and wheat prices in Lima rose from two or four pesos per bushel to over twenty or even thirty pesos.[58] To avert the possibility of famine and to stabilize prices, merchants imported large quantities of Chilean wheat, which came to dominate the Lima market by the 1690s.[59] Agricultural suppliers along the central coast never recovered from the natural disasters of 1687; as late as 1745 local farmers complained of the dominance of Chilean wheat in the Lima market.[60] Ironically the earthquakes of 1687, which devastated the central coast, proved a boon to the hacendados of Valparaíso, Santiago, Concepción, Coquimbo, and Arica. The net result was to transform Chile from a struggling frontier province into the principal wheat producer of Spanish Peru.

The economic decline of the central coast had far-reaching consequences for Spanish Peru. Credit organizations such as merchant banks and clerical bodies undoubtedly lost on many of their investments after the economy entered a recession. Even the powerful Jesuit colleges complained that numerous bankruptcies and defaults by their *censo* (long-term loans) holders occurred after 1687.[61] In addition, the order's own economic ventures suffered from a temporary scarcity of capital and a fall in land values. These problems were hardly confined to the Jesuits. When the crown demanded a renewal of annuity sales and forced donations during the 1690s, for example, the viceroy was forced to admit that Lima was too poor to meet its quotas.[62]

In all, it was a bleak period for the economy of central Peru.

Apart from Chile, another region which gained some advantage from the economic eclipse of Lima and the central coast of Peru was the Río de la Plata. Buenos Aires, the region's chief city, had become a thriving center of contraband trade with the Portuguese and later the Dutch and the English. The city had grown from only 1,000 inhabitants in 1615 to over 7,000 by 1700.[63] The crown had allowed register ships of two hundred tons each to sail from Seville in 1624, but in the 1630s merchants in Lima complained that these ships only provided a cover for a lively clandestine trade at Buenos Aires, which included the importation of 3,000 slaves each year.[64] The city used its favorable location on the Atlantic and the lower-priced contraband goods to compete for markets in Upper Peru. As early as 1620, contemporaries estimated that over 100,000 pesos in illicit silver flowed through the port.[65] Even before the great earthquake, the region was so prosperous that the Portuguese founded their own colony across the estuary at Colonia do Sacramento, in 1680. In spite of this Portuguese competition, however, merchants in Buenos Aires continued to exploit the economic weakness of Lima and made considerable strides toward capturing the lucrative markets of Upper Peru.

After the earthquake, Lima was an important but declining city. By the end of the century, the recession in the Atlantic trade, the fall in mining output, the growth of competing regional economic centers, and the earthquake of 1687 all worked to undermine the power and influence of the viceregal capital. How this eclipse of Lima affected the development of Spanish Peru in the eighteenth century is uncertain, but it seems likely that it produced many internal economic and political changes. Some areas, like the Río de la Plata, undoubtedly benefited, while others, like Quito, even declined. The erosion of the power and influence of Lima may well have led to a more cantonal viceroyalty by the next century. The basis for these changes was laid in the period from 1625 to 1687, however, when the regional economies of Spanish Peru grew more diverse, self-sufficient, and stable.

The Stimuli for Economic Change

Several factors combined to stimulate the shift from mining to a more diversified economic base in Spanish Peru. A sluggish aggregate demand for locally produced commodities hindered such diversification in the sixteenth century. A small home market, an overreliance on mining, and a dependence on Europe to supply most of the manufactured goods and luxury items needed in the colony all retarded any substantial growth of aggregate demand. By the seventeenth century, however, the high productivity of the silver lodes began to drop, and economic problems in Spain rendered the metropolis an unreliable and expensive source of commercial goods. In response to these problems, patterns of consumer demand, investment, government spending, and trade shifted during the century. The economic balance between mining and other sectors achieved in the sixteenth century was not the only one possible for Spanish Peru. Enterprises like agriculture and industry now absorbed more of the investment capital that had previously gone to mining or had been drained off to Europe. The net result was a restructuring of the economy in Spanish Peru, characterized by increasing self-sufficiency, diversification, and the growth of interregional trading systems to supplement the faltering commercial ties with Europe.

An important element in this economic diversification was the growth of the European population. Although the number of Europeans remained smaller than in New Spain, even the most conservative estimates indicate that over 245,000 people had left the Old World to settle in the viceroyalty by 1650.[66] The Europeans formed the upper crust of colonial society, and the growth of this group led to an increase in consumer demand for local products. This was particularly true after the decline of the transatlantic trade curtailed the supply of European goods. Even more crucial for this rise in demand was the concentration of the white population in urban areas such as Potosí and Lima. Sketchy census data for Potosí indicate that the city's population may have peaked at 160,000 by 1650.[67] More reliable data for Lima show less spectacular urban growth, although by midcentury the overall total of European residents may have been larger than at Potosí. In 1619 Lima had a total of 24,902 inhabitants, with the European segment forming the largest component, at 46 percent of the total.[68] Before the earthquake of 1687, some estimates of the capital city's population demonstrate that it may have reached 80,000.[69] This impressive growth in both Lima and Potosí meant that both cities had to draw food and supplies from many parts of the viceroyalty.[70] According to one contemporary in 1630, Lima alone imported and consumed more than 200,000 jugs of wine, 20,000 jugs of honey, 6,000 jugs of rice, 75,000 pounds of sugar, 17,500 pounds of ice, 10,000 pounds of almonds, 150,000 bushels of wheat, 3,500 head of cattle, 200,000 *carneros* (llama, alpaca, and vicuña), 25,000 head of sheep and goats, and 7,000 pigs.[71] In addition to Lima and Potosí, urban centers like Saña, Huánuco, Quito, Huamanga, Cuzco, Arequipa, and Buenos Aires developed, attracting immigrants from Spain and other parts of the realm.

Another stimulus to consumer demand was the gradual integration of the European and Amerindian populations. After the Toledan reforms in the late sixteenth century regularized the tax and labor obligations of the Amerindians in Spanish Peru, this process of integration had a progressively more important impact on the colonial economy. Even along the Peruvian coast the native population did not decline as dramatically as in Mexico, and in the highlands it stabilized at over 500,000 by the 1630s.[72] In some areas of Spanish Peru, such as Quito, the Amerindian population even grew, from 144,000 in 1591 to 273,000 by 1690.[73] By the seventeenth century these substantial Amerindian communities throughout Spanish Peru paid tribute in specie and in kind, which forced them to take part in the market economy of the Europeans. Substituting money payments for tribute in kind protected harvests and animals needed for the survival of the traditional communities (*ayllu*).[74] In addition the Spaniards often demanded that taxes be paid in products such as wheat, cattle, or pigs, which were not indigenous to the Americas. This forced the Amerindians to alter their own patterns of agriculture or to buy the commodities from Europeans. Moreover, the crown also required some

Amerindian communities to serve as forced laborers in the obrajes or the mines, which also drew them into the money economy. Some mitayos decided to stay on as wage laborers, while others were willing to hire substitutes to work in their place. Apart from working as wage laborers or mitayos, Amerindians also migrated to Spanish farms or towns to find work. Census data for the districts (*repartimientos*) of Huacho and Végueta, for example, in the valley of Chancay, indicate that Amerindian males commonly traveled great distances to supply the seasonal demand for labor on the wheat haciendas.[75] In short, crown tax and mita policies along with the overall development of the economy forced the Amerindians to participate as producers and consumers in Spanish Peru.

The rising number of African slave laborers imported during the seventeenth century eased potential labor shortages and helped stimulate economic diversification in Spanish Peru. Portuguese and Spanish merchants provided a steady flow of slaves from West Africa to work on the sugar, wheat, and grape-producing estates along the coast, where the labor shortage was most severe. The black population of the viceroyalty grew from only 3,000 in 1550 to over 60,000 by 1650.[76] These freedmen and slaves had to be clothed, fed, and housed, which spurred internal demand, and they aided in increasing production through their labor.

A vital stimulus to economic growth during the seventeenth century was investment capital, much of which was supplied by clerical organizations. The Church received bequests from wealthy believers, dowries from women entering convents, and money from the tithe and sale of indulgences, which it invested in local enterprises. According to one viceroy, the conde de Chinchón (1629–39), clerical bodies had gained control over some of the best farmland in the realm.[77] The Society of Jesus was particularly successful in its agricultural and commercial ventures during the seventeenth century. The order began investing heavily in enterprises producing sugar, wine, yerba mate, livestock, wheat, and even textiles. Like many clerical investors, the Jesuits could rely on a large and centralized source of capital, enjoyed certain tax exemptions, and enforced cooperation rather than competition among their various regional holdings.[78] Furthermore, clerical organizations like the Jesuits had such extensive resources that they could absorb temporary losses until they finally turned a profit.[79] In the 1630s, for example, several Jesuit colleges complained that overinvestment in heavily mortgaged land, high operating costs, and mismanagement had cut into profits.[80] Within a decade, the society had overcome these setbacks and could once again expand its holdings. Many of these holdings in the seventeenth century, such as the large sugar estate at Villa, produced returns of 10 percent by the 1670s, which compared favorably with the profits of the best Jamaican plantations of the day.[81] By the end of the century the Jesuits and other clerical investors had acquired profitable holdings throughout Spanish Peru, giving them considerable economic power.

The Church also served as an important source of credit during the century. Ecclesiastical bodies frequently negotiated long-term loans with laymen, in the form of a censo agreement. These censos usually provided for 5 percent interest, subject to a mortgage guarantee by the borrower and his promise to make regular interest payments.[82] Most often the loans went to rural landowners, who offered their holdings as collateral for the loan. The administrators of convents and monasteries handled requests for censos, while loan applications from chantries or pious works were made to the Juzgado de Capellanías y Obras Pías of the local archdiocese, which administered the endowments given to the tribunal by the faithful.[83] If the borrowers failed to keep up their interest payments, their collateral reverted to the agency granting the loan. As a result the loans provided the Church with a profitable and secure outlet for its surplus capital, and also allowed clerical bodies to gain control over land either repossessed or donated by borrowers who wished to repay the debt. Regardless of whether the censos were repaid or the land taken over by the lenders, these transactions probably provided the largest source of rural credit in Spanish Peru.

Not all investment capital for economic development came from censos. Most commercial, industrial, and mining ventures relied on merchant banking houses for credit, rather than on censos. Clerical organizations offered funds to borrowers only when they became available and favored low-risk ventures with substantial collateral. Most business groups, however, engaged in riskier enterprises, offered little as collateral, and needed consistent sources of funding, which forced them to rely on the higher-interest loans offered by the banks. These agencies often maintained a very tenuous existence. Between 1613 and 1629, for example, eight important merchants and three banks declared bankruptcy.[84] Defaults on loans, general economic downturns, demands by the crown for *donativos,* poor management, and fraud by the merchants themselves all contributed to the failures. Even the establishment of a merchants' guild in Lima, with the authority to supervise the banking industry, did not always insure stability. In the famous bankruptcy of Juan de la Cueva, in 1635, for example, the consulado of Lima recorded claims of 1,068,248 pesos against his bank. Most were never repaid.[85] In fact, the viceroy, the conde de Chinchón, blamed this and other bank failures for a temporary economic downturn during the 1630s.[86] In spite of this instability, merchant banks like that of Juan de la Cueva held large deposits and financed many local economic enterprises during the seventeenth century, reducing the need to rely on metropolitan sources of credit.

This growing self-reliance in banking and credit was supplemented by the steady rise in direct government spending. As table 1 indicates, despite the decline in total government receipts from the 1660s, the viceregal treasury spent an increasing share of its income within the realm. Between 1591 and 1600, the treasury retained under 12,000,000 pesos or 36 percent of its income, in the colony, while in the decade from 1681 to 1690, these same officials spent over 20,000,000 pesos, or 95 percent of the government's revenues, within the viceroyalty. Most of these funds were earmarked for defense projects such as subsidies to frontier provinces, maintaining the Pacific fleet and the fortress at Callao, and support for the shipyards at Guayaquil. These government monies not only stimulated arms production, local shipbuilding, and metal foundaries, but also

Table 1. Public Revenues from the Central Viceregal Treasury of Lima Retained in the Indies, 1591–1690 (in pesos de ocho reales)

Decade	Total Revenue	Revenue Retained in Peru	% to Castile	% Retained in Peru
1591–1600	31,407,730	11,450,254	64	36
1601–1610	37,976,256	20,726,850	45	55
1611–1620	33,242,788	21,323,078	35	65
1621–1630	33,105,674	20,916,697	37	63
1631–1640	32,894,130	18,055,639	45	55
1641–1650	33,720,680	19,452,359	42	58
1651–1660	35,887,968	24,126,862	33	67
1661–1670*	20,325,261	17,298,253	15	85
1671–1680	26,060,453	26,060,453	16	84
1681–1690	24,078,352	22,806,459	5	95

*Accounts for the years 1662–64 are missing from the AGI and the AGN, Lima

agriculture and artisan industries, as food and supplies were stockpiled to support local garrisons. Furthermore, the expenditures provided an important boost to the economy of frontier regions, such as Chile, as the viceregal capital supplied funds to maintain military outposts and protect isolated settlements. While the rise in yearly spending from government sources is not large by modern standards, it provides another example of how local capital came to be redirected to support economic growth in Spanish Peru.

Despite its decline during the 1620s, the Atlantic trade did not atrophy during the seventeenth century and still retained an important, albeit diminishing, role in the commercial life of Spanish Peru. In fact, the Lima treasury sent over 100,000,000 pesos in public revenues to Seville during the period.[87] Figures on the amount of private capital passing between Portobelo and Seville are not available, but in all likelihood it too reached impressive levels. In addition, tax-farming contracts negotiated between viceregal authorities and the Lima consulado to collect the sales and port taxes steadily rose in value during the century, an indication at least that trade from Callao was not yet moribund.[88] Also, foreign consuls in Seville and Cadiz frequently wrote of Lima merchants, called *peruleros*, who circumvented the Seville monopoly and royal taxes by trading directly with foreign and Spanish merchants.[89] These consuls also reported that the decline in legal remissions of bullion from Peru could be explained, in part, by a dramatic rise in contraband trade in the Spanish harbors themselves. Galleons from the Indies often unloaded most of their cargo onto foreign ships in the harbor before docking at Seville or Cádiz.[90]

In spite of these reports of contraband in the Atlantic trade, an overall recession in commerce with the metropolis made trade in the Pacific an attractive alternative to colonial merchants. Merchants from Guayaquil sent tropical woods, charcoal, cacao, and cloth to markets in Lima, Central America, and Mexico. Producers in central and southern Peru shipped wine, brandy, sugar, olive oil, wheat, textiles, and silver to Pacific ports from Chile to Acapulco. Soap, sugar, textiles, cotton, and tobacco were sent from Quito and northern Peru to markets in Lima and New Granada. Finally, Chile sent wine, wheat, meats, salt, tallow, and commodities from the Río de la Plata, such as hides and yerba mate, to Lima.[91]

Among the most profitable maritime exchanges in the Pacific were those between Peru and New Spain. The more developed economy of New Spain contributed textiles, clothing, jewelry, leather goods, and books from Mexico, while Central America sent considerable amounts of indigo for the obrajes of Quito and Peru.[92] In addition, Lima merchants exchanged silver, mercury, wine, and cacao for these goods and luxuries from the Orient. In some years estimates indicated that oriental goods may have accounted for 90 percent of the commodities sent from New Spain in exchange for Peruvian silver.[93] Each year or so the Manila galleons left Acapulco, loaded with Spanish silver and bound for the Philippine Islands. Here Spanish traders exchanged the specie for silks, porcelains, musk, tapestries, pepper, ivory, jade, damask, and other luxuries.[94] When the oriental products reached New Spain, they were either sold in Mexican markets or sent to eager Peruvian buyers. In fact the demand for these commodities exceeded the supplies carried on the Manila galleons, and peruleros from Lima and other coastal ports even sailed directly to Manila to carry on the trade.[95]

The crown attempted to exert controls over the trade with Manila and the drain of specie from the Indies to the Far East. In 1582 royal edicts ordered an end to all direct navigation between the Philippines and South America and prohibited the sale of goods from Manila in Peruvian markets. In 1593 the Madrid government even ended the reexport of Chinese goods transshipped from Mexico.[96] The crown restricted trade between New Spain and Peru to three ships of three hundred tons each in any given year. The legislation aimed to limit the legal value of trade between the two viceroyalties to approximately from 150,000 to 200,000 pesos each year.[97] By 1631 the crown ordered an end to all trade between New Spain and Peru.[98]

Royal sanctions failed to end the drain of silver to the Far East. Chinese traders still flocked to Manila, and by 1650 that city had an estimated 30,000 Chinese residents.[99] China needed silver during the seventeenth century and Chinese merchants exchanged silver at rates much higher than those paid in Europe, which was in the midst of its price revolution.[100] In addition, ships from other Asian nations, such as Japan, Indochina, Indonesia, India, and the Moluccas, docked at Manila to exchange their products for silver from Indies. These oriental goods brought high prices in Lima and Mexico City, which insured the prosperity of merchants who circumvented the authorities and avoided punishment. In all likelihood, the legal prohibitions were more successful in increasing contraband than they were in curbing the trade. Compliant officials in Acapulco, Callao, Paita, and Guayaquil were probably more interested in extorting bribes from the contrabandists, or even in taking part in the illicit traffic themselves, than in enforcing the royal edicts. In fact the cabildo of Mexico City even admitted publicly that in peak years during the 1590s, the value of the trade was over 5,000,000 pesos.[101] The cabildo of Lima petitioned the crown to legalize the trade in oriental goods in 1638, explaining that over 600,000 pesos of contraband Chinese cloth entered the city an-

Table 2. Silver and Merchandise Entering the Philippines from Mexico and the Far East, 1591–1700 (in pesos de ocho reales)

	Privately Owned Silver from Mexico**	Public Revenues from Mexico*	Approximate Value of Far Eastern Goods Entering the Philippines**
1591–1600	578,170	466,016	1,379,550
1601–1610	3,516,513	1,174,782	2,597,333
1611–1620	5,048,118	2,541,652	5,752,000
1621–1630	5,423,822	3,620,573	870,050
1631–1640	3,509,871	3,672,874	1,077,133
1641–1650	1,759,706	2,206,810	1,017,517
1651–1660	2,015,681	1,508,388	168,950
1661–1670	1,726,151	1,379,509	97,717
1671–1680	2,230,883	1,628,439	192,900
1681–1690	876,528	1,952,190	802,350
1691–1700	171,954	1,661,385	1,199,566

*From John J. TePaske and Herbert S. Klein, "The Seventeenth-Century Crisis in Spanish America: Myth or Reality," *Past and Present* 90 (February 1981), 133.
**From Pierre Chaunu, *Les Philippines et le Pacifique des Ibériques (XVIe, XVIIe, XVIIe siècles): Introduction méthodologique et indices d'activité, Ports-Routes-Trafics* (Paris, 1960), 12:136–43; 14: 200–216.

yway. The alderman estimated the total value of the Asian trade at 2,000,000 pesos each year, and stated that the taxes accruing to the crown from the trade, if it were legalized, would contribute significantly to ending the financial woes of the viceregal treasury. Finally, the members of the cabildo asked to expand the trade in wine with Mexico, which they estimated would allow local producers to sell at least 4,500,000 bottles each year in the northern viceroyalty.[102]

Additional evidence for the continuation of the trade in oriental goods is provided in table 2. These trade figures indicate that the flow of public money from Mexico to support the soldiers, administrators, and clergy in the Philippines reached more than 3,500,000 pesos by the 1640s. Likewise, the shipments of private funds that accompanied the Philippine subsidy peaked at over 5,000,000 pesos a decade earlier. Sketchy figures on the value of oriental goods taxed at Manila also demonstrate that the value of these imports reached 5,752,000 pesos by the second decade in the century.[103] These officials records, which do not measure contraband goods, point to a rise in the trade in silver and oriental goods in the Pacific until the 1640s. Either the trade itself declined after this time or it fell into the hands of peruleros and other contrabandists. In fact, as late as 1704, the Viceroy of Peru and the Audiencia of Lima issued a joint edict calling for an end to the extensive contraband trade in oriental goods with New Spain.[104]

Not all of the Pacific trade involved oriental goods or products from New Spain. At least fifty ships departed Callao each year during the century, and most went to Valparaíso, Panama, Arica, Guayaquil, and other viceregal ports.[105] In addition, during the first third of the seventeenth century, over 150 vessels sailed from other South American ports. The tonnage of these ships was probably less than those leaving Callao, but nevertheless they supplied a host of locally produced products from Pisco, Cañete, Trujillo, Chancay, Huaura, La Barranca, and other regional centers.[106] Indeed, the traffic in legal and illicit goods continued within Spanish Peru itself, and goods from New Spain, Europe, and the Far East still entered the viceregal ports, particularly after the legal fleet system began to break down. In 1686, for example, some contemporaries estimated that the legal fleet system supplied only one-third of the goods traded in the Spanish Indies.[107] The growth of the viceregal merchant marine from 35 or 40 vessels in 1590 to over 70 ships by the end of the seventeenth century provides a further indication that mercantile activity continued to flourish after the 1620s.[108] This expanded merchant fleet also helped other commercial centers to take a larger part in the legal and contraband trade in Spanish Peru, often to the detriment of the mercantile monopoly of the Lima merchant community.

By the 1690s, the consulado was complaining most bitterly about the illicit trade flowing through Buenos Aires, which it claimed was drawing off large amounts of public revenues from Potosí, in exchange for contraband European merchandise.[109] An investigation of the problem of contraband forty years earlier had found widespread evidence of the trade at Callao as well as regional centers like Buenos Aires, and even implicated members of the Lima consulado itself. The viceroy, the conde de Salvatierra, despaired of ever stopping the illegal traffic completely and recommended easing certain unenforceable trade restrictions and lessening the penalties for violators.[110] These sentiments were also echoed in Madrid in a special meeting on commercial violations in 1677, when several key government officials agreed it would be better to permit more legal avenues for trade in the Pacific. No concrete changes in royal commercial policies occurred, however, and the contraband continued.[111] It would only worsen during the secession crisis in 1700, when French merchants would enter the Pacific and dominate colonial markets until 1724.[112]

A series of overland trade routes had developed by the seventeenth century, to aid the internal flow of goods from the coast and the interior provinces. The large mining town of Potosí, for example, received luxury goods, wine, brandy, fish, and fruit from coastal Peru, and sugar, preserves, fruit, wine, wheat, corn, meat, cotton, and clothing came from inland centers like Cuzco, Chucuito, Tucumán, Paraguay, Santa Cruz, Cochabamba, Chaqui, and Matoca.[113] Throughout Spanish Peru the internal circulation of goods as well as the Pacific trade aided in the progress of economic diversification during the seventeenth century.

Conclusion

The economic structure established by the crown in the sixteenth century gave way to a more diverse and self-sufficient economy in Spanish Peru. The retention of more mineral wealth in the colony, the growth of the Spanish population, the closer integration of the European and Amerindian economies, larger investments by clerical and merchant groups in local enterprises, the development of credit facilities, and the Pacific trade all stimulated the aggregate demand for locally produced goods. This rise in demand removed many of the old impediments to internal capital formation and encouraged the development of sectors other than mining.

In preindustrial societies like Spanish Peru, annual capital formations of from 3 to 6 percent were usually sufficient to promote growth and diversification.[114] After all, most enterprises were small-scale undertakings, and investments in agriculture or industry were generally modest. As a result, agricultural and stock-raising ventures developed in the coastal and highland valleys to supply the major urban markets of the viceroyalty. Local industries also evolved to provide the textiles, wine, brandy, and artisan goods previously imported from Spain. Luxury goods still came from Europe, but trade expanded beyond the confines of the legal system to include merchandise illegally imported from other European countries and the Far East. In addition, intercolonial trade facilitated the exchange of local goods and stimulated regional economies.

As time progressed, more of this development was funded by local banking and financial operations rather than by metropolitan investors. Less silver left the provinces and local bankers served as conduits for capital from those with savings to those in need of credit. Much of this investment and regional development began to expand and encompass regions formerly peripheral to the economy of Spanish Peru, such as Chile, Quito, and the Río de la Plata. Whether these internal changes led to an overall rise or fall in the total economic output of Spanish Peru remains uncertain. These developments might appear to imply an "autonomy of stagnation," but this is misleading.[115] The local economies were welded more tightly together and were more diverse than in the past, and there is no evidence of a sustained depression or malaise; nor do Europeans appear to have lived any less well, at least until the earthquake of 1687. The economy of Spanish Peru was simply becoming more diverse, stable, and self-sufficient. As in any other period the process undoubtedly had its ups and downs, with different regions experiencing cycles of depression and recovery.

In this era of transition from mining to a more diversified economic base, one of the principal problems facing local elites in Spanish Peru was the accumulation and control of capital. Adequate capital accumulations existed in the viceroyalty to finance economic change, and elites wisely directed it to growing sectors like agriculture, industry, and the Pacific trade. This period of change, from the 1620s until the 1690s, was bound to be accompanied by a hardening of attitudes among the elites, anxious to protect their vulnerable investments. The colonials needed low taxes, more government spending within the viceroyalty, and freedom from excessive government regulation and interference. But the needs of the crown in the Indies were quite different. The seventeenth century was a time of crisis in Spain, when the crown demanded more money from the Indies to advance the imperial ambitions of the Habsburgs in Europe. As a result, the Madrid government sought to raise taxes and tighten imperial controls. The financial needs of the crown and the economic adjustments in Spanish Peru put Madrid on a collision course with the most powerful citizens in the viceroyalty. This struggle between the crown and colonial taxpayers formed the central political issue in the seventeenth century. Both sides in this conflict looked to a powerful group within the empire to protect their interests—the officials attached to the viceregal treasury, centered in Lima. These bureaucrats had the responsibility for enforcing any controversial tax policies of the crown, and their response would ultimately determine the outcome of this conflict of interest within the seventeenth-century Spanish Empire.

3 *Treasury Policy and the Fiscal Crisis*

The seventeenth century saw great changes in the structure of royal finance in the Viceroyalty of Peru. From the 1620s the decline of the silver-mining economy in Peru and Upper Peru and the recession in the Atlantic trade began to undermine the tax base of the viceregal treasury and make it increasingly difficult to meet the crown's demands for more money. At the same time, the treasury also had to pay larger amounts of revenue to meet the increasing military and administrative costs of the viceroyalty. The central problem facing treasury officials during the seventeenth century was finding new sources of income to counterbalance the shrinking tax base of the realm and ease the burden of rising expenditures.

The key to understanding the response of treasury officials in the Viceroyalty of Peru to this problem lies in a detailed examination of the accounts (cuentas) from the central treasury office in Lima. These accounts list the income from taxes collected in the Lima district itself and the remissions of revenue sent from the other treasuries of the realm. The Lima office then used these monies to pay the various expenses of viceregal administration. As a result the Lima treasury was the financial hub of the viceroyalty, and its accounts provide a detailed picture of the financial position of the government and the fiscal policies pursued by treasury officials throughout the seventeenth century.

These treasury records reveal that officials in both Lima and

Madrid were unsuccessful in maintaining the fiscal solvency of the viceregal government. Despite imposing a host of new permanent tax levies and utilizing several temporary financial expedients, income levels began to drop drastically by the 1660s.[1] Although these fiscal policies allowed treasury officials in Lima and elsewhere in the viceroyalty to meet their immediate financial needs, they never provided a consistent or stable source of funds to replace the declining yield of taxes on commerce and mining. The net result was the onset of a worsening fiscal crisis in the 1660s that lasted until the middle of the eighteenth century.

The Structure of Viceregal Finances

Of all Spain's vast American possessions the Viceroyalty of Peru remitted the most substantial quantities of revenue until the 1670s, when it was overtaken by New Spain. The economy of Spanish Peru had grown rapidly after the conquest and by the seventeenth century had undergone considerable diversification. In order to tap the resources of the Peruvian provinces, the crown maintained a large staff of officials (*oficiales reales*) attached to the royal treasury (*hacienda real*). These officials were distributed in a series of treasury offices (*cajas reales*) located in the key economic centers of the realm. The crown maintained local offices in all major mining centers, ports, agricultural regions, and places of particular political or strategic importance. Royal officials in each of these treasuries had the responsibility of collecting and distributing the income according to the demands of the metropolitan government in Madrid.

Treasury offices in the major political and bureaucratic capitals, such as Lima, usually acted as clearing houses for funds sent from other subtreasuries (*cajas subordinadas*). Each of these subtreasuries, at regular intervals, sent its fiscal accounts and surplus income to the central, or matrix, office (*caja principal*, or *caja matríz*).[2] The matrix caja then used the money to pay the various expenses of viceregal administration. What remained was put on the ships of the royal armada and sent to Spain. After 1607 annual accounts from all the treasury offices were sent to the tribunal of accounts (*tribunal mayor de cuentas*) in Lima, the body responsible for auditing the final accounts of each caja and for sending a summary report of its findings to the Council of the Indies in Spain.

The principal, or matrix, caja for Peru and Upper Peru was in Lima. The provinces which composed Tierrafirme, Santa Fe, Quito, Chile, and the Río de la Plata were separate political and bureaucratic units within the viceregal treasury; they never remitted income to Lima.[3] Surplus income from the cajas of Potosí, Oruro, La Paz, San Antonio de Esquilache (Chucuito), Otoca, and Carangas in Upper Peru, along with revenue from Huánuco, Cuzco, Cailloma, New Potosí (Bombón), Trujillo, Castrovirreyna, Arequipa, Arica, Piura, and Loja continually flowed into the central treasury office in Lima.[4]

In keeping with the procedures of the royal treasury in the seventeenth century, royal officials in Lima kept detailed accounts of all income and expenditures for the office. Royal officials recorded all debits and credits in a common workbook (*libro común*), which they kept collectively.[5] In addition the officials maintained other, separate journals, recording the various daily transactions of the caja.[6] The accountants closed out all of the account books at the Lima office before the departure of the armada and sent copies of the final treasury accounts both to the tribunal of accounts and to Spain.

Royal officials in Lima recorded income from every individual tax in its own section (*ramo*) of the account, and entered each category of expenditure separately in its own particular divisions (see Appendix 1). As a whole, the taxes recorded in the Lima accounts may be divided into the following categories: levies on the Amerindian population, taxes on commerce and production, bureaucratic taxes, mining duties, charges on royal monopolies, clerical taxes, loans, and temporary or miscellaneous taxes.

In the caja of Lima, treasury officials collected four separate taxes from the Amerindian population in the district—*tercias de encomiendas, tributos vacos, lanzas,* and *tributos reales*. All four represented one single tax or tribute—a head tax imposed by the first Spanish conquerors on the Amerindian communities of the Viceroyalty of Peru. Royal officials in Lima were not responsible for collecting this tax. Instead a network of local magistrates (*corregidores de indios*), with the aid of the local priest and the Amerindian clan leaders (*kurakas*), actually gathered the money twice each year, at St.John's day (in June) and at Christmas.[7] The tax rates (*tasas*) for each village varied in these districts (repartimientos) according to the material wealth of the area and the population of the community. In any case all adult males between the ages of eighteen and fifty paid a specified share of the town's assessed rate.[8] After collecting the tribute, the corregidor deducted his own salary and expenses, as well as those of the priest (*sínodo*) and the kuraka. The rest was sent to the Lima treasury office.[9] If the corregidor collected the tribute from an area under the jurisdiction of an encomienda grant, the law required that one-third of the total be sent to Lima and entered in the ramo for tercias de encomienda.[10] Tribute collected from areas where the encomienda grants had fallen vacant reverted to the crown and was recorded as tributos vacos or *vacantes de encomiendas*. Between 1554 and 1619 the crown set aside tribute revenues from certain designated vacant encomiendas to pay the salaries of the viceregal guard (*guarda de lanzas y arcabuces*). This money was entered in the ramo of *lanzas* until 1619, when the guardsmen, whose positions were largely honorific, agreed to perform their duties without pay. These tribute rents then reverted to the crown. Income from regions under the direct jurisdiction of the treasury appeared in the accounts as tributos reales. The exact amount of money remitted to Lima from tributos vacos and tributos reales was not fixed by law, but treasury officials usually expected to receive between one-third and one-fifth of the total amounts collected in the repartimientos.

The major taxes on production in the Lima treasury office were the *novenos*, the *composiciones de pulperías*, and the *alcabala*. Novenos were that portion of the ecclesiastical tithe going to the crown.[11] In 1501 Pope Alexander VI gave the Spanish crown the right to collect the tithe, a 10 percent tax on virtually all agricultural, livestock, and dairy products in the Indies.[12] Composiciones de pulperías, established in 1623, was a levy of between thirty and forty pesos each year on all new pulperías—shops selling both wine and provisions. The law limited the number of such shops after 1623, and anyone wanting to own and operate a new store had first to pay this special licensing fee.[13] The alcabala, imposed in 1591, was a sales tax of 2 percent on most salable goods collected at the first and each subsequent sale of the merchandise.[14] Amerindians and the clergy were exempted by law from paying the tax, as long as they did not engage in large-scale merchant enterprises.[15] A host of articles were also exempt from the alcabala, including grain, corn, bread, horses, books, bullion, and all inherited goods.[16]

The crown established commercial taxes very early in the Lima district. The *almojarifazgo,* an import-export duty, was first collected in 1567. Goods from Castile paid 5 percent of their market value upon arrival in Callao.[17] Materials from within the viceroyalty or from any other Spanish possession licensed to trade with Peru likewise were subject to a 5 percent duty after entering the port city.[18] Unlike Castilian merchandise, goods sent from elsewhere in the Indies were charged another 2½ percent of their market value when they left the port for reexport to another colonial city.[19] Goods passing from Callao to another region with higher prices than those charged in Lima for the merchandise also paid an additional entry tax, at the point of sale, of 5 percent of this price differential for the almojarifazgo.[20] Customarily, the masters of the entering ships paid the almojarifazgo in cash to the customs inspector at the port. In addition to these import-export duties, the *avería* was charged at Callao after 1589.[21] The crown used the proceeds from this tax, calculated at 1 percent of the total value of the goods carried in the armada, to pay for the maintenance of the armada.[22] Customs inspectors at Callao also collected the avería.

The last levy on both commerce and production in the Lima district, the union of arms, appeared in 1638. It consisted of a tax of one *real* per bottle of Peruvian wine imported into Lima, and surcharges of 1 percent on the avería and 2 percent on the alcabala.[23] The entire tax package was imposed as part of the conde duque de Olivares's plan to have every area of the empire contribute to the defense of Spain.

Treasury officials in Lima usually leased the right to collect levies on commerce and production. In some cases prominent citizens contracted to administer the levies, but most of the contracts (*asientos*) went to private or public organizations, such as the local cabildo or the consulado. As early as 1649 the cabildo of Lima held the contract to collect the tax on pulperías, while the consulado held the asiento to collect the alcabala, the union of arms, and the port taxes for most of the seventeenth century. In the smaller cities in the district, such as Pisco or Arnedo, these taxes were usually administered by the local cabildo or a prominent citizen. In all cases the terms of the contract varied with the economic status of the region. Such tax farming was very common in Europe and other parts of the empire, and it proved a convenient way to avoid the difficulties of administering the taxes with the small staff of the treasury offices. In addition the asientos could be quite profitable to tax-farmers and acted as a form of subsidy from the treasury to prominent local groups, such as the consulado.

The taxing of bureaucratic officeholders was another integral part of the fiscal structure of the Lima treasury. The practice of selling public offices in the Spanish Indies began in the 1550s, and by the seventeenth century the crown commonly sold minor posts such as those of scribes, notaries, and even municipal officers through the colonial treasuries. Debtors and minors could not purchase offices, and credit purchases were likewise forbidden.[24] All salable offices of this type (*oficios vendibles y renunciables*) could also be renounced, or passed on, to a chosen successor, provided the person could pay the treasury one-half of the market value of the office. If the office had been renounced once before, then only one-third of the value of the office had to be paid.[25] All sales had to be approved by the Council of the Indies in Spain within six years. Whether an office had been sold or granted on merit, however, after 1632 the crown required the holder to pay the *media anata,* a tax of one-half of one year's salary and one-third of any benefits related to holding the office. This money was due in two equal parts within the first two years of taking office and was often paid in installments.[26]

Mining production was also an important source of taxes. At most mines the *quinto*, or one-fifth of all the gold or silver mined, was paid to the crown. The crown also charged an additional tax of 1½ percent of the refined ore, called the *cobo*, for smelting costs.[27] In some marginal areas where the quality of the ore was low or transportation costs were unusually high, the main tax by the crown could be lowered to one-eighth or even one-tenth, as at the small mines at Bombón. The cobo was supposed to be charged in all areas. Miners had the responsibility of taking the metal to the nearest treasury office for smelting, registration, and taxing. Wherever possible the nearest treasury officials or the local corregidor saw that the miners complied with the law.[28]

For additional income the crown also established royal monopolies for the distribution and sale of certain commodities. In Peru monopolies were established for (*naipes*) playing cards in 1572, *solimán* (bichloride of mercury, used as an antiseptic and in some cosmetics) in 1616, *nieve* (snow) in 1634, and *papel sellado* (stamped paper) in 1638. Treasury officials in Lima did not administer these monopolies directly.[29] The exclusive right to sell playing cards or snow in the city was usually rented out to a prominent citizen. The collection of the tax on stamped paper, required for all legal letters and documents, was administered by a commissioner and a treasurer in each audiencia, who sent the proceeds to the nearest treasury office. Finally, the tax on solimán was administered by a professor of medicine at San Marcos University.[30]

The treasury employed four separate types of transactions for borrowing money. Loans (*emprestidos*) were collected from individuals or wealthy corporate groups, such as the consulado, at an established rate of interest and usually for a limited period of time.[31] Censos were another common form of borrowing. In these transactions the treasury received money, usually from the Indian community chests (cajas de communidad). A censo, however, was seldom repaid quickly. Instead the treasury office made regular interest payments to the creditor over an extended period of time.[32] Another form of borrowing, similar to a censo transaction, was the sale of annuities (*juros*). A juro was a contract whereby a person, corporate group, or institution advanced capital to the treasury in return for an annual pension, paid from certain specified government revenues. In the case of the Viceroyalty of Peru, juros were sold in 1608, 1639, 1640, and 1641, largely to clerical organizations.[33] Strictly speaking the final borrowing transaction utilized by the viceregal treasury, forced donations (donativos, or *servicios graciosos*), were not really loans. They were instead contributions forced from certain wealthy individuals or groups in Peru to support the immediate needs of the treasury.

In addition to loans another source of income in Lima were two clerical taxes, the *bulas de la santa cruzada* and the mesada. The cruzada was a yearly sale of papal indulgences, begun in 1573. The pope originally granted the crown the right to sell indulgences in the Indies to aid in propagating the faith among the Amerindians, but by the seventeenth century officials in the viceroyalty viewed it as merely another source of public funds. A committee composed of both clerical and lay officials called the tribunal of the holy crusade (tribunal de la santa cruzada) administered the sales in the audiencia district of Lima for the treasury. The committee consisted of a commissioner general (*comisario general*) appointed in Madrid, an *oidor* and *fiscal* of the audiencia, a treasurer, a comptroller, an *alguacil*, a scribe, a solicitor, and a porter. It met three times each week.[34] The committee coordinated the activities of a series of subdelegates (*subdelegados*) and treasurers sent out once each year to sell the indulgences.[35] The crown required each citizen of means to buy an indulgence, but the price varied according to the type of indulgence granted and the wealth of the purchaser. The subdelegates sent the funds to the nearest treasury office, which forwarded the money to Lima.[36] The second clerical tax, the mesada, was easier to administer. After 1629 the treasury simply compelled each new clerical appointee to pay one month's salary directly to the nearest caja.[37]

Several taxes collected in Lima fit into no single category. *Venta y composición de tierras*, for example, was a tax collected from the sale of all land and land titles issued in the viceroyalty. Although land grants could be made by the viceroy, the provincial governor, or the local cabildo, the legal title for these grants was taxed by the government and the proceeds sent to the nearest treasury office. Other miscellaneous taxes included *comisos* (confiscated contraband goods), *alcances de cuentas* (collected debts or back taxes), *extraordinarios* (extraordinary income that fell into no single category), *situado de Chile* (usually payments from men buying deferments from military service in Chile), and *multas* (fines). The final miscellaneous entry, *depósitos* (deposits), was used to hold intestate funds or goods in escrow until they could be properly classified and disposed.

Income of the Lima Treasury

The sum of all these taxes collected in the Lima district and the funds remitted from the subtreasuries (*venido de fuera*) comprised the total income flowing into the principal treasury caja each year. Since these funds supplied the operating money to the central government in Lima, the fiscal accounts of this central treasury office provide the most precise picture of the yearly financial position of the viceregal government. This yearly income recorded at the Lima caja was plotted for the century, in order to examine the general trends for the viceroyalty (see graph).[38] These years may be divided roughly into three separate time periods. During the first period, from 1600 until 1621, income levels remained stable, dropping off only slightly in the last two years. By contrast the years from 1622 until 1660 were a time of expansion and contraction, as income rose unevenly from approximately three million pesos to heights of over four million pesos and then fell to just over three million again. Income levels in the first half of the century experienced relatively modest cyclical fluctuations: a stable period until 1620, a short recession in the 1620s, recovery until 1636, decline lasting until 1638, sustained growth to 1643, contraction until 1647, and a fitful recovery until the 1660s. By the third period, however, beginning around 1660, a serious downward trend started, lasting until the end of the century. This uneven decline in royal revenues became progressively more serious as income levels in Lima dipped to barely two million pesos, the lowest

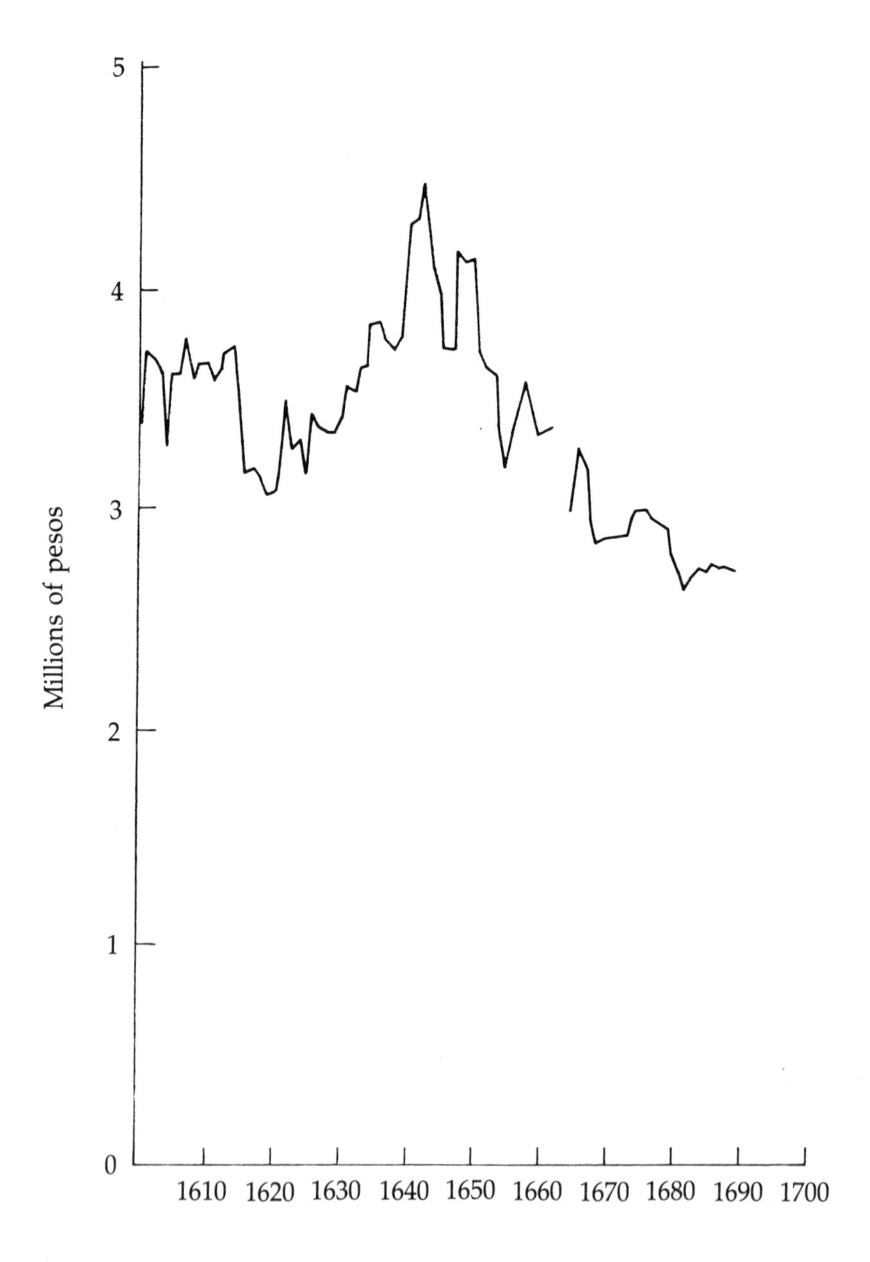

Graph of Three-Year Moving Average of Total Income Recorded in Lima Treasury, 1607–90 (in pesos de ocho reales)

recorded levels since the silver-mining boom began in the sixteenth century. Indeed the overall decline in royal income may be characterized as a fiscal crisis of major proportions.

In years of both prosperity and crisis during the seventeenth century, the most important components of the total income in the Lima treasury were taxes on commerce and production, borrowing, and remissions from the subtreasuries. As can be seen in table 3, these three major tax categories alone generated nearly 80 percent of the total income entering the royal treasury in Lima.

The most important single source of revenue for the Lima office was remissions from the other cajas. The Lima office was able to obtain 64 percent of its total income from such remissions from these outlying subtreasuries of Peru and Upper Peru, testimony to the importance of economic regions outside of the capital. Clearly Lima was essentially a bureaucratic and trade center, receiving and later distributing most of its funds from other revenue-producing centers of the viceroyalty. In spite of this reliance on the subtreasuries, however, the Lima district still emerged as a major source of tax revenue in its own right. From 1607 to 1690 the average yearly income of the Lima office, excluding remissions from other cajas was over one million pesos. The central treasury of Lima siphoned off the largest share of its tax receipts from other offices, but it was still an important generator of raw income in the Viceroyalty of Peru.

The largest percentage of the total income generated in the Lima district itself derived from taxes on commerce and production and from borrowing. The trade and productive centers supplying the populous viceregal capital were well developed, and taxes on their activities naturally produced significant amounts of revenue. This was particularly true of the alcabala, almojarifazgo, and the union of arms, which together provided over 18,600,000 pesos during the period. Loans, forced donations, and juros also supplied nearly 7 percent of the total income in Lima and netted over 19,000,000 pesos. The ability of the treasury office to draw large amounts of money at short notice through such borrowing practices provided needed financial relief in meeting immediate problems.

Table 3. Royal Income by Type of Tax, Caja of Lima, 1607–90 (in pesos de ocho reales)

Category and Type of Tax	Amount Collected	Percent
I. Commerce and production	23,731,881	8.4
Estanco de sal	17,677	
Alcabala*	8,233,651	
Almojarifazgo	7,194,500	
Avería	3,091,109	
Novenos	1,726,423	
Pulperías	288,233	
Unión de armas	3,180,296	
II. Indian Tribute	1,721,810	.6
Tercias de encomiendas	380,068	
Tributos	903,569	
Lanzas	438,172	
III. Bureaucratic	6,538,560	2.4
Media anata	2,873,294	
Oficios	3,605,003	
Real del ducado	31,599	
Sala de armas	2,648	
Salarios	26,015	
IV. Mining	764,516	.3
V. Royal Monopolies	1,745,462	.6
Naipes	914,936	
Nieve	58,827	
Papel sellado	768,504	
Solimán	3,195	
VI. Clerical	4,372,450	1.6
Cruzada	3,717,821	
Espolios	64,042	
Mesada	368,080	
Vacantes de obispados	222,505	
VII. Loans and Forced Contributions	19,338,203	6.9
Donativos	1,880,950	
Préstamos	15,877,032	
Juros	1,580,221	

Table 3. (continued)

Category and Type of Tax	Amount Collected	Percent
VIII. Miscellaneous	43,174,234	15.8
Alcances	2,986,271	
Comisos	250,525	
Estranjeros	8,263	
Tierras	912,344	
Multas	186,627	
Depósitos	2,646,548	
Extraordinarios	23,722,062	
Limosnas	4,715	
Situaciones	422,531	
Situado de Chile	121,158	
Visitas	32,429	
Trueques de barras	11,880,757	
IX. Venido de Fuera	109,955,270	64.0

*After 1672 the alcabala and the unión de armas were recorded as one ramo in the Lima accounts.

Neither mining taxes nor tribute were important sources of funds in Lima. Taken together they do not even comprise 1 percent of the caja's income. This stands in marked contrast to the situation in a major mining region like Potosí, where levies on mining production constituted nearly 60 percent of the local treasury office's yearly receipts.[39] In spite of its importance in other areas of the viceroyalty, mining obviously was not a major economic sector within the jurisdiction of the Lima office. Likewise tribute yielded an average of only 20,500 pesos each year to the Lima treasury, or just over 1/2 percent of the total income. Once again this differs considerably from amounts raised in highland treasuries, where the Amerindian population remained dense. Sketchy evidence from the Cuzco office, for example, indicates that tribute paid by Amerindians produced nearly 45,000 thousand pesos each year.[40] In addition, Potosí, with its large pool of mita and minga laborers, sent approximately 44,000 pesos each year to its local treasury office in tribute.[41] The catastrophic decline in the central-coast Amerindian population in the sixteenth century is clearly evidenced by the meager tribute returns collected in the district of Lima.[42]

Clerical taxes and charges on royal monopolies made important, but not overwhelming, contributions to the income of the royal treasury in Lima. Nearly 4,400,000 pesos flowed into the office from the sale of indulgences, the mesada, *espolios,* (goods belonging to recently deceased clergyman) and vacant archbishoprics (*vacantes de obispados*).[43] Among the royal monopolies, the sale and distribution of playing cards was the most important revenue producer, followed closely by stamped paper. The sale of snow and solimán produced insignificant sums.

The remaining 15 percent of the Lima treasury's income derived from miscellaneous impositions. The sale of land and land titles produced over 900,000 pesos. The most significant contribution in this tax category, however, was made by extraordinary revenues. Nearly 24,000,000 pesos accrued to the treasury from receipts of this ramo between 1607 and 1690.[44]

The roots of the financial problems faced by the Lima treasury office during the seventeenth century may be determined by breaking down the tax revenues that flowed into the caja by decade, as in table 4. Despite the income collected by the crown each decade in the district of Lima and the subtreasuries, inspection of table 4 indicates that the relative importance of the various taxes in making up the total income in Lima changed, sometimes significantly, over time. Levies on the clergy, royal monopolies, Amerindians, miners, and commerce and production remained relatively stable sources of revenues. Some of the most important revenue sources, however, such as loans, miscellaneous income, and remissions from other treasury offices varied considerably. In addition these lucrative sources of revenue showed the sharpest declines after 1660.

Characteristically taxes on royal monopolies and levies on commerce and production were among the most consistent sources of revenue over time in the Lima district. Since all of these levies were tax farmed for an established yearly price,

Table 4. Income and the Percentage of Total Income by Decade from the Major Tax Categories in the Caja of Lima, 1607–90 (in pesos de ocho reales)*

	1607–10	1611–20	1621–30	1631–40	1641–50	1651–60	1661–70	1671–80	1681–90
Commerce and Production	775,789 (4.7%)	1,685,187 (5%)	2,193,570 (6.6%)	2,460,007 (6.7%)	3,061,412 (8.4%)	3,086,369 (8.4%)	1,832,976 (9.2%)	5,292,444 (15%)	3,344,124 (13.4%)
Indian Tribute	68,128 (.4%)	166,876 (.5%)	219,471 (.7%)	290,172 (.8%)	263,748 (.7%)	136,342 (.4%)	73,318 (.3%)	262,723 (.8%)	241,029 (.9%)
Bureaucratic	141,224 (.9%)	356,454 (1%)	399,851 (1.2%)	1,117,912 (3%)	1,033,453 (2.9%)	1,376,611 (3.8%)	582,707 (3%)	882,855 (2.5%)	647,488 (2.6%)
Mining	19,757 (.1%)	66,554 (.2%)	211,923 (.6%)	88,376 (.2%)	165,016 (.5%)	136,931 (.4%)	8,741 (.04%)	33,813 (.1%)	33,402 (.1%)
Monopolies	81,066 (.5%)	157,268 (.5%)	176,213 (.5%)	192,929 (.5%)	300,875 (.9%)	301,663 (.8%)	173,645 (.8%)	246,599 (.7%)	115,203 (.5%)
Clerical	241,245 (1.5%)	532,921 (1.6%)	545,091 (1.6%)	500,870 (1.4%)	448,089 (1.3%)	661,748 (1.8%)	327,087 (1.6%)	727,737 (2%)	387,658 (1.6%)
Loans	984,601 (6%)	2,326,695 (7%)	2,836,312 (8.6%)	2,217,506 (6%)	3,288,844 (9%)	4,845,249 (13%)	600,088 (3.3%)	1,378,824 (4%)	800,082 (3.2%)
Misc.	2,216,633 (13.5%)	4,868,552 (14%)	3,620,959 (11%)	2,252,248 (6%)	4,876,657 (14%)	4,208,723 (11%)	2,570,787 (12.8%)	8,104,372 (22.5%)	5,767,799 (23%)
Remissions	11,903,495 (72.4%)	24,215,773 (71%)	23,195,602 (70%)	28,981,745 (76%)	22,371,811 (63%)	23,156,143 (61%)	13,766,227 (68.8%)	18,962,544 (53%)	13,658,918 (55%)

*Accounts for the years 1662–64 are missing from the AGI (Seville) and the AGN (Lima)

the funds they sent to Lima remained stable. Tax-farming contracts were never granted for a permanent or even an indefinite period of time, and most lasted only for from three to five years. Contracts were also renewable. The consulado of Lima, for example, held the asiento for the avería, alcabala, almojarifazgo, and later the union of arms at Lima and Callao, for most of the century, through a series of such short-term contracts.[45] Whenever these tax-farming asientos were renewed, the treasury was free to demand better terms for the next contract, and the consulado could ask for a cheaper price for the privilege. The conde de Santisteban, viceroy from 1661 to 1666, boasted to the crown that when the consulado's contract expired in 1664, he was able to renegotiate the asientos for the avería at 100,000 pesos in years that the armada sailed, and annual rates for the almojarifazgo and the union of arms at 113,000 pesos and the alcabala at 139,500 pesos.[46] Altogether, the amounts paid were significantly higher than the previous contracts.

As can be seen from table 4, the rising contribution of these taxes to the total income in the Lima treasury reflects the efforts of administrators to negotiate higher rates. In spite of such increases in the value of the asientos, however, the treasury undoubtedly lost some money by making contracts with the consulado to collect these levies on commerce. In the armada of 1662, for example, the avería netted 154,333 pesos for the consulado, yet the guild sent less than 80,000 pesos that year to the Lima treasury. Such tax-farming contracts also curtailed the flexibility of the government in raising taxes in the short run to meet pressing financial emergencies. The ability of treasury officials to raise the tax rates depended variously on their political power at the moment the contract negotiations took place, local economic trends, and the willingness of local individuals or groups to invest in the asientos. Despite these shortcomings the advantages of a secure income from the tax farmers and the inconveniences of administering the taxes with the small staff of the Lima caja led the crown to continue the practice throughout the seventeenth century.

Clerical and bureaucratic taxes remained another consistent source of royal revenue. The levies on the clergy yielded between 1.3 percent and 2 percent of the total revenue in the office.[47] Likewise bureaucratic taxes fluctuated between slightly under 1 percent and 3.8 percent of the total. The continual turnover in personnel in the bureaucratic capital of Spanish South America kept this tax category a consistent but modest source of income.

Two other steady contributors to the Lima treasury were mining taxes and tribute. Since neither category generated significant sums, however, they had little impact on the decline in treasury receipts after 1660.

The fluctuations in the amounts of capital received from loans, donativos, censos, and juros did have a serious long-term impact on the structure of royal finance in the district of Lima. This category varied from a low of 3.3 percent in the 1660s to a high of 13 percent in the previous decade. In the five year span between 1643 and 1649, the treasury managed to scrape together 22 percent of its total income from these sources.[48] Yearly fluctuations were extreme. Peaks of over 600,000 pesos in 1642 and 1644, for example, were followed by declines to under 100,000 pesos by 1649.[49] Apparently the treasury could extract large amounts of money in loans, donations, censos, and juros, but not on a consistent, year-to-year basis. This was particularly true after 1660, when loans never supplied more than 4 percent of the treasury's total income. Like its counterparts in Spain, the Lima treasury office came to depend heavily on borrowing, a dangerously inconsistent source of revenue.

In addition to their inconsistency, measures like borrowing and juro sales encumbered the treasury with debts and made the government increasingly dependent on the goodwill of local elites to remain solvent. Public borrowing usually went to fund immediate and pressing financial needs, such as sending money to Spain, paying the salaries of public officials, sending subsidies to the frontier provinces, and meeting the military emergencies that arose from time to time, such as the English invasion of Panama in 1670. As a result the failure to secure such funds could put the government in a very difficult short-run position. As reward for their services, the lenders demanded and most often received prompt repayment of the loans and steady interest payments on their juros. They also gained considerable political and financial leverage within the government.[50] In most cases the lenders received offices, an appointment to one of the knightly orders, a pension, or occasionally even direct government assistance in the form of tax abatements or government contracts.

From the 1620s, for example, the crown routinely received large loans at no interest from two prominent merchant-bankers, Juan de la Cueva and Bernardo de Villegas. In 1620 alone these two men provided a total of 280,000 pesos to meet the pressing needs of the royal treasury.[51] Not surprisingly Villegas and de la Cueva gained considerable favor at the viceregal court. Juan de la Cueva, in particular, took large deposits of government silver into his bank; in his famous bankruptcy of 1635, the consulado recorded claims of 1,068,248 pesos against his bank, including funds deposited from the treasuries of Potosí, Oruro, Cuzco, and Huancavelica. The bankruptcy of Juan de la Cueva illustrates the dangers of relying too heavily on a few credit sources, and after 1635 the Lima accounts reveal that the crown received broader support in negotiating loans. Although the treasury never again became as dependent on a single lender, it still depended heavily on loans, which too often proved unreliable and further tied the government to the interests of local elites. This was particularly true in the 1640s, when the Lima treasury relied most heavily on borrowing and juros, rather than on direct taxation, to forestall the erosion of the tax base of the government as remissions from the mining regions declined. The ultimate failure of this policy became all too apparent by the 1660s, with the onset of the fiscal crisis.

Although miscellaneous income apparently proved a more stable source of funds than loans over the long run, it too was unpredictable on a yearly basis. For much of the century these ramos regularly returned between 11 percent and 14 percent of the treasury's income. The only exception to this trend was during the 1630s, when receipts fell to 2,252,248 pesos, or only 6 percent of the total income. Despite this apparent stability, extraordinary income, which formed the largest portion of the miscellaneous category, showed more instability on a yearly basis. This ramo fluctuated from a low of under 100,000 pesos in 1640 to a high of 500,000 pesos ten years later.[52] As a consequence over long periods of time extraordinary income did not change greatly; but from year to year it could fluctuate considerably.

The contributions of the treasury offices outside of the Lima district also varied greatly over time. According to table 4, in the period from 1607 to 1650, remissions from the interior accounted for over 70 percent of the total income in Lima. In the second half of the century, however, that figure fell to between 53 and 68 percent. An examination of the remissions from each of the subtreasuries presented in table 5 indicates that the largest contributor of surplus income, Potosí, also became increasingly erratic in its shipments from 1660. In addition fluctuations of 200,000 pesos from one year to the next were commonplace. Apparently royal officials in Lima could never predict with precision how much Potosí and the other subtreasuries would send them in any given year.

Table 5 also illustrates that the serious declines in remissions to Lima were the principal cause for the shortage in royal funds after 1660. Remissions fell from a high of 28,000,000 pesos in the 1630s to under 13,700,000 pesos in the 1680s. Such disastrous declines were most severe in the three largest contributors of surplus income, Potosí, Oruro, and La Paz.[53] As early as the administration of the conde de Chinchón (1629–39) the decline of the key mining districts of Potosí and Oruro did not pass unnoticed. Explanations such as the shortage of Amerindian laborers, mercury, and high-grade ore, in addition to water in the mineshafts, and the increasing indebtedness of the miners, were all advanced to explain the general decline of the silver-mining industry. By 1662 this decline had become acute. A report from the viceroy, the conde de Santisteban, indicated that the surplus income from mining taxes had fallen from 6,186,043 pesos in the period from 1648 to 1654 to only 4,691,645 pesos in the years from 1654 to 1661.[54]

The secondary cajas of Bombón, Castrovirreyna, Trujillo, Arica, Pasco, Piura, and Arequipa also registered declines as the century progressed. Only cajas in the newer mining regions,

Table 5. Remissions from the Subordinate Cajas to Lima Each Decade (in pesos de ocho reales)*

Caja	1607–10	1611–20	1621–30	1631–40	1641–50	1651–60	1661–70	1671–80	1681–90	Totals
Potosí	9,820,148	17,595,547	12,416,212	17,255,323	12,754,553	14,643,632	7,477,579	10,583,003	7,409,272	109,955,270
Oruro	1,360,634	4,393,706	4,341,929	4,102,599	3,634,287	1,494,150	507,923	1,147,437	772,798	21,755,465
La Paz	276,214	450,365	578,708	1,101,938	1,450,300	935,415	394,415	1,033,661	604,796	6,825,700
Castrovirreyna	140,365	688,493	688,988	481,182	286,456	227,027		78,160		2,590,674
Arequipa	103,929	217,404	401,381	743,244	567,079	617,716	164,177	567,731	357,549	3,740,313
Trujillo	59,584	24,015	110,150	270,707	322,721	345,168	114,510	265,634	151,892	1,664,384
Arica	36,735	262,549	252,196	193,840	173,193	134,677	17,609	36,464		1,107,726
Cuzco	105,884	591,064	1,252,722	1,890,842	1,576,586	1,417,922	834,866	1,526,268	954,802	10,150,979
Huánuco and Pasco		1,820	31,379	56,412	41,058	64,157	22,157	138,879	76,609	433,472
Piura			24,989	30,322	15,182	3,975	9,528	13,988	49,519	147,513
Bombón			198,019	407,412	301,571	226,209	43,505	111,699	108,399	1,396,817
Cailloma				2,447,859	1,508,360	1,546,096	690,516	1,261,473	949,300	8,403,603
San Antonio de Esquilache						978,958	3,543,292	1,605,215	1,774,419	7,901,885
Carrangas						521,412	172,626	338,534	261,898	1,294,472
Otoca								357,066	216,660	573,726
TOTALS	11,903,495	24,215,773	23,195,602	28,981,745	22,371,811	23,156,143	13,766,227	18,962,544	13,658,918	180,212,258

*Accounts for the years 1662–64 are missing from the AGI (Seville) and the AGN (Lima)

such as San Antonio de Esquilache, contradict this downward trend. By the end of the century, however, these regions had fallen off considerably in their yearly remissions to Lima. As a result even silver from the new mining provinces could not, in the long run, compensate for the decline in shipments from the other cajas, particularly those of Potosí and Oruro. In large part this decline in remissions was linked to the fall in silver-mining output, but at least some of the evidence points to other factors. Data on mining taxes at Potosí, for example, indicates that these receipts from the quinto fell from 4,475,142 marks of silver in the 1650s to 3,569,098 marks in the next decade, a drop of 20 percent.[55] During this same time period, remissions from the caja of Potosí to Lima fell from 14,643,632 pesos to 7,477,579 pesos, or a drop of 49 percent.[56] Obviously the treasury in Potosí was withholding a larger share of the revenues taken from mining and spending it within the district.

Much more data on the relationship between the total income from the subtreasuries and their remissions to Lima must be compiled before any firm conclusions can be reached, but the data from Potosí suggest that the subtreasuries abetted the fiscal crisis in Lima by sending less each year to the colonial metropolis. If such a condition were indeed widespread, it would be strong evidence that Lima's control over the interior had also begun to erode by the 1660s. In any case it is clear that from the 1660s the central treasury in Lima received a steadily diminishing flow of money from the subtreasuries, which seriously undercut the solvency of the viceregal government.

With the gradual decline of remissions from the subtreasuries, royal officials in Lima needed other sources of revenue to maintain total income levels. By the 1660s many of these had already been depleted. From 1639 to 1648 the viceroy, the marqués de Mancera, and the treasury had supervised the collection of 3,221,561 pesos from temporary sources such as land sales, loans, and the sale of new public offices.[57] Similar sources of income, bolstered heavily by fines levied from an inspection tour at the mint at Potosí, yielded the viceroy's successor, the conde de Salvatierra, only 1,272,979 pesos from 1648 to 1654.[58] By the viceregency of the conde de Alba de Liste (1654–60), revenues from these same sources had shrunk to only 767,468 pesos.[59] Along with the decline in remissions from the subtreasuries, the drop in these temporary levies were chiefly responsible for the onset of the fiscal crisis. Clearly the treasury's ability to draw income from the traditional tax structure slowly declined during the second half of the century. Lucrative new levies on commerce, agriculture, industry, or the church might have forestalled the crisis, but they were never enacted. The result was a serious fiscal crisis for the treasury system in Lima.

Expenditures of the Lima Treasury

Throughout the seventeenth century the expenditures of the Lima treasury kept pace with total income. Each year the office spent virtually all of its funds meeting the varied expenses of the government. The caja of Lima was responsible for supporting the military and bureaucratic costs of the entire viceroyalty as well as its own administrative costs. Any income remaining after expenses had to be shipped to Spain, since the crown continually pressed treasury officials in Lima to minimize all local expenses and maximize the yearly remissions to the metropolis. During periods of expansion in the treasury's income, such as the period from 1622 until 1660, the government had more revenue to dispense. After the 1660s, however, royal officials had to make hard decisions about just where to cut costs.

According to the data presented in table 6, between 1607 and 1690 remissions to Spain formed the largest single component of the treasury's expenditures, at 32 percent of the total. Defense expenditures for the maintenance of fortifications, the South-Sea Armada, and subsidies to the shipyards at Guayaquil or frontier regions like Chile were the second largest outlay, at 28 percent. The repayment of loans, payments to the mercury miners at Huancavelica, administrative expenses such as salaries, and miscellaneous costs all varied between 8.5 percent and 12.5 percent of the total expenses. With such heavy yearly obligations, the Lima treasury could never generate any surplus income, despite the large amounts of revenue produced within

Table 6. Royal Expenditures in the Caja of Lima, 1607–90 (in pesos de ocho reales)

Category and Type of Expenditure	Amount	Percent
I. Remissions to Spain	82,654,673	32
II. Defense	73,192,141	28
Situado de Guayaquil	885,742	
Armada	1,643,671	
Guerra	40,391,173	
Situado de Chile	23,088,430	
Situado de Panama	3,746,486	
Situado de Valdivia	3,436,638	
III. Huancavelica	24,401,889	9.4
IV. Loan Payments	22,551,139	8.6
Juros	4,109,018	
Préstamos	18,442,120	
V. Administration	25,124,573	10.0
Sal	2,341	
Alcances	365,619	
Avería	32,572	
Cruzada	1,376,955	
Comisos	297,110	
Donativos	54,633	
Pulperías	63,050	
Tierras	52,945	
Condenaciones	23,559	
Espolios	85,204	
Visitas	5,075	
Lanzas	165,951	
Limosnas	434,234	
Media anata & mesada	331,153	
Novenos	1,280,144	
Oficios	2,249,410	
Salarios	13,586,039	
Situaciones & mercedes	3,621,701	
Tributos	521,286	
Unión de armas	100,000	
Vacantes de obispados	475,531	
VI. Miscellaneous	32,580,887	12.5
Depósitos	3,394,921	
Extraordinarios	29,232,300	

the district each year. Without the inflow of money remitted from the subtreasuries of Peru and Upper Peru, Lima would have faced hopeless yearly deficits. When these remissions of silver declined, and the total income of the office began to drop after 1660, treasury officers in the capital faced the difficult choice of cutting needed local expenditures or curtailing remissions to Seville, at precisely the time when the crown needed funds to shore up its sagging fortunes in Europe.

Despite repeated demands by the Madrid government for larger shipments of silver from Peru, the figures presented in table 7 indicate that remissions to the metropolis suffered more serious declines during the century than any other expenditure. During the reign of King Philip IV, when Spain was most in need of funds to support its war effort in Europe, the royal treasury was most successful in responding to the metropolitan demands for funds. Between 1630 and 1650, for example, the Lima treasury sent nearly 30,000,000 pesos to Seville. Still these sums were considerably lower than the goals set by the crown, which felt that the treasury should send more than just 40 percent or 45 percent of its total income to Spain, as Lima did during those two decades. When income levels dropped by the 1660s, however, authorities in Lima became ever bolder in ignoring metropolitan demands, by withholding larger sums from Spain to meet local colonial expenses. While the marqués de Mancera, viceroy from 1639 to 1648, sent an average of 1,677,386 pesos each year to Madrid, less than twenty years later the conde de Santisteban, viceroy from 1661 to 1666, managed to put a yearly average of only 237,717 pesos on the armada for Spain. In addition, between the 1650s and the 1660s, remissions to Spain fell from 33 percent of the treasury's total income to only 14.9 percent. By the last decade of the period, that figure had shrunk to only 5 percent of the total receipts of the Lima office. Clearly the king's own ministers were sacrificing the pressing needs of the metropolis in order to meet local expenses.

While remissions to Spain declined during the seventeenth century, expenditures for viceregal defense proceeded to rise unevenly. The intrusion of Dutch and English traders and buc-

Table 7. Major Expenditures and the Percent of Total Expenditures by Decade, Caja of Lima, 1607–90 (in pesos de ocho reales)*

	1607–10	1611–20	1621–30	1631–40	1641–50	1651–60	1661–70	1671–80	1681–90
Remissions to Spain	8,075,373 (51%)	11,919,710 (35%)	12,188,977 (37%)	14,838,491 (45%)	14,268,321 (42%)	11,761,106 (33%)	3,027,008 (14.9%)	5,303,792 (16.9%)	1,271,893 (5%)
Defense	2,620,180 (16.5%)	8,185,297 (24%)	10,179,033 (31%)	7,153,033 (22%)	8,882,599 (26%)	9,057,803 (25%)	7,001,459 (34.5%)	9,827,566 (32.5%)	10,346,848 (43%)
Huancavelica	1,216,156 (7.6%)	3,922,254 (11.6%)	2,369,799 (7%)	3,086,663 (9.4%)	2,957,510 (9%)	3,151,577 (9%)	977,511 (4.8%)	3,726,994 (11.9%)	2,993,420 (12.4%)
Loans	869,505 (5.5%)	2,377,422 (7%)	4,844,620 (15%)	2,192,818 (6.6%)	2,679,590 (8%)	4,744,366 (13%)	1,282,656 (6%)	2,210,797 (7%)	1,309,361 (5.4%)
Administrative	1,138,203 (7.2%)	3,438,037 (10%)	2,733,227 (8%)	6,552,959 (10.8%)	2,444,802 (7%)	3,289,219 (9%)	2,390,787 (11.8%)	4,305,320 (13.7%)	2,404,672 (10%)
Miscellaneous	2,022,324 (12.7%)	3,400,068 (10%)	749,699 (2%)	2,070,166 (6.3%)	2,487,858 (7%)	3,883,397 (11%)	5,645,840 (27.8%)	5,988,776 (19%)	5,752,158 (24%)

*Accounts for the years 1662–64 are missing from the AGI (Seville) and the AGN (Lima)

caneers forced officials in Lima to expend large sums each year to protect the realm. As can be seen from table 7, defense spending rose from 7,000,000 or 8,000,000 pesos each decade early in the century to over 10,000,000 pesos by the 1680s. In addition, as royal income declined from the 1660s, treasury officials in Lima continued to spend money lavishly on defense. By the 1680s these outlays had reached a high of 43 percent of the total royal income. This ongoing commitment to achieve self-reliance in defense was the single most important cause for the dramatic decline in remissions to Spain, as funds previously sent to the crown were retained within the viceroyalty.

The largest share of the defense expenditures went to pay directly war-related bills, such as those for coastal fortifications, provisioning land forces, and the upkeep of the small Pacific fleet (Armada del Mar del Sur). From 1607 to 1690 these expenditures totaled 42,034,844 pesos or 57 percent of the total defense outlays for the period (see table 6). The most serious military threat to the viceroyalty early in the century came from the Dutch, as expeditions under Joris Speilbergen in 1615, Jacob L'Hermite in 1624, and Hendrick Brouwer in 1643 entered the Pacific.[60] Problems with the English came later in the period, culminating in 1670 with the attack on Panama by the pirate Henry Morgan and the appearance of an English fleet off the coast of Valdivia.[61] The obvious need to protect the extended South American coastline and to secure the sea-lanes for the silver fleets from Arica to Lima and Panama made such expenditures an urgent and costly necessity.

As the threat from foreign invaders increased during the century, the treasury had to finance an ever more costly effort to upgrade the viceregal fleet. Until 1615 the Pacific fleet consisted of only four modest warships.[62] The invasion of Speilbergen in that year, however, forced the viceroy, the marqués de Montesclaros, to divide this small fleet by sending two ships with the silver shipment and the remaining two smaller vessels to meet the Dutch invaders. When the Spaniards were vanquished in the ensuing sea battle off Cañete, only the vacillation of the Dutch commander saved the Peruvian coast from devastation.[63] As a result of this near disaster in 1615, the Lima treasury increased its defense spending to over 1,000,000 pesos annually, in order to enlarge the fleet to eight ships. These large expenditures brought censure from the crown by 1619, as officials in Madrid demanded that such funds be directed to the metropolis.[64] The defense of the sea-lanes still proved inadequate in 1624, when the Dutch fleet under L'Hermite nearly captured Callao and the silver shipment.[65]

In the 1630s the viceroy, the conde de Chinchón, decided to let the war fleet languish and relied instead on a less expensive policy of using galleys to protect the coastal waters.[66] Inspection of table 7 demonstrates that the viceroy was successful in curtailing costs to slightly over 7,000,000 pesos in the 1630s, but in the long run the galleys proved unreliable on the open sea and were less effective in meeting the defense needs of the realm. His successor, the marqués de Mancera, completely reversed this parsimonious program, embarking on an ambitious policy of upgrading the viceregal defenses. Mancera was a military man who had little faith in Chinchón's unseaworthy galleys. In addition he ruled during a period (1639 to 1648) when treasury receipts in Lima reached a peak for the century. Mancera used this additional capital to expand the fleet by adding larger vessels with over sixty guns.[67] He also worked to improve coastal defenses. The most important of these ventures was the construction of the wall and fortifications at Callao from 1640 to 1645, which probably cost over 1,500,000 pesos.[68] The administration of the marqués de Mancera began a trend toward rising defense expenditures in the viceroyalty that continued for the rest of the century.

Apart from providing for coastal defenses, the Lima treasury also sent large yearly subsidies to peripheral provinces of strategic importance. The largest of these subsidies (*situados*) from 1607 to 1690 was the more than 23,000,000 pesos sent to support the Spanish garrisons in Chile (see table 6). For this Chilean subsidy alone, outlays reached as high as 13 percent of the treasury's total expenditures in the period from 1658 to 1662, when the nearly perpetual war with the Araucanian Indians became more heated. In addition to these sums, from the 1650s the Lima treasury sent separate remittances to support the garrison town of Valdivia, on the frontier of southern Chile. Valdivia had always been a weak link in the viceregal defenses, subject not only to repeated Araucanian attacks, but also to raids from Dutch and English intruders. When the Dutch under Brouwer entered the Pacific in 1643, they landed at Valdivia in an unsuccessful attempt to join forces with the Araucanians and raze the Spanish outpost. After the local Spanish forces succeeded in forcing the Dutch to leave, officials in Lima were quick to recognize the need for supporting the garrison. They then began sending separate subsidies to the region, which totaled 3,500,000 pesos for the period from 1607 to 1690 (see table 6).

In addition to this support for Chile, the Lima treasury also sent similar subsidies in times of emergency to Panama. From the 1670s these funds were dispatched from Lima to expell the English pirate Henry Morgan and then to help rebuild and maintain the defenses of the region.[69] Subsidies also went to Guayaquil in the first half of the seventeenth century to pay for the purchase of vessels from the local shipyards outfitted for the Pacific fleet, as well as to shore up local defenses. Like Panama and Valdivia, Guayaquil and its lucrative shipyards proved an irresistible lure to foreign intruders, who attacked several times between 1624 and 1687.[70] One reason for Lima's failure to continue supporting Guayaquil after 1650 was that this responsibility was taken over by the port city's highland neighbor, Quito.[71] As a consequence, Guayaquil drifted away from its dependency on Lima, while Chile and Panama did not.

Subsidies to the outlying provinces served economic as well as military ends for the Lima government. Securing the trade routes to Panama, for example, served the interests of Lima merchants taking part in the Portobelo fairs. In addition the shipyards at Guayaquil provided merchant vessels as well as warships. Of course this gave both the merchant community and the treasury an equal stake in protecting the region. Finally the rich farmland in central Chile provided wheat for Lima, particularly after the earthquake of 1687. As these peripheral areas grew and developed economically, they played a larger role in the economic life of the viceroyalty. The subsidies protected the strategic interests of the viceroyalty and thus stimulated the development of these regions, which were also important to commercial interests in Lima. Yearly support from the Lima treasury was a form of economic aid from the colonial capital to the periphery that benefited both the outlying provinces and the merchant class in Lima, which needed secure trade routes and new markets for its own economic expansion.[72]

Despite this overall importance to the viceroyalty, defense expenditures undoubtedly produced a steady drain on the resources of the Lima treasury, particularly after the 1640s. As an examination of table 7 shows, most of this money came from funds that had been sent to the metropolis in earlier years, when a larger share of the treasury's income was retained in the colony to meet these expenses. The Madrid government sought to reverse this trend and alter the priorities of treasury officials in Lima, but it was unable to do so. At the same time the crown was also unable or unwilling to underwrite the cost of defending the viceroyalty itself. As long as the silver fleets sailed with regularity, Madrid ignored the threat of foreign invaders and the costly Chilean war. The result was to saddle its treasury office in Lima with the expensive task of providing for the defense of the viceroyalty.

Another costly responsibility of the Lima treasury was the yearly subsidy to the mercury mines at Huancavelica. Mercury was essential for silver refining, and the crown wanted to keep the mines at Huancavelica, the only major source of mercury in the Indies, operating at high levels of productivity. The treasury office in the region was established to check the operation of the mines, to keep the supply of quicksilver flowing to the silver mines, and to dispense the funds sent from Lima. This money was used to pay the Amerindian laborers, buy supplies for the mines, pay the bureaucrats, purchase mercury, and the transportation costs of moving the quicksilver to warehouses in the city of Chincha.

These treasury remittances to Huancavelica composed between 4.8 percent and 12.4 percent of the Lima treasury's budget from 1607 to 1690. The data in table 7 demonstrate the amount of money paid each year remained relatively uniform, aver-

Table 8. Percent of Total Expenditures of Lima Treasury from Emprestidos, Juros, and Censos, 1633–60

	1633–38	1638–43	1643–48	1648–53	1653–58	1658–62	1664–69*
Loans (total)	6	7	10	6	11	14	8
Juros y Censos	.5	.6	1.4	2	2.6	2.6	2.7
Emprestidos	5.5	6.4	8.6	4	8.4	11.4	5.3

*Complete accounts for the years 1662–64 are missing from the AGI (Seville) and the AGN (Lima).

aging from 240,000 pesos to 300,000 pesos. The vital importance of these mines is reflected in the steady and high levels of support provided by the Lima treasury.

Despite the support from Lima, reports from Huancavelica frequently complained of the inadequacy of the subsidy to meet the rising costs of mining. As the quality of the ore declined and production costs rose, the miners demanded larger subsidies. By the 1660s the Lima treasury was faced with the dismal prospect of either paying larger subsidies to keep the mines productive or having severe mercury shortages at the silver mines. Interestingly officials in Lima chose to continue support for Huancavelica at traditional levels, rather than increase it after the problems began at the mineheads. Production at the mercury mines did decline, and the silver industry, the crown's favored economic sector, suffered.

Rising defense costs and the burden of the subsidy to Huancavelica could not be funded entirely by withholding funds from Spain. As we have already seen in table 4, the government also relied heavily on borrowing and juro sales to maintain total income levels and meet expenses, particularly in the period from 1640 to 1660. This reliance on borrowing, however, further increased the treasury's yearly expenditures in the long run. Loans, after all, had to be repaid. Money expended on repaying loans more than doubled from 6 percent to 14 percent in the period from 1633 to 1669 (see table 8). Of particular interest is the rise in the treasury's debt to annuity holders from .5 percent to 3 percent of the total yearly expenditures.[73] Most purchasers were clerical organizations; unlike loans, which were repaid quickly at little or no interest, the debt to the church from annuities was a long-range commitment with interest payments extending over many years. This indebtedness never exceeded reasonable limits or threatened to bankrupt the government, as it did in Spain, but the rising debt did increase the treasury's dependence on local interest groups and undoubtedly gave lenders greater political leverage over this key institution of the viceregal government.[74]

The burdens imposed by paying the various administrative and miscellaneous costs of the Lima office fluctuated wildly from one year to the next. According to figures in table 7 administrative expenditures varied from approximately 2,400,000 pesos in the 1640s to over 4,300,000 pesos in the 1670s. Miscellaneous expenses, on the other hand, shifted from a low of 750,000 pesos in the 1620s to more than 5,750,000 pesos in the last decade of the period. This increase of 5,000,000 pesos marked a swing from only 2 percent of the total expenses of the Lima office to 24 percent of the yearly expenses in the later period.

Administrative payments, which consisted largely of bureaucratic salaries and supplies, varied most often as a result of the crown's policy of selling high government appointments in the viceroyalty. The Madrid government began selling posts on the tribunal of accounts and the treasury offices of the viceroyalty in 1633; in 1687 it even extended the practice to audiencia posts.[75] In times of acute financial distress the Madrid government also sold future appointments to these key agencies to individuals who then had to wait for an opening before assuming their duties. Since many of these future officeholders in Lima received a portion of their salary from the treasury until they took possession of their post, the financial burden of having five or six extra men on the payroll, each waiting to assume his duties, could be quite heavy. On the other hand once these men took office, the burden of the extra salaries could lighten, if the crown refrained from selling any further futures.

The wild fluctuations in miscellaneous payments are more

difficult to explain. These expenditures were commonly unexpected military costs, bureaucratic salaries or expenses, or even additional payments to Huancavelica or the Lima consulado. The exact cause for the variations in payments from this ramo differed each year.

Ironically the very fiscal bureaucracy established by Spain to oversee the extraction of wealth from the Indies became more costly to operate as the seventeenth century progressed. Most of the money to support the rising cost of operating the government and defending the realm came from loans and funds that had traditionally been earmarked for Spain. The caja of Lima remitted over 2,225,000 pesos to Spain in 1640, yet by 1659 less than one-third of that amount sailed with the treasury fleet from Callao. In precisely the period when the Spanish monarchy faced grave military threats in Germany, Flanders, and Italy, as well as the revolts of Catalonia and Portugal, remissions of silver from Peru began their inexorable decline. Demands from Madrid became more strident, yet contributions from Lima continued to diminish.

Conclusion

Treasury accounts from the Lima office reveal that the seventeenth century marked a watershed in the relationship between Spain and the Viceroyalty of Peru. Between 1607 and 1621 the gradual decline of the silver-mining industry and the erosion of the transatlantic trade led to a series of long-range financial difficulties in the colony. At the outset of the century, as much as 70 percent of the royal income came from provinces outside of Lima, particularly from the mining centers. In addition many of the port taxes and the sales tax collected in the capital were themselves supported by the trade in gold and silver that flowed into the capital each year from the highland mining zones. The declining productivity of these very mining areas, and in all likelihood, the retention of more money to meet local expenses in the subtreasuries, led to a fall in the yearly shipments of silver to Lima. This trend forced officials in Lima and Madrid to consider imposing other levies to expand the tax base of the viceroyalty and counterbalance the fall in tax remissions from the mining zones.

On the other hand viceregal elites had sound reasons for attempting to resist any new levies at a time of economic transition from mining and the Atlantic trade to other economic enterprises. As a result levies such as the union of arms and royal monopolies such as that on stamped paper, enacted between 1621 and 1660, failed to place the Lima treasury on a sound financial basis. Consequently treasury officers in Lima relied instead on less controversial measures to raise revenue, more acceptable to local taxpayers, such as borrowing, withholding funds normally sent to Spain, and the sale of juros, land titles, and public offices. Although these expedients allowed treasury officials to meet immediate fiscal needs until 1660, they never provided a consistent or permanent source of funds to counter the decline in mining taxes. In addition measures like juro sales and borrowing encumbered the treasury with debts and made officials more dependent on the goodwill of local elites to remain solvent.

As even these sources of funds became scarce by the 1660s, government income levels began to drop. Even after the decline began, however, treasury officials in Lima failed to cut expenditures or impose any permanent new levies on the clergy, landowners, merchants, or other elites. As a result the fiscal crisis in the viceroyalty deepened. The viceregal government slowly became poorer and imperial ties with Spain weakened. In essence treasury officers in Lima and elsewhere, entrusted with implementing royal financial directives and maintaining a steady flow of silver from the highland mines of Peru and Upper Peru to Seville, failed in their duties. This failure was not inevitable. The Viceroyalty of Peru suffered no prolonged economic depression during the century. Indeed the crisis of the seventeenth century in Spanish Peru was not economic but rather fiscal and administrative. Somehow the institutions of the viceregal government and the men who staffed them failed their sovereign by sacrificing the needs of the metropolis and the solvency of the colonial government itself during the imperial crisis of the seventeenth century.

PART TWO

The Treasury System and the Forces of Change

4 *The Crisis and the Administrative System*

Institutional weaknesses within the viceregal treasury system posed fundamental problems for the Spanish crown in its efforts to raise money and reverse the fiscal crisis of the seventeenth century. The administrative structure of the viceregal treasury had been established in the sixteenth century to restore order among the unruly conquerors and to organize and tax the chief economic enterprises of interest to the crown—silver mining and the trade with Europe. As receipts from these sectors declined during the next century, crown officials had to enact new permanent levies in the viceroyalty, shifting more of the tax burden to powerful magnates such as merchants, landowners, manufacturers, and the Church. These royal efforts to raise taxes and expand the power of the crown beyond what had been its traditional limits evoked strong protests within the viceroyalty.[1] They also led to tensions within the viceregal treasury, as officials struggled to mediate between the financial needs of the crown and the resistance of local taxpayers to new government levies. In short the crown's attempts to reverse the fiscal crisis required a stronger, more centralized, loyal bureaucracy, capable of changing the distribution of economic resources within the empire. The Madrid government embarked on this difficult enterprise, however, without attempting to strengthen in any significant fashion the administrative structure of the treasury, which had been developed generations earlier to meet more modest political goals.

The governmental apparatus in the Viceroyalty of Peru simply proved inadequate in dealing with the crisis of royal revenues in the seventeenth century. The decentralization of political power, in both Spain and the viceroyalty, among a series of public administrative agencies continually hindered efforts to devise and implement a workable tax package to stem the fiscal crisis. Administrators working in Spain and Peru lacked a clearly defined set of duties, and relations between superiors and subordinates were informal and poorly defined under the law. This ambiguity within the legal code allowed officials to choose from a variety of technically legal policy options and gave them considerable autonomy in the decision-making process.[2] As a result jurisdictional conflicts, bureaucratic infighting, and inefficiency abounded, and action on legislation could be delayed. This was particularly true whenever the crown imposed controversial policies. Such changes could cause serious conflicts at all levels of the ponderous fiscal bureaucracy. Compromise and consensus were essential in implementing such new policies, but they were difficult to attain, particularly where new taxes were concerned. In the end this decentralization of political power within the treasury system undermined the implementation of vigorous new programs designed to alter the tax structure of the viceroyalty and increase remissions of revenue to Spain.

The administrative dimension of the problems posed by the fiscal crisis proved insurmountable for the Spanish imperial government. In order to counter the decline in royal revenues at the Lima treasury, the crown had to exercise an unprecedented degree of control and discipline over the system of administration in the viceroyalty. To achieve this control the crown had to work at transforming the structure of the imperial bureaucracy to give it at least some of the more important characteristics of what Max Weber has termed rational-legal authority.[3] Somehow Madrid had to bind colonial officials to a stricter and less ambiguous legal order and establish a clearly defined hierarchy of authority, with each official given a specific sphere of authority. Moreover officials had to be appointed more strictly on the basis of talent and technical training, have substantial fixed salaries, and no other outside activities. Finally bureaucrats could have no social or economic ties with the local population and must retain a strong sense of discipline and honesty.[4] This more modern model of a disinterested and loyal professional bureaucracy emerged in part during the seventeenth century, but these traits were never sufficiently present. As a result the crown could not attain the administrative power necessary to reverse the fiscal crisis during the period. The colonial government had passed from the control of the conquerors, but it had not yet become a professional civil service operating under the strict rule of law.

Royal Advisory Bodies

The most powerful of the government institutions advising the crown on colonial finances was the Council of the Indies, created by Charles I in 1524. The authority of the council extended to every sphere of government—legislative, judicial, military, ecclesiastical, commercial, and financial.[5] To deal with financial matters, four councilors from this body formed the important subcommittee on finance (*contaduría*). The specific duties of the contaduría included dispatching inspectors to the treasury districts of the Indies, eliminating corruption and fraud, and auditing treasury accounts. In addition the contaduría had extensive powers over tax-farming contracts, mining policies, and Amerindian affairs. In all areas the contaduría and the full council exercised full legal powers.[6]

As a check on the extensive powers of the Council of the Indies, the crown gave two additional agencies certain specific administrative powers over the colonial treasuries—the Council of Finance of Castile (Contaduría Mayor de Castilla) and the House of Trade (Casa de Contratación). From 1556 the Council of Finance and the Council of the Indies exercised joint control over the allocation of tax revenue collected in the Indies. Both agencies had to approve all requests for outfitting fleets, extraordinary expenditures, and funds for general administrative duties. The House of Trade, established in 1503, exercised control over the receipt of money from the Indies and audited the accompanying treasury accounts. It also supervised the sale of taxes collected in kind sent from overseas and received a security bond (*fianza*) from any treasury officer leaving for the Indies.[7] Their power over the royal treasuries of Peru, however, was clearly inferior to that of the Council of the Indies.[8]

Despite their powers the councils were always hampered by the system of checks and balances. The crown consciously diffused political power over financial policy among three separate government agencies. This system led to the accumulation of massive amounts of useless documentation, jurisdictional conflicts, excessive debates, indecision, and outright procrastination. Compromises were hard to reach, even with the direct intercession of the monarch. Even a strong sovereign like Philip II, the quintessential bureaucrat-king, found it difficult to master the details of government and to control and coordinate the activities of the councils. Less capable kings such as Philip III, Philip IV, and Charles II, had to rely on a chief minister or *válido,* to perform the task.

The most enterprising of these ministers in coordinating royal policies for both Spain and the Indies was the conde duque de Olivares. During his tenure, from 1621 until 1643, Olivares managed to take the key post of *gran canciller* in the Council of the Indies for himself, and to place his political allies in other important conciliar positions.[9] When necessary he even worked to circumvent the councils by establishing special ad hoc committees (*juntas*).[10] During Olivares's tenure members of these councils managed to reach substantial agreement on at least one important issue: more money had to be extracted from the Indies. The councilors still disagreed at times over the best specific policies to achieve this goal, but they all recognized the need to raise taxes in the empire and curtail bureaucratic corruption and inefficiency. During the first half of the century, the councils framed a series of new tax levies for the overseas empire; when these failed, they relied on an extensive *visita general* (inspection tour) to regain control over the resources of the Viceroyalty of Peru. At no time, however, did the councils recommend any substantial changes in the institutional framework of the viceregal treasury, which remained virtually unchanged throughout the century.

Viceregal Decision Makers

The royal treasury system in the Viceroyalty of Peru played the crucial role in implementing the policies framed by the councils in Madrid. Throughout the seventeenth century, treasury officials collected the taxes that financed the empire and distributed this income according to the needs of the viceregal administration and the demands of the metropolitan government. They also served as judicial officials, who formulated and implemented all fiscal policies at the local level. Particularly during periods of financial distress, these treasury officials were among the most powerful members of the viceregal government.

The administrative hierarchy of the treasury in the Viceroyalty of Peru was even more ponderous and decentralized than it was in Spain. Political power was divided between major administrative bodies (*administración por mayor*), such as the viceroy, the audiencia, the tribunal of accounts, and the provincial governors (*gobernadores*); and minor administrative agencies (*administración por menor*), such as the treasury offices, the cabildos, the corregidores, and the tax farmers.[11] The administración por mayor usually established basic policy guidelines and supervised the administration of the royal finances. The administración por menor implemented policy decisions. In practice the functions of these two groups frequently overlapped. Members of the audiencia, for example, served on tribunals that actually collected taxes; officers in the Lima treasury office served on the policy-making committee of finance (*junta de hacienda*). As in Spain this decentralization of administrative power made quick energetic responses to the fiscal crisis difficult.

The titular head of the viceregal treasury system and the man directly responsible for resolving the financial difficulties of the realm was the Viceroy of Peru, in Lima. He ensured that any appropriate fiscal policies were enacted and supervised the overall administration of the treasury. Specifically the viceroy could issue laws (*bandos*) by himself or in conjunction with the audiencia. He also possessed supreme executive powers over the enforcement of all legislation. In the administrative sphere the viceroy had the final voice in determining the number, location, and jurisdiction of all treasury offices. He also had the power to make interim appointments to all treasury positions, subject to confirmation by the Council of the Indies. Even specific issues such as tax-farming contracts, the distribution of mercury, the administration of royal monopolies, and the collection of donativos fell to the viceroy.[12] In short he was the most powerful and trusted representative of the king in the viceroyalty. The crown usually chose older, trustworthy, and experienced officials to fill the position, most often high-ranking members of the peninsular nobility. Despite his extensive powers, however, the viceroy served only a limited tenure during the seventeenth century, and his success usually depended on his ability to dominate the more experienced officials serving in the viceroyalty. During periods of political and financial crisis, in particular, the burdens of office were onerous. Like the King of Spain, the viceroy relied on many administrative agencies to run the royal treasury system.

One of the principal agencies of the administración por mayor was the audiencia. The audiencia possessed a mixture of legislative, executive, and judicial powers over the administration of the royal revenues in its district. Along with the viceroy it could initiate fiscal legislation and distribute laws issued in Spain. The audiencia possessed additional powers over the enforcement of laws in the viceroyalty. In cities such as Lima, which had both an audiencia and a royal treasury office, members of the audiencia supervised many details of the fiscal administration. When treasury officials put taxes collected in kind up for public auction, a justice (oidor) and an attorney (fiscal) of the audiencia had to be present. An oidor also assisted the treasury officers in writing periodic accounts for the tithe collections.[13] Lastly the audiencia even had to approve any official or personal trips made by treasury officers outside of the jurisdiction of their caja.[14]

In addition members of this body commonly served on committees that actually collected taxes in the viceroyalty. An oidor and fiscal of the audiencia, for example, served on the tribunal of the holy crusade, which sold papal indulgences; an oidor also served as the judge for intestate properties (*juzgado de bienes de difuntos*).[15] In short, judges of the audiencia in Lima worked both on the formulation and implementation of financial policies for the viceroyalty.

In spite of the audiencia's extensive powers, the crown imposed distinct limits on the tribunal's authority. Most important legislative decisions, for example, were made in Spain. The audiencia only investigated the treasury offices under its jurisdiction after authorities in Spain, the viceroy, or the tribunal of accounts had requested such assistance. In any judicial cases involving the treasury, the audiencia was not the court of first venue; it heard only appeals from lower courts. Also the crown entrusted many important administrative powers, such as the right to audit treasury accounts, to the tribunal of accounts. In many ways the audiencia played a passive role in resolving the financial problems of the viceroyalty during the seventeenth century, acting in conjunction with other colonial agencies.

After 1607 the crown entrusted the final audit of all treasury accounts in Peru to a special tribunal of accounts, located within the gates of the viceregal palace, along with the Lima treasury caja and the audiencia chambers.[16] Although technically a chamber (*sala*) of the Audiencia of Lima, this tribunal was largely independent of the other governmental agencies of the city. Its decisions could not be appealed, even to the Council of the Indies. Each treasury caja in the Audiencias of Lima, Charcas, Quito, Panama, and Chile sent copies of their fiscal accounts to this tribunal for final audit. The agency also examined the final accounts of corregidores de indios and tax farmers.[17] After completing these periodic audits, the tribunal sent a summary report of its findings and copies of the final accounts themselves to the Council of the Indies, keeping copies for its own files in Lima.

When the original legislation establishing the tribunal of accounts was issued in 1605, it provided for only three senior auditors (*contadores mayores*), two lower-ranking auditors (*contadores ordenadores*), and a few minor functionaries to serve on the agency.[18] A backlog of unfinished accounts had accumulated by 1630, and the crown modified this original plan to add two new auditor positions (*contadores de resultas*) to finish back accounts and collect debts.[19] Still the workload of the agency proved too much for the staff, and by 1651 the viceroy added two more interim contadores ordenadores and enlisted the aid of the supernumeraries and the future appointees waiting to take a permanent seat on the tribunal.[20] Finally in 1682 the viceroy, the duque de la Palata, added an additional four contadores.[21]

Apart from keeping abreast of their yearly audits, the tribunal collected the debts that had accumulated at the treasury offices. The law obligated the auditors to recover these unpaid taxes from the debtor, the treasury officers, or their bondsmen. After collecting the money, the auditors deposited the funds in the local treasury office and recorded the transaction in their workbooks. The law further required the senior auditor to make periodic inspection tours of the various treasury offices in the realm, to check on the accumulation of debts. The crown also demanded the contadores mayores, in rotation, to visit such important treasury offices as Potosí every three years.[22] The collection of unpaid taxes at the many cajas under the jurisdiction of the tribunal occupied much of the time and energy of the auditors.

The tribunal had the power to rule on all cases involving treasury debts, and they frequently instituted such proceedings to recover royal funds.[23] If the matter was particularly controversial or if the plaintiff contested the verdict, the viceroy could name a special commission to try the case, composed of four oidores and a fiscal of the audiencia. Two senior members of the tribunal also sat on the commission to act as consultants and to cast a vote on the final verdict. The proceedings were secret, and appeals could be made to the Council of the Indies only with the approval of the entire audiencia.[24] Even the viceroy was bound by its verdict. The commissioners usually dispatched a judge (*juez executor*) to enforce their ruling and collect the debt.[25]

During the years of financial turmoil in the viceroyalty, the tribunal had to cooperate closely with the viceroy and the audiencia, and the successful operation of the treasury depended on this cooperation. The viceroy, for example, served as president of the tribunal and had to approve any actions concerning the cabildos, treasury offices, corregidores, or audiencias.[26] Special commissions to hear cases involving treasury debts included members of the audiencia, and any judges sent to collect unpaid taxes had to be commissioned by the audiencia and the viceroy.[27] When such cooperation did not occur, friction arose. Shortly after the foundation of the tribunal of accounts, for example, the viceroy and authorities in Madrid had to remind members of the Audiencia of Lima not to interfere in the auditing of accounts taken in the *residencias* (judicial reviews) of the corregidores. That task now fell under the jurisdiction of the tribunal of accounts, whose members had complained about this interference from the audiencia.[28] The opposite problem could also occur. In a letter of July 15, 1646, members of the tribunal of accounts complained to Madrid that the Audiencia of Lima failed to cooperate fully in recovering debts and back accounts from the treasury offices.[29] To settle such problems the viceroy and one oidor of the audiencia met in special sessions with a senior member of the tribunal.[30] When cooperation could be achieved, the administrative functions of the treasury could proceed more effectively. If conflicts arose, as they too often did, the diffusion of political power among the viceroy, the audiencia, and the tribunal of accounts led to indecision, conflict, and inefficiency. All hindered efforts to deal with the fiscal crisis.

Jurisdictional conflicts with the viceroy and the audiencia were not the only problems faced by the tribunal's auditors. The task of examining the accounts from the widely scattered cajas under their jurisdiction was immense. In 1634, for example, the tribunal explained that it received accounts from twenty-four separate cajas each year. Since government employees received approximately 125 days of vacation each year, that left only 10 days to audit and duplicate each account and collect debts.[31] This did not include the time the auditors spent in planning sessions with the audiencia, the viceroy, and the treasury officials; nor the time spent hearing court cases or preparing the voluminous daily correspondence carried on with other administrators. Visiting distant cajas such as Potosí, Oruro, and Castrovirreyna every three years also took manpower away from the main task of auditing the accounts. In fact on one such mission the contador Alonso Martínez Pastrana remained in Potosí for five years, trying to put the accounts of the office in order.[32]

In 1548 Pedro de la Gasca established local councils of finance (juntas de hacienda) throughout the viceroyalty to deal with this important problem of coordinating the efforts of the agencies of the administración por mayor and the administración por menor. The most important of these councils met on Wednesday and Thursday afternoons in Lima, to facilitate cooperation between the tribunal of accounts and the treasury cajas. It was comprised of the viceroy, the senior oidor and fiscal of the Audiencia of Lima, the senior auditor (*contador mayor decano*), of the tribunal of accounts, and treasury officers of the Lima district.[33] In regions of the interior the governor and treasury officials met weekly for the same purpose.[34] When special emergencies arose, an ad hoc meeting of these juntas usually convened to decide on a course of action.

The sessions of the junta de hacienda rarely dealt with the daily administrative problems of the treasury offices. This was the duty of the local treasury officers. Instead it established general goals and priorities for the treasury. Problems of jurisdictional conflict, debt collection, the periodic remission of accounts to the tribunal in Lima, increasing the number of salable offices, approving new expenditures, and dispatching inspection tours were the activities most commonly handled by the junta de hacienda. After reaching an agreement, the council sent its decision to the proper officials for execution.

Despite the efforts of the junta de hacienda, too many of its decisions were not carried out effectively. The most obvious example of this shortcoming was the continual problem of friction between the tribunal of accounts and the treasury offices. A major source of conflict was the failure of the cajas to send their yearly accounts to Lima. Without yearly audits it became virtually impossible to supervise the treasury, and in 1651 the junta de hacienda issued a special order demanding that all missing accounts be sent to Lima. When local officials ignored even this order, the viceroy, the conde de Salvatierra, ordered special investigators to enforce it.

Francisco Nestares Marín, the president of the Audiencia of Charcas, reported from his visita of Potosí that no accurate records of income and expenditures in the office had even been kept since 1630, which particularly unsettled members of the junta de hacienda.[35] Potosí was the most important caja in Upper Peru, which allocated tax revenue each year to pay the salaries of the Audiencia of Charcas, the treasury officers, the local corregidor, the governors of Tucumán and Paraguay, and the subsidy to Buenos Aires. In addition the law required these officials to control the flow of contraband silver from the rich Potosí mines. Without accurate treasury records, no one in either Lima or Madrid could keep abreast of the activities of the caja. Results from the other important economic centers of the realm were equally dismal. The tribunal of accounts either failed to receive or to audit thirty-two accounts from Oruro, forty-one from Cuzco, and twenty-nine from Arequipa.[36] The junta de hacienda managed to involve key officials from the administración por mayor and the administración por menor in the decision-making process, but too often it failed to resolve the administrative breakdowns within the treasury system.

The Cajas Reales and Fiscal Policy

The responsibility for implementing all royal fiscal policies during the seventeenth century fell on officials working in the treasury offices. The crown established these cajas reales in every major mining, agricultural, commercial, administrative, and strategic center of the realm; officials serving in them carried out the daily administrative chores of collecting taxes and paying the government expenses in their district. Each office was the center of an administrative orbit of considerable importance. Indeed the operation of local government depended on the honesty and efficiency of the officials attached to the treasury offices.

The economic and political needs of the viceregal government determined the location of a treasury office. Whenever the viceroy or the junta de hacienda in Lima wanted to tap the economic wealth of a region, treasury officials were dispatched and a caja established. When the mines at Cailloma began producing at a high level in 1631, for example, a new office with its own regulations (*ordenanzas*) was founded.[37] Treasury offices could also be withdrawn from an area. During the sixteenth century a separate treasury office operated at the port of Callao. In time authorities in Lima deemed it unnecessary to maintain offices in both cities. In 1613 they closed the Callao office and placed the port under the jurisdiction of Lima.[38] The site of a treasury office might also change from one location to another, as the economic needs of the region evolved. The caja at Huánuco was established in 1568, moved to the province of Conchucos in 1644, came back to Huánuco in 1660, shifted to Pasco in 1669, and finally went to Jauja in 1785, were it remained.[39] As regions experienced cycles of prosperity and stagnation, the junta de hacienda established or closed treasury offices in them.

When treasury offices closed down or opened in new areas, jurisdictional lines changed.[40] In 1653, for example, when the mines at Carangas began producing large silver yields, the junta de hacienda separated the region from the Oruro office so that it could be supervised more easily.[41] Likewise in that same year the Lima government ordered the establishment of a new caja at the rich mines of San Antonio de Esquilache, and took the province from the control of the La Paz office.[42] The jurisdiction of an office could extend through several entire provinces or only a few leagues. The caja of Bombón, founded in the province of Canta in 1627, had jurisdiction over just the immediate territory surrounding the silver mines in the region. The rest of the province fell within the orbit of the larger office in Lima. When a new treasury office opened in a frontier zone such as Buenos Aires or Tucumán, its jurisdiction was usually vague and took more definite form only as the region developed and became more closely integrated into the mainstream of the viceregal economic and administrative system.[43]

When the Spanish conquerors established the principal, or

matrix, treasury of Lima in 1535, its jurisdiction was wide but largely undefined. Slowly, as the conquest proceeded and other regions developed, new districts were carved from the Lima office. For most of the seventeenth century the Lima treasury controlled the broad central coast of Peru, including the provinces of Cajatambo, Canta, Cañete, the Cercado, Chancay, Huaylas, Ica, Jauja, Yauyos, and parts of Huarochirí and Conchucos (see map).[44] In the case of certain ecclesiastical taxes, such as the tithe, the provinces of Huánuco, Tarma, and Santa also sent income to Lima. Normally Huánuco and Tarma remitted income to the Huánuco office, and Santa sent its tax revenue to the caja at Trujillo.[45] Since Lima was the principal treasury office for the viceroyalty, all of the subordinate offices in Peru and Upper Peru also sent their surplus income and annual accounts there. Like all of the treasury offices of the realm, the authority of the Lima office changed over time to meet the needs of viceregal officials.

The administrative organization of the Lima treasury was relatively simple during the seventeenth century. Three senior treasury officials collected the taxes, a comptroller (contador), a treasurer (tesorero), and a business manager (factor). The comptroller supervised the income and expenditures of the caja, while the treasurer actually handled the receipt and payment of all authorized funds. The business manager sold all goods confiscated by the government and all taxes collected in kind at public auction, kept the armories in Lima and Callao stocked, and attended to any other commercial transactions involving the king's money. One of these three senior officials also served, in rotation, at the port of Callao to operate the customs house and keep an accounting of the military expenses of the port. In this last duty, however, the treasury officers frequently received aid from the supernumerary (*supernumerario*) of the office, who served as an adjutant in the office until one of the senior positions became vacant. In addition the three senior officials had a number of subordinates to aid them in dispatching their duties. All of the treasury officials worked together, and the crown held them collectively responsible for the honest and efficient administration of the treasury office.[46]

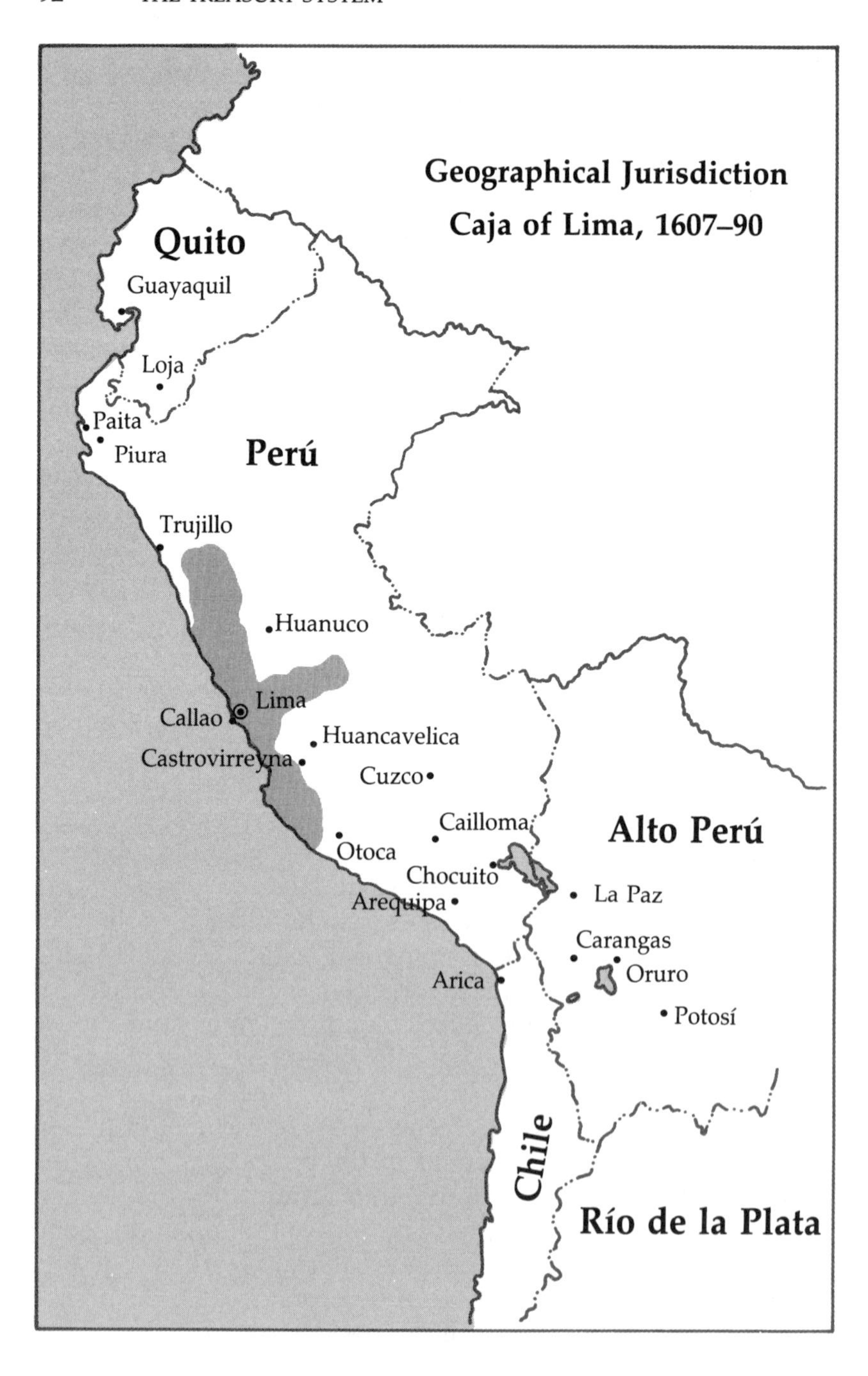
Geographical Jurisdiction
Caja of Lima, 1607–90
Quito
Guayaquil
Loja
Paita
Piura
Perú
Trujillo
Huanuco
Lima
Callao
Huancavelica
Castrovirreyna
Cuzco
Cailloma
Otoca
Chocuito
Arequipa
Alto Perú
La Paz
Carangas
Oruro
Potosí
Arica
Chile
Río de la Plata

Before taking office treasury officials in Lima had to satisfy a number of legal requirements. Candidates for office had to be loyal subjects, free from any debts or binding contracts with merchants or the government, and have some experience in the imperial bureaucracy.[47] Most importantly they needed sufficient wealth to pay the media anata and to post a cash bond, or fianza, paid to the caja as assurance of their honesty. If convicted of any malfeasance in office, the treasury officer forfeited the bond. Usually a candidate for office secured the assistance of one or more prominent acquaintances to act as his bondsman (*fiador*). Although the exact terms of the fianza differed, the bondsmen usually agreed that the bond would be forfeited to pay any fines, debts, or replace any shortages of funds in the caja, should the guilty officer be unable to meet the obligation from his personal resources. No treasury officer could take office without paying his fianza. If a bondsman died or declared bankruptcy, the tribunal of accounts suspended the treasury officer until he found a new fiador.[48] Every ten years the bonds had to be checked by the tribunal of accounts and reaffirmed by the concerned parties.[49] In 1683, for example, as part of a general inspection tour of the entire viceregal treasury system, a thorough check was made of fianzas of the officers serving in the Lima caja.[50]

If the treasury official happened to reside in Spain before taking office, he guaranteed his bond before the Council of the Indies and paid it at the House of Trade in Seville. When the official was living in Lima, the bond was offered to the tribunal of accounts and the money held in deposit by the Lima treasury office. After the bond had been settled, the new official swore an oath of loyalty, honesty, diligence, and confidentiality, signed the inventory of goods in the caja, and took office.

Once treasury officials in Lima took office, a complex of laws and local customs regulated their six-day workweek. Monday was spent meeting with the audiencia and hearing court cases concerning fiscal matters. On Tuesday and Saturday they supervised the smelting, marking, and taxing of all shipments of precious metals. In addition each Saturday the three senior treasury officers opened the strongbox (*caja fuerte*) to receive tax revenue remitted from tax farmers.[51] Debt collection, tribute lists, and the accounts of the corregidores de indios occupied officials on Wednesday, and on Thursday morning they paid salaries, pensions, and other debts. In the afternoon members of the treasury office attended meetings of the junta de hacienda. On Friday taxes in kind and illegal goods confiscated by the crown and taken as fines were sold at auction.[52]

Another responsibility of treasury officials was the supervision of the mining industry. The smelting, marking, weighing, and taxing of all precious metals mined in the district and the distribution of mercury to the miners was a vitally important duty, particularly for officials working in the great mining regions of the viceroyalty. In Lima a special mining inspector, the *ensayador y balancario,* did the routine work in the smelting process, under the supervision of the treasury officials. Treasury officers insured that no illegal smelting took place within the district, and any personal or business ties between crown officials and miners were strictly forbidden. Since mining was less important in Lima than in other districts such as Potosí or Cailloma, treasury officials spent less time and energy supervising its activities. Most of their work in this area involved checking the remissions of silver bars and coins sent from the subordinate offices.

Apart from their duties administering royal revenues in the caja, after 1587 treasury officials in Lima were the court of first instance in all fiscal suits.[53] During the seventeenth century treasury officials commonly ruled on cases involving debts, taxes, abuses of the law, corruption, and any other fiscal matter.[54] A tribunal composed of all three senior treasury officers heard the case together and had to reach a unanimous ruling. No single official could sentence an offender without the written consent of his colleagues.[55] Even the corregidores de indios and local governors had to yield in all fiscal cases to the treasury officers. In practice, however, treasury officials usually had to rely on the active cooperation of local magistrates to enforce their decisions or to bring the accused to court.

The most troublesome problem in Lima was the collection of tax debts. Each year various individuals or groups were unable or simply refused to meet their tax obligations. The limited staff of the caja and its large geographical jurisdiction made this problem difficult to resolve. Officials in Lima continually attempted to collect these back taxes in cash instead of sequestering the personal possessions of the debtors, which involved the time-consuming process of selling them at public auction. Often their efforts were ineffective. In these cases the treasury officers petitioned the audiencia and the viceroy to send out special judges or direct local magistrates to collect the debt and send it to Lima. As with their judicial proceedings, treasury officials had to rely on the cooperation of local officials as well as that of the viceroy and the audiencia. This cooperation was often difficult to obtain, unless the debt was large. As a result debts accumulated in the Lima caja during the seventeenth century.[56]

There were also limits set on the authority that treasury officials in Lima exercised over the subordinate offices in Peru and Upper Peru. The treasury office in the capital merely served as a clearing house for funds sent from the subordinate offices, and the Lima officials had no direct control over the collection and disbursement of tax monies in these subtreasuries. After they had collected the royal taxes and met their administrative expenses each year, officials in the subordinate offices (or their appointed representative) brought the surplus and their fiscal accounts to Lima. Officials in the Lima caja only counted and weighed this money, checked the amounts against the enclosed accounts, and sent a receipt (*carta de pago*) to the subtreasuries. Even the disbursement of these funds from the interior was regulated by the junta de hacienda and the royal legislation.

Only in rare cases could treasury officials in Lima demand that their colleagues in the subordinate offices pay outstanding debts. On April 30, 1665, for example, the factor of the Lima office sent a letter to the treasury caja of La Paz ordering Luis César de Escocola, the corregidor of Chilques y Másques, to pay 208 pesos he owed for the media anata.[57] Since the law required royal officials in Lima to keep detailed records of all income in Peru and Upper Peru from certain taxes, such as the media anata, the mesada, and papel sellado, the factor of Lima had the authority to require the payment of this money. The Lima treasury office could not overtly interfere in all phases of the administration of royal revenue in the subordinate offices. In fact it could not demand accounts or income from another district without the permission of a superior authority. Officials in Lima frequently tried to have these restrictions overturned. In a letter to the crown on April 28, 1623, they argued that Lima should have undisputed jurisdiction over certain taxes, such as tercias de encomiendas, collected in the other offices. In addition these treasury officials requested the right to collect debts owed to their office by individuals living outside the Lima district.[58] In practice, however, the crown usually ignored such requests from Lima, and limited the power of the principal office over the other cajas to those specific issues which influenced the administrative activities of the Lima treasury.

The administrative authority of Lima treasury officers was curtailed even within their own district by the large number of taxes collected by tax farmers. Of the forty-two separate levies that appeared in the financial accounts of the Lima office during the seventeenth century, treasury officials collected only ten themselves.[59] The rest were handled by the various public and private individuals or organizations holding the tax asientos. Often these tax farmers failed to keep accurate accountings of their activities for the Lima caja and the tribunal of accounts. Since the district of Lima covered a large geographic area, it was virtually impossible to keep close watch over the many subordinates working to collect taxes for the caja. An inspection of Callao in 1634, for example, indicated that those supplying the military installations in the city had been consistently cheating the government. Treasury officers in Lima never received accurate accountings from these merchant suppliers in Callao, however, and failed to uncover the fraud until the inspection.[60]

Conflicts between treasury officials and tax farmers could make even routine tax collection duties a tortuous and complex task for the royal officials. In 1647, for example, officials in Lima tried to collect 500 pesos owed by Alonso Ortíz Pariago to the account of the cruzada for indulgences purchased in 1640. Since the affair concerned the purchase of indulgences, the treasury tried turning the matter over to the tribunal of the holy crusade. The body was slow to take action, however, and only decided to perform its duty after a rebuke from the Council of the Indies. When it finally sent commissioners to Cañete and Ica to collect this debt and others, the corregidores and other local officials resented this intrusion on their own jurisdiction and impeded the commissioners. The mission ultimately failed, and the frustrated treasury officials in Lima angrily complained in a letter to the Council of the Indies dated July 21, 1647, that "regardless of the laws and orders that this tribunal (caja) possesses, each day we find ourselves with new obstacles like this concerning our jurisdiction because of the impediments that the judges and tribunals of this city and outside of it place before us, much to the harm of your majesty's treasury."[61]

The matter was not resolved until the Council of the Indies reprimanded the tribunal of the holy crusade for its obstreperousness.[62] Without the active support of the tax farmers and the help of local officials, the treasury officers in Lima were helpless. Legal provisions issued in 1565, 1620, 1626, and 1636 reaffirmed the right of officials in Lima to demand the aid of subordinates in the provinces in collecting debts, but many such officials guarded their own powers and prestige more closely than the laws of the realm.[63] Incidents like these in Cañete and Ica made a mockery of the authority of officials in the capital.

Jursidictional conflicts and professional antagonisms between treasury officials and corregidores were particularly intense. These magistrates had extensive political, judicial, and military power in their provinces; in all areas except finance they were more powerful local forces than the treasury officials. Whenever treasury officials opposed the corregidores, they found it difficult to enforce their will. In 1643 treasury officials serving at the caja of Bombón, then located in Huarochirí, charged the local corregidor with embezzling silver owed to the office. The corregidor and his lieutenants in Huarochirí normally collected silver from the mines and had it transported to San Mateo, the seat of the treasury office.[64] Several miners and Amerindian workers at the mineheads alleged that much silver was taken to Lima instead and sold illegally by the corregidor, Diego Moreno de Zárate, and his cohorts.[65] It was even hinted by some in Lima that a justice of the Lima audiencia, Antonio de Calatayud, took part in this traffic in contraband silver.[66]

When the treasury officers finally confronted Moreno de Zárate about the charges, a brawl erupted, injuring several of the participants. Relations between the corregidor and the treasury officers, which had always been strained, then broke down completely. The case proved difficult to resolve when it came before the Audiencia of Lima, in all likelihood because some justices, such as Calatayud, wanted to cover up the incident. Litigation continued until 1649, and although the treasury officers eventually received a favorable verdict, the administration of royal finance suffered in the region.[67] According to later accounts the smuggling of contraband silver from the area continued, although further incidents of violence were avoided.[68] This conflict in Bombón, although acrimonious, was not an isolated incident. Similar problems between corregidores and treasury officials occurred throughout the century.

Even institutionalized efforts to eliminate bureaucratic conflicts, corruption, and inefficiency, such as the visita and the *pesquisa,* often proved ineffective. The visita was an inspection tour that could cover any aspect of viceregal administration, in a single institution or in the entire viceroyalty.[69] The pesquisa was more limited in scope. It reviewed a particular scandal or crisis and usually focused on the activities of a single institution in a limited geographic area.[70]

Both the visita and the pesquisa, however, had many defects. For one thing the investigations could be very costly. A series of inspections ordered in 1647 of Bombón, Castrovirreyna, Cuzco, Cailloma, Carabaya, Arequipa, Trujillo, Huánuco, and Buenos Aires accumulated expenses totaling 108,000 pesos.[71] Another problem was the reliability of witnesses. Powerful local officials could easily coerce witnesses into altering their testimonies, and personal prejudices or grudges also motivated some witnesses. Even the bias of the judge could influence the outcome of an investigation. Furthermore the inquiries always disrupted the routine of the administrators and frequently caused much confusion and inefficiency. Tribunals or individual officials spent more time supplying the visitadores with documentation than in discharging their duties. Finally, tension and jurisdictional conflicts between local officials and the visitadores could intervene and further disrupt the investigation. Too often the visita and pesquisa proved cumbersome and even ineffective as mechanisms for increasing royal control over the viceregal treasury.

The residencia was another potentially powerful but often ineffective tool for regulating the administration of the treasury. This was a judicial review, conducted after an individual left office, on every bureaucrat who held a post with a legally limited tenure. Viceroys and corregidores were subject to a residencia, for example, while members of the tribunal of accounts and the treasury office were not. Anyone in the tribunal or a treasury caja served for an indefinite period at the discretion of the crown and so were not obligated to undergo a residencia.[72] The crown and the Council of the Indies or the viceroy and the audiencia named an official judge (*juez de residencia*) to conduct the inquiry. When an official left office, the judge traveled to the region and gave public notice of the time and place of the trial. Anyone could testify. Once evidence had been collected and a verdict reached, the decisions of the residencia could be appealed only to the Council of the Indies.[73]

Generally the residencia was less costly and caused less confusion than the visita, because the official under investigation was not holding office. Still the procedure had many shortcomings in practice. Local prejudices, unreliable witnesses, and uncooperative local officials frequently undermined the investigation. The most glaring defect in the system, however, was the frequent bias of the judges. The crown commonly appointed the successor to the official under investigation to head the inquiry. Too often these men had a stake in covering up the mistakes of their predecessors. In 1637, for example, a visitador in the province of Arica found that a string of local corregidores had committed a wide range of crimes never uncovered in their successive residencias. The magistrates had commonly leased Amerindian laborers to Spanish ranchers, farmers, and merchants in the area for lucrative kickbacks. The corregidor and his lieutenants had so abused this practice that there were not enough Amerindians left behind to work the fields, and crop yields and tribute returns suffered. In addition the corregidor and his lieutenants further supplemented their income in Tarapacá, Tacna, and Locumba by operating illegal wine shops and other stores selling goods at highly inflated prices to their Amerindian charges.[74] The abuses apparently continued unexposed, because each new corregidor in the region was loath to unmask abuses of the law that they themselves hoped to continue after taking office. As a result the residencias in Arica and elsewhere had turned into hollow rituals that left abuses uncorrected.

Conclusion

During the seventeenth century the administrative system in both Spain and Peru proved inadequate to meet the pressing financial needs of the crown. The entire imperial treasury apparatus was based on a system of checks and balances, with authority divided among the king, his advisory councils, the viceroy, the audiencia, the tribunal of accounts, the treasury officials, and the various tax farmers. No clear lines of authority separated their powers and responsibilities, and each supervised the actions of the other. This administrative overlap was deliberately constructed during the sixteenth century, when the chief aim of the crown was to control the strife-torn colony and extract the precious metals of the highland regions. It was an inherently conservative system, based on compromise and consensus, and proved ill suited to meet the fiscal needs of the Madrid government for additional revenue a century later. Any new revenue policies would provoke the opposition of local elites and divide the already decentralized bureaucracy.

Officials were caught between two conflicting royal standards: the need to satisfy the crown and their responsibility to appease local taxpayers and preserve the cohesion of the empire. The diffusion of political authority allowed these local officials to preserve a delicate balance of political power, playing off the needs of both parties. In essence the course of events was often determined by these local treasury officials, who had the power to choose from a number of different options in implementing crown directives. Distance from Madrid or even Lima, the ambiguities in the legal system, and the decentralization of power all worked to their advantage. The net result was often a marked disparity between the letter of the law and its observance.

To end the financial crisis, the crown first had to correct the structural defects of its bureaucracy. Otherwise any deviation from the traditional patterns of behavior, such as widening the tax base and imposing a stricter adherence to the wishes of the crown, was certain to cause conflicts, political infighting, competition, and inefficiency, rather than the desired changes. To secure the successful implementation of any meaningful financial reforms, the crown had to expand in a dramatic fashion the power of the state in the viceroyalty and transform the colonial bureaucracy from a decentralized, patrimonial system to a more rational-legal one.[75] It is not surprising that when the Bourbon kings in the eighteenth century undertook their reforms of the imperial system, they learned from the experiences of their predecessors and attempted a more integrated attempt at bureaucratic, financial, and commercial reform.

5 *Royal Authority and the Sale of Fiscal Offices*

The decentralization of the viceregal bureaucracy allowed treasury officials to serve as a key link between colonial elites and the crown in all matters of imperial finance. These bureaucrats had direct responsibility for transmitting and implementing all fiscal directives sent from Madrid. In all ways they were well suited to accomplish this task. Ties of loyalty, professionalism, and seniority in the crown's service encouraged them to respect the needs of the metropolis, while economic and social connections to local elites also made them sensitive to the impact of royal legislation. As a result the demands of local taxpayers, the crown, and the needs of the bureaucrats themselves all played a role in the decision-making process. In periods of financial distress, such as the seventeenth century, these viceregal officials served as political brokers within the empire, maintaining the political balance of power essential for imperial unity.[1] Any measure that weakened the loyalty and efficiency of these officials could alter dramatically the political balance of power within the empire.

During the struggles over taxation policy, the crown unwittingly undermined its own position in Peru and helped tip the balance of power in favor of local elites in 1633, when it approved the systematic sale of all high-ranking treasury appointments.[2] The sales allowed a group of generally inexperienced, inefficient, and dishonest officials, with strong local connections, to gain control of the two chief agencies of the viceregal treasury—the tribunal of accounts and the central treasury in Lima. These venal officeholders became *radicado en país,* or firmly rooted to local interests. In the end venality and corruption became institutionalized, thwarting royal efforts at imposing heavier taxes in the viceroyalty.

Political changes brought about by the sales proved particularly damaging to royal authority in the Viceroyalty of Peru during the seventeenth century. Partisan groups in the viceroyalty had long tried to forge alliances with local bureaucrats in order to influence the decision-making process. At the same time treasury officials traditionally found it convenient and even lucrative to keep such ties to local groups. The sale of offices, however, encouraged this process and contributed to a dramatic rise in local influence, as representatives of local interests even gained high offices themselves. As a result the sales contributed to a steady decline in royal control over these officials, whose family, business, and political ties to elites in the viceroyalty proved stronger than their allegiance to the crown.

Treasury Appointments before 1633

Before 1633 the crown and the Viceroy of Peru controlled the appointment of officials to the tribunal of accounts and the treasury caja in Lima. The king maintained the legal right to name all officials to the viceregal treasury, but before the sales began in 1633, officials in Madrid recruited only six men from the ranks of the peninsular bureaucracy to serve in Lima.[3] The rest went to residents of the Indies.[4] In these cases the crown commonly relied on the advice of the viceroy. As treasury positions fell vacant, the viceroy exerted his influence in Madrid to insure that his friends and retainers (*criados*) staffed these important jobs. Empowered to make any necessary interim appointments to the treasury, subject to royal approval, viceroys frequently offered suggestions to the crown about final appointments to these agencies. This influence over key bureaucratic appointments greatly strengthened the viceroy's political position in Lima, and usually made for a more pliable bureaucracy. Although the power of patronage proved useful to the viceroy, it also provoked criticism from local residents. Partisan interests often complained that the viceroys too often favored newly arrived peninsulars over native sons and *radicados.* As the creole apologist Fray Buenaventura de Salinas y Córdoba scornfully wrote of recent immigrants from Spain, "The South Sea baptises them, and places a 'don' upon each: after arriving in this City of the Kings (Lima), all are dressed in silks, descended from don Pelayo and the Goths and Visigoths. They proceed to the palace of the viceroy to claim pensions and office."[5]

Despite Fray Salinas y Córdoba's remarks, not all members of the viceregal entourage in Lima received an office immediately after arriving in Lima. Some courtiers waited many years before receiving an appointment, while others never managed to secure a post. On the other hand, gaining office without viceregal connections was difficult. Even experienced officials found it easier to win a treasury appointment if they had connections in the palace. Fernando Bravo de Lagunas, for example, had a distinguished record as treasurer of the Lima caja, as well as the favor of the viceroy, the conde de Chinchón, when he was promoted to contador mayor of the tribunal of accounts, in 1638.[6]

Despite his considerable patronage power, however, the viceroy often found it prudent at least to consult with local authorities before making his interim appointments or recommending candidates to the crown. In a letter of May 22, 1638, the conde de Chinchón told of soliciting recommendations for treasury posts from the cabildos of every major city in Peru and Upper Peru.[7] In any case, whether the viceroy consulted widely before making his recommendation to the king or simply named a favorite, he exercised considerable power of appointment over these two agencies of the treasury. For the most part the king, his advisors in Madrid, and the viceroy successfully used this power to name competent and dedicated men, likely to respond to the financial needs of the metropolis.

Before the systematic sale of appointments to the tribunal of accounts and the Lima caja in 1633, the crown usually favored Spanish-born candidates with few previous ties in the city. Between 1607 and 1633 authorities in Madrid named only two creoles, Hernando de Santa Cruz y Padilla and José de Jaraba y Arnedo, to the tribunal of accounts. Both were prominent native sons of the city. Santa Cruz y Padilla was a successful merchant and a founder of the consulado in 1613, while Jaraba utilized the good name of his father, Pedro de Jaraba y Vivar, a former treasury officer in Lima, to obtain his appointment.[8] Likewise in the twenty years before the sale of appointments to the Lima treasury office, the crown named only two creole ministers, Leandro de Valencia and Juan de Guzmán. Valencia came from a prominent limeño family who arrived in Peru with the Pizarro expedition, while Guzmán came from a notable Huánuco family with a tradition of government service.[9]

The remaining appointees apparently came from Spain. At least one, Pedro de Jaraba y Vivar, was a man of some importance and influence in the mother country. He belonged to the royal household (*cámara*) of King Phillip III, and his wife, Juana de Arnedo y Péres, was an attendant (*azatea*) of the queen.[10] The other Spaniards who served in the tribunal and the treasury office were men with fewer connections. Most decended from the gentry (*hidalguía*) and had only limited opportunities for achieving wealth and fame in Spain. Bartolomé Astete de Ulloa, for example, came from the less prominent Miraveche branch of his family, and Fernando Bravo de Lagunas descended from the Huelva line of his family, which became more prominent in Peru than it had been in Spain.[11] For these men government service in the viceroyalty provided a better opportunity to achieve wealth, status, and professional advancement than in Spain, where they probably would have remained minor members of the Spanish gentry.

The members of the tribunal of accounts and the treasury office in Lima were usually experienced bureaucrats of proven ability. This is hardly surprising. Since both agencies were involved in the administration of royal finance, the crown attempted to screen applicants for the positions very carefully.

A clear indication of this is the strong credentials of the twenty men who served in the tribunal of accounts before 1633. It was not unusual for an official like Juan Bautista de Aramburu to serve for two decades as a functionary in the *Contaduría Mayor de Hacienda* before receiving a post on the tribunal. Other accountants gained their experience in the viceroyalty. Diego de Meneses and Fernando Bravo de Lagunas, for example, served terms as treasury officials in the Lima office, before taking a post as contador mayor.[12]

Even viceregal criados usually had considerable training and experience before being elevated to the tribunal. Typical of this group was Pedro de Gordejuela Castro, who received his promotion to the agency after twenty-six years of government service in Spain.[13] Unlike the viceregal audiencias, however, which usually recruited men with advanced degrees, the contadores of the tribunal seldom boasted strong academic credentials. One exception was José Suárez de Figueroa, a prominent legal mind of his day, who taught at San Marcos University and published scholarly works in Spain.[14] In a similar manner the crown and the viceroys stressed practical experience over academic training in making appointments to the Lima treasury office. Most of the men serving in the Lima office over the twenty years preceding the sales had considerable government experience in Spain or Peru, but little advanced academic training. They had usually worked as corregidores, provincial governors, functionaries of an accounting or judicial tribunal, aldermen, or treasury officers in a subtreasury before being promoted to Lima.

By the seventeenth century the crown had established relatively clear patterns of promotion (*ascenso*) to the treasury office in Lima. Only one official, Juan López de Hernani, had gained this experience in Spain, where he served in lower echelon posts in the Contaduría Mayor de Quentas and the Council of the Indies.[15] In addition a few criados or friends of the viceroy could move directly into the Lima office after some government experience. Most appointees, however, had served for many years in a variety of lesser positions in the Indies, usually in some post in the viceroyalty outside of Lima. The career of

Bartolomé Astete de Ulloa is in many respects typical. In 1598, at the age of twenty, Astete migrated to Peru; two years later he received an appointment in the Pacific fleet. After his military service Astete took a series of minor bureaucratic posts in the viceroyalty, and by 1606 he was made treasurer in the Potosí district. In 1613 Astete served as factor of the office until ten years later, when he received an appointment as corregidor of the entire province. Not until 1628, after nearly thirty years of government service, did the crown name him comptroller of the Lima office, a post he held until his death, in 1662.[16]

Few appointees to the Lima caja served the crown quite as long as Astete, but most had to earn a spot in the capital after proving themselves elsewhere. Competition for posts in Lima was fierce. Once an official earned a place there, he had the opportunity to impress the viceroy and perhaps even gain a more lucrative promotion. Before 1633 two treasury officers in Lima, Diego de Meneses and Fernando Bravo de Lagunas, were elevated to the tribunal of accounts, and the treasurer Sebastián Hurtado de Corcuera managed to secure an appointment as president of the Audiencia of Panama.[17]

The ascenso was not clearly established in the tribunal of accounts before the crown began selling these appointments, in 1633. The agency had only begun operating late in 1607, giving the crown little time to develop clear lines of recruitment and promotion. Like the treasury office, however, the majority of the men appointed to the tribunal had served in the viceregal government. In fact only four men can be identified as having been recruited from the peninsular bureaucracy. The remainder were viceregal retainers or officials who had spent time serving in treasury offices, lower echelon posts in the audiencia, and also as corregidores and governors. Opportunities for promotion within the tribunal itself also showed no consistent pattern. Between 1607 and 1633 the crown elevated only one man serving in the tribunal, José Suárez de Figueroa, to the post of contador mayor.[18] It was certainly not automatically assumed in either Madrid or Lima that a vacancy in the position of contador mayor should be filled by someone holding one of the lesser posts in the tribunal, contador de resultas or contador ordenador. Similarly not a single contador mayor in the tribunal of accounts in Lima moved up to a higher post in either Spain or the Indies. This is not surprising, however, since the office of contador mayor was the highest office in the viceregal treasury hierarchy. Moreover there were only three similar tribunals for all of the Indies, and colonial officials rarely received direct promotions to high-ranking posts in Spain.

Although promotions might be difficult to attain, officials in the tribunal of accounts and the treasury office in Lima had ample opportunity to gain important titles, honors, awards, and additional offices for themselves or their children. During his brief stay as treasurer of the Lima caja, for example, Sebastián Hurtado de Corcuera used his influence with the viceroy, the conde de Chinchón, to become a general of the prestigious cavalry unit in Callao and later to sit on the viceroy's council of war (*junta de guerra*).[19] Since holding more than one government office was not unknown, some treasury officials in Lima obtained several additional offices for themselves and their families. Bartolomé Astete de Ulloa held the office of ensayador mayor of Barca in Upper Peru, while serving as comptroller of the Lima caja.[20] Later he secured the same office for his son, Nicolás, in Potosí.[21] Similarly Pedro de Jaraba y Vivar used his influence in Spain and Peru to have his son, José de Jaraba y Arnedo, named contador mayor of the Lima tribunal.[22] These offices and honors served as a form of informal reward for loyal treasury officials in the viceroyalty.

To curb the considerable power of treasury and tribunal officers, the crown imposed a host of laws regulating their behavior. Although many of the regulations were ignored during the seventeenth century, they served as a model of conduct for crown officials of the period. Fiscal officers could not, by law, hold another bureaucratic office, an encomienda grant, or serve in any public or private position that might hinder them from discharging their duties effectively.[23] Personal ties among members of the bureaucracy were forbidden, and intermarriage among the families of government officials was particularly discouraged.[24] Furthermore the law prohibited treasury officers from engaging in any commercial ventures. They could not borrow any money or own mines, sugar mills, or land without the consent of their superiors.[25] Authorities in Madrid adamantly forbade these fiscal officials to use their political position for personal gain or to turn royal funds to their own use.[26] Most of these prohibitions extended to the wives and sons of bureaucrats. The contadores of the tribunal could not meet collectively outside the chambers of the viceregal palace. Even a short trip beyond their district had to be approved by the viceroy or the president of the audiencia.[27] When accused of violating any of these laws, fiscal officials in Lima received a suspension from office until the charges were resolved. If found guilty an official could forfeit his office, his personal property, or even his life.

Before the sales began in 1633, government officials in Spain and Lima tried to exercise care in scrutinizing the records of fiscal officers in the capital. Treasury officers had to satisfy their debts and responsibilities from any previous assignments before taking office. On one occasion during the seventeenth century, the tribunal of accounts prohibited Bartolomé Astete de Ulloa from taking office in Lima for thirteen months. He had been ordered by the caja of Potosí to pay 65,000 pesos in uncollected taxes from his tenure as corregidor of the region. After several exhausting court sessions to settle the account, the tribunal ordered Astete put in jail until he paid the fine. Finally Astete was allowed to take office, but only after he agreed to hand over 28,000 pesos to the treasury at Potosí and to pay the remainder within the next six years.[28] Had officials in Madrid known of Astete's debt, it is doubtful that he would have been selected to serve in Lima. Still the crown was reluctant to remove any fiscal officer, once his appointment had been confirmed in Madrid. Not a single treasury official in the first half of the seventeenth century suffered any permanent loss of his office or a long-term jail sentence for misconduct. Crown discipline could be harsh in principle, but in practice once an officer received his título from Madrid, he was likely to retain the post.

Despite legal prohibitions and crown scrutiny, links between fiscal officials and the local citizenry definitely occurred during the first three decades of the seventeenth century. In fact some of these ties solidifed even before the bureaucrats took office. Each employee in the treasury had to pay a security bond, or fianza, before taking possession of his office.[29] Since the fianzas usually ranged from 20,000 pesos to 40,000 pesos, the treasury officer often found it impossible to pay the entire amount from his personal savings. Occasionally relatives or friends in Spain helped to post the bond, but more frequently prominent local citizens in Lima performed the favor. Eight contributors, for example, met the fianza of 37,500 pesos presented by Juan de Guzmán, in 1626. Tomás de Paredes, an alderman of the Lima cabildo, and Bartolomé González, one of Lima's most successful merchants and a future head (*prior*) of the consulado, were the two largest contributors.[30] Although the payment of a fianza did not necessarily wed the treasury officer to the interests of his bondsmen, it provided an obvious link between government officials and prominent citizens in Lima.

Men holding positions in the tribunal of accounts and the royal treasury office found it easy to establish close personal ties with members of the local citizenry. A few were native sons of Lima, who already had strong community connections; but most peninsular-born officials used marriage to solidify their social and economic position in the city. Bartolomé Astete de Ulloa took a prominent young widow, Petronilla Dávila y Zuñiga, for his first wife; when she died prematurely, in 1630, he contracted a second marriage, to another well-connected Lima widow, Inés Bravo de Zárate.[31] Astete's second wife was a cousin of Fernando Bravo de Lagunas, who served in both the treasury office and the tribunal of accounts in Lima. This second marriage, like the first, took place with great ceremony in the city cathedral.

In addition to his own marriages, Astete arranged favorable matches for his sons Nicolás and Melchór with young ladies of notable Lima families. While the Spaniard Astete tried successfully to advance his social position in the capital through favorable marriages, some bureaucrats were already married before arriving in Lima. Pedro de Jaraba y Vivar had married in Spain, and Juan de Guzmán took a prominent Cuzco woman for his bride.[32] Jaraba, however, arranged the marriage of his son, José de Jaraba y Arnedo, in 1630 to Constanza de Valencia, daughter of the former treasury officer Leandro de Valencia.[33] The family alliance between the Jarabas and an old conquistador family like the Valencias undoubtedly proved helpful to José de Jaraba in winning his post as contador mayor of the tribunal of accounts. The crown naturally tried to forestall these political marriages by forbidding unions between fiscal officers and members of their district unless granted a special dispensation, but in practice these dispensations were frequently awarded or sold. When they were not the couples usually married in defiance of the law. The longer a fiscal official served in Lima, the more likely it became for him to develop strong local connections.

Economic as well as social ties linked treasury officials in the caja and the tribunal of accounts with important citizens of Lima. Over one-third of the taxes collected by the treasury office were administered by tax farmers. Private individuals or organizations such as the consulado usually held these lucrative contracts. Officials serving in the caja and the tribunal had considerable influence in awarding the contracts, supervising the activities of the tax farmers, and negotiating contract renewals. For these crown officials the possibilities for favors, kickbacks, and the advantages derived from making these personal connections were tremendous. In short fiscal officials serving in Lima had the political power to be very useful to prominent local citizens. The potential, at least, existed for turning this political power into personal gain.

Members of the tribunal of accounts and the central treasury office could not function apart from the society where they lived and worked, but before 1633, at least, they were not the pawns of local elites. They were experienced officials with strong ties of loyalty to the crown. Indeed the appointment procedure of the crown produced a strong and relatively unified political establishment in Lima, revolving around the chief financial officer of the king, the Viceroy of Peru. In a time of political tension within the empire like the seventeenth century, the task of reconciling the often divergent aims of the crown and local taxpayers in Lima placed considerable strain on this political establishment. Only by maintaining a political balance of power could the officials of the viceregal treasury preserve their own power, status, and privileges. This state of affairs began to change after 1633, however, when the crown began the systematic sale of all high-ranking treasury appointments.

The Coming of the Sales

Authorities in Madrid recognized many of the dangers in selling treasury appointments and only reluctantly approved the policy, on April 27, 1633.[34] Debate on the measure was most heated in the Council of the Indies. Members of the council warned the king that the sales would allow unqualified, incompetent, or corrupt men to gain these important offices. The councillors cautioned the king to weigh the "merits" of the purchasers against the "considerable amounts of money" offered to meet the "urgent needs" of the financially hard-pressed treaury.[35] In addition the council recognized that the policy was a sharp break with the past. The crown had openly sold some hereditary and transferable offices (oficios vendibles y renunciables) at public auction since 1559, but these sales involved only minor posts such as scribes, notaries, and some municipal offices. Treasury officers, however, had extensive financial and judicial powers and received high salaries.[36] Ultimately the councillors approved the sales only under pressure from Philip IV and the conde duque de Olivares. Faced with bankruptcy and impending military defeat in Europe, the government decided to sell treasury appointments regardless of the consequences.[37]

The crown derived considerable income from the sales and continued them throughout the seventeenth century. It was able to command particularly high prices for seats on both the tribunal of accounts and the central treasury office in Lima. Sales were made through individual private transactions, rather than at auction, and the receipts went directly to the Spanish treasury. Since there was no predetermined price list, the amounts charged for each position varied considerably over the years. In fact the price of a post in the Lima treasury office fluctuated between 5,375 pesos and 18,750 pesos.[38] In the tribunal of accounts the office of contador mayor commanded the highest prices—from 9,000 pesos to 20,000 pesos.[39] The lesser positions of contador de resultas and contador ordenador cost between 2,500 and 8,750 pesos.[40]

Since all senior offices in the Lima caja were legally equivalent, no such price differential existed there. In fact if no position in the office was vacant, the buyer could purchase a future, which enabled him to assume the first available opening in the office, whether that of treasurer, comptroller, or factor. Purchasers of positions in the tribunal, on the other hand, usually received a future for one of the three specific contador positions. In the caja other considerations, such as the immediate financial position of the crown, the political influence of the purchaser, his past record, his qualifications, and his eagerness to buy an appointment were the factors that influenced prices. In 1646, for example, a Spaniard, Dr. Bartolomé Torres Cavallón, purchased a future in Lima for 6,000 pesos, but he had an advanced academic degree and boasted a distinguished record of government service in Spain and the Indies.[41] On the other hand, a young native son of Lima, Francisco Antonio de los Santos, paid 14,400 pesos for his future in 1680.[42] This was consistent with the crown's policy of discouraging native sons from serving in the highest echelons of the colonial bureaucracy. In short each transaction was negotiated separately and the receipts received by the crown varied, within limits, according to the individual circumstances involved.

Despite the considerable income accruing to the crown from the sale of treasury offices in Peru, opposition to the practice continued in the Council of the Indies. Although the councillors recognized the king's legal right to sell offices in any of his kingdoms, they feared the sales would allow dishonest, inept men to gain high office in a particularly difficult time in Spain's fiscal affairs, which was bound to damage the efficiency and responsiveness of the viceregal treasury. In 1667 the president of the council, the conde de Peñaranda, seemed obsessed with the problem. In secret instructions to the viceroy-designate, the conde de Lemos, Peñaranda warned him to beware of opponents on the tribunal of accounts in particular, because "I know little of the subjects who are on it, the offices were bought, and thus the officials show no respect for you."[43] The situation, Peñaranda feared, could undermine the viceroy's position in Lima, hinder attempts to reform the treasury, and ultimately weaken the entire imperial system.

Treasury Appointments after 1633

The Council of the Indies had good reason to fear the consequences of selling appointments to the tribunal of accounts and the royal treasuries of Peru. The crown's deteriorating financial position, which led to the sales in 1633, eventually resulted in officials in Madrid reducing their vigilence in the recruitment and promotion of crown ministers. As a result inexperienced men with strong local connections came to dominate these two agencies and to prejudice their operation during the years when the Spanish crown most desperately needed greater contributions from the Indies to shore up the position of its treasury.

In Lima one unforeseen effect of the sales was to undermine the viceroy's patronage power over the appointment of treasury officials. Although the king could legally name officials to serve in the viceregal treasury, the viceroys often used their power to make interim appointments. Historically the viceroys also exercised their influence in Madrid in place their own criados and friends in the jobs. After the sales began, however, treasury appointments were negotiated through private transactions between the crown and the purchaser. In some cases the viceroy was not even consulted. In 1634 a prominent Lima merchant, Juan de Quesada y Sotomayor, went to Spain on business, where he used the opportunity to negotiate the purchase of the treasurer's post in Lima without the prior knowledge of the viceroy, the conde de Chinchón. When word of the appointment finally reached Lima, in 1637, Chinchón wrote a stormy letter to Madrid denouncing Quesada. He objected to merchants serving in the treasury, especially Quesada, who had many outstanding debts in the city and little real training or talent for the job.[44] Quesada's generous offer of 18,750 pesos for the post impressed authorities in Madrid, however, and they overruled Chinchón's objections.[45]

In other cases the crown worked more closely with the viceroy in filling fiscal appointments, and a few viceregal criados still received the posts. José de Bernal, a former secretary of the viceroy, the duque de la Palata (1681–89), received a position as contador mayor of the tribunal in 1697, but he was an exceptionally well-qualified man and was not obliged to pay for his appointment.[46] Too often viceregal criados like Bernal could not outbid wealthy radicados and native sons for the powerful and prestigious posts. As the financial distress of the crown grew, authorities in Madrid were more likely to sell the offices for the highest possible price, regardless of the man's qualifications or the recommendations of the viceroy. As a consequence the Lima elite stood a good chance of putting their own candidates in office, even without the support of the viceroy. In all likelihood, as these native sons and radicados became less dependent on the viceroy for their appointments, they also became less responsive to his will. This indirect curtailment of the viceroy's patronage power and influence probably hindered efforts to raise taxes in the viceroyalty.

The sale of appointments to the Lima treasury office also led to a significant increase in the number of local personnel recruited to serve the crown. The Madrid government relaxed its rules against admitting candidates with strong local connections and freely allowed native sons and radicados to buy offices. Among the first purchasers were two radicados, Baltásar de Becerra and Juan de Quesada y Sotomayor, both wealthy merchants who had long resided in the city.[47] By the end of the century the crown also routinely approved sales to native sons of Lima. In fact the last three appointments to the treasury office in the century went to the limeños Cristóbal de Llanos Jaraba, Francisco Antonio de los Santos, and Francisco de Arnao y Granados.[48] Apparently the financially destitute government of Charles II had little choice but to sell these offices to eager native sons of Lima, willing to pay higher prices for the honor and prestige that went with the appointments.[49]

The sale of fiscal offices had a direct impact on the staffing of the tribunal of accounts. After 1633 the crown sold so many futures to the tribunal that by 1653 six purchasers were waiting to take a post as contador.[50] Most of these futures went to creoles. Of the twelve men who purchased an appointment to the tribunal between 1633 and 1660, only two were peninsulars.[51] Like their colleagues seeking a post in the treasury office, creoles and especially native sons were apparently willing to outbid peninsular claimants for the posts. The higher prices they were willing to pay also led officials in Madrid to ignore any legal obstacles to their holding office. One *limeño,* Alonso Bravo de la Maza, purchased an appointment in 1649 while holding an encomienda in the district, a clear violation of the law.[52] Another, Álvaro de Alarcón, received a dispensation from the crown to buy an appointment to the tribunal while his father, Sebastián de Alarcón, served as an oidor in the Audiencia of Lima.[53] By the second half of the century, when these purchasers gained numerical superiority in the tribunal of accounts, it had become a stronghold of local power and authority in Lima.

Most of the men who bought positions on the tribunal of accounts and the treasury were younger and less experienced than their predecessors. The new appointees to the tribunal usually had little training in government accounting matters; most only had limited experience as soldiers, aldermen, or in a few cases, as corregidores. It was not unusual that a young native son, such as Alonso Bravo de la Maza, should have used his family's considerable wealth and influence to secure an appointment as contador mayor, despite his lack of experience and training. The same problems appeared in the Lima treasury office. Of the nine men who bought appointments in Lima during the century, only Bartolomé Torres Cavallón and Cristóbal de Llanos Jaraba had strong bureaucratic backgrounds.[54] The rest had little preparation. As the financial plight of the crown worsened, particularly after the revolt of the Catalan and Portuguese provinces in 1640, officials in Madrid became even less selective in screening purchasers. In 1641 the father of Sebastián de Navarrete even managed to purchase an appointment for his fifteen-year-old son, with the understanding that the boy would not begin serving until his twenty-fifth birthday.[55] Some of these inexperienced officials, such as Navarrete, had to serve an apprenticeship as supernumeraries in the caja, but by the end of the century even this precaution was ignored.

The entry of inexperienced men into the Lima treasury office clearly disrupted the ascenso. Before the sales began, members of this agency had usually served outside of Lima in a number of lesser posts before moving to the capital. After 1633 wealthy influential young men could avoid serving in these minor positions and directly purchase a post in the caja. In addition the sales made it difficult to gain a promotion on merit alone. From 1633 not a single purchaser received a promotion from the treasury office. The net result was that members of the treasury office usually received their jobs at a younger age and held them for longer tenures, until their retirement or death. Before the crown began selling these appointments, officials had usually spent from three to ten years in office; after the sales commenced, purchasers held office for twenty years or more. The only exception was Baltásar de Becerra, who died less than a year after assuming his duties in Lima.[56] After taking the post his father had bought him, Sebastián de Navarrete served for nearly thirty years in Lima (but he died in disgrace after being exiled to Mexico for malfeasance in office).[57] Although treasury officials served at the king's pleasure, after purchasing an office in Lima most held the post for life. To gain a promotion an official needed money and influence, rather than a strong service record. Consequently officers in the caja of Lima had little incentive to work honestly, efficiently, and loyally.

The crown did not have enough time between 1607 and 1633 to establish a clear-cut ascenso for the tribunal of accounts, but problems similar to those found in the treasury office emerged after the sales began. Again appointments generally went to younger men, who served long terms in office. In addition only two men who began serving in the agency before 1633, (and thus did not buy their jobs), Juan Bautista de Aramburu and Francisco Gómez Pradera, received promotions to the post of contador mayor, the pinnacle of the viceregal treasury hierarchy. All others holding that position bought it outright, without first serving in one of the lesser jobs in the tribunal. As in the treasury office, money and influence came to outweigh ability and experience in gaining a post.

Purchasers of offices used their long tenures to develop and sustain strong political, social, and economic ties in Lima. In time most bureaucrats probably had little desire for a promotion, because it meant leaving behind these important connections in the capital. Lima was a prosperous city that served as the bureaucratic and commercial center of the Viceroyalty of Peru. Social mobility was less restricted than in Spain, and limeño society offered many opportunities for advancement for the young radicados serving in the treasury. The salary of a senior treasury officer in Lima by 1650 was 3,000 pesos; a contador mayor of the tribunal of accounts earned 3,500 pesos. While these incomes alone did not insure a life of luxury, they did provide considerably more than the 250 pesos to 600 pesos that contemporaries considered adequate to maintain a comfortable standard of living.[58] In addition their government positions provided high social standing and access to political power. Local interest groups eagerly sought personal and professional alliances with these powerful officials, to gain influence over government policy. This was particularly true during the political and financial turmoil of the seventeenth century. Treasury officials were also eager to augment their wealth and power by expanding ties to important local citizens. All these factors had existed before 1633, but the deteriorating financial position of the crown, the longer tenure of most officials in Lima, the limited opportunities for professional advancement in the bureaucracy, and the entry of native sons and radicados all facilitated the integration of these officials into colonial society.

Like their predecessors before 1633, the men who bought treasury offices established or reinforced ties to local residents in Lima through the fianza. Among the ten bondsmen of Cristóbal de Llanos Jaraba in 1665 were several merchants, family members, and two judges of the audiencia, Juan de Retuerta and Martín de Zavala.[59] Of course the payment of a fianza did not necessarily bind this young native son to the interests of his fiadores, but it did provide an important link between government officials and local magnates. Native sons such as Jaraba already had such ties before they took office, but reinforced them through the fianza.

Family and marriage ties formed an even more important bond between treasury officers and local interests groups. Officials frequently had relatives among the most important families of Lima. Among those who were not native sons of the city, Juan de Quesada y Sotomayor had the strongest family connections in the capital. Members of his clan preceded him to Peru; by the early seventeenth century, several of them had accumulated fortunes of over 200,000 pesos.[60] When fiscal officers lacked these strong family ties or simply wished to extend them, they frequently searched for favorable marriages. The power and influence of the officials made them attractive matches for the daughters of the rich and powerful in Lima. Young Francisco de Colmenares, for example, married a rich widow, Silveria Hermosa de Chillón. The marriage was apparently arranged for political and economic reasons, because gossips in Lima continually whispered of their frequent quarrels and the beatings Colmenares meted out to his wife. Furthermore, the young official was a notorious rake, who lived openly with his mistress.[61]

Apart from marrying for money, officials also chose their mates in order to cement political alliances. Sebastián de Navarrete's wife was the granddaughter of Juan de Loayza Calderón, an oidor in the Lima Audiencia; and Juan Fermín de Izu, a contador mayor in the tribunal of accounts, married Antonia de Ibarra, the daughter of Gregorio de Ibarra, a prominent merchant and a lay member of the Inquisition. Her brother, Álvaro de Ibarra, would later become the most influential politician of his era, serving as an oidor of the Audiencia of Lima, visitador general of Peru, and confidential advisor (*privado*) to at least two viceroys.[62] Family ties were also evident within the staff of the treasury itself. Cristóbal de Llanos Jaraba was the factor of the Lima caja at the same time that his first cousin,

José de Jaraba y Arnedo, served as contador mayor of the tribunal of accounts. In short treasury officials developed a network of interpersonal relationships after 1633 that helped bind them to prominent politicians, merchants, miners, and clergymen.

There is also evidence that the native sons and radicados serving in the central treasury office and the tribunal of accounts participated directly in illegal economic ventures. Juan de Quesada y Sotomayor provides only the most obvious example of such activities. Before he assumed his duties as treasurer of the Lima caja, in 1637, Quesada was a notable merchant in the city. He lived ostentatiously, and when his daughter María married, in 1636, he provided a dowry of 25,000 pesos.[63] This was an exorbitant sum for a man about to assume an office that paid only 3,000 pesos in annual salary. After holding office for only one year, however, Quesada used his influence to become an admiral of the Pacific armada, and in 1648 he even gained command of the treasury fleet to Panama.[64] These positions allowed the enterprising merchant the opportunity to supplement his salary by consorting with contrabandists operating in the Pacific, smuggling unregistered silver from Callao, and extorting bribes from his fellow merchants trading in both legal and contraband goods.

The Decline of Royal Authority

The sale of treasury appointments in 1633 set in motion a series of political changes that contributed directly to a steady erosion of royal authority in the Viceroyalty of Peru. During the first half of the seventeenth century, the declining position of the Habsburg monarchy in Europe led officials in Madrid to attempt an overhaul of the Peruvian tax system. To undertake any major reforms, the crown needed loyal dedicated servants in the chief agencies of the fiscal bureaucracy—the tribunal of accounts and the treasury office in Lima. At this juncture, however, crucial financial decisions in Lima were entrusted to officials who often proved inefficient, corrupt, and strongly tied to local partisan interests hostile to new tax levies. As the metropolis declined, treasury officials drew closer to local magnates in order to maintain their own wealth and status. Treasury ministers became immersed in local political issues, which accentuated divisions at all levels of the government. Furthermore as the political establishment became more divided, administrative corruption and inefficiency abounded. In the end royal authority over the viceregal treasury deteriorated, and the fiscal crisis deepened.

A major administrative problem resulting from the sale of offices was a decline in efficiency, particularly in the tribunal of accounts. The tribunal had never proved as effective in supervising the treasury as officials in Madrid had hoped, but problems intensified after 1633. In 1664 royal inspectors reported that officials serving in the tribunal of accounts were not capable of performing their duties. The inspectors found Andrés de Mieses, a contador mayor, incompetent and other members, for instance Joseph de Bolívar, seldom came to work in the tribunal chambers.[65] Most of the work at the agency was either left unfinished or completed by supernumeraries or other future-holders, working on a part-time basis. The morale of the tribunal as a whole was appalling. The influx of less-competent auditors and the tolerance of absentee officials made it impossible for the Madrid government to maintain adequate checks on the activities of the royal treasury during these vital years.

Similar problems plagued the treasury office in Lima. In 1659 royal inspectors found several officials incompetent. Bartolomé Astete de Ulloa was knowledgeable, but at sixty-two he was too old and sickly to serve as the comptroller without the aid of his colleagues. The inspectors judged these men—Bartolomé Torres Cavallón, Sebastián de Navarrete, and Francisco de Colmenares—too stupid, inexperienced, or lazy to work effectively in the office.[66] All except Astete had purchased their appointments. Further proof of these problems came in 1696, when the visitador general Juan de Peñalosa reported that debts owed the Lima treasury had increased dramatically by 1650.[67] As can be seen in table 9, those who purchased their appointments after 1633 were primarily responsible for this large accumulation of debts. The declining standards of efficiency after the

Table 9. Treasury Debts Accumulated by Officials in Caja of Lima, 1620–79

Treasury Official	Years of Service	Debts in Pesos de Ocho Reales
Cristóbal de Ulloa	1620–25	750 pesos 6 1/2 Reales
Juan López de Hernani	1620–26	1,120 pesos 7 1/2 Reales
Leandro de Valencia	1613–26	470 pesos 1 Real
Gerónimo Pamones	1625–28	370 pesos
Bartolomé de Osnayo	1628–31	1,309 pesos 3 Reales
Fernando Bravo de Lagunas	1633–38	1,095 pesos 4 1/2 Reales
Pedro de Jaraba	1638–48	13,310 pesos 5 Reales
Bartolomé Astete	1638–62	22,753 pesos 2 3/4 Reales
Baltásar de Becerra*	1648–49	9,754 pesos 5 Reales
Bartolomé Torres Cavallon*	1649–63	10,805 pesos 1 1/2 Reales
Juan de Quesada*	1638–72	39,983 pesos 6 1/4 Reales
Bartolomé de Solórzano**	1650–57	1,761 pesos 6 1/2 Reales
Sebastián de Navarrete*	1650–82	27,516 pesos 6 Reales
Francisco de Guerra*	1650–72	6,712 pesos 2 Reales
Francisco de Colmenares	1658–85	29,421 pesos 4 Reales
Cristóbal de Llanos Jaraba*	1666–85	20,864 pesos 1 3/4 Reales
Francisco Antonio de los Santos*	1679	4,496 pesos 6 1/2 Reales
TOTAL		192,497 pesos 5 3/4 Reales

*Men who purchased their appointments

**Bartolomé de Solórzano served these seven years as supernumerary of the office. Before an opening developed for one of the senior positions, he was promoted to the tribunal of accounts.

sales began exacted a considerable price in lost revenues, a price the crown could ill afford to pay.

The sales also encouraged divisions within the bureaucracy, as the new venal officeholders broke into the inner circle of the Lima political establishment. These more locally oriented officials sometimes clashed with their colleagues over policy making within the colonial government. This was the case in the notorious confrontation between the volatile viceroy, the marqués de Mancera, and Juan de Medina Avila, a wealthy merchant and member of the tribunal of accounts. The controversy began with the circulation of an anonymous document in both Lima and Madrid, charging the entire viceregal bureaucracy with nepotism and fraud. Among its principal allegations were the following: intermarriage among families of the political establishment, the arbitrary appointment of viceregal criados to important government posts, the misappropriation of tax revenues, the smuggling of mercury and silver, illegal commerce along the Peruvian coast, fraud in the recent sale of land and land titles, and wasteful defense expenditures. In addition the document charged Mancera with using government-funded projects to enrich himself and his cronies in the political establishment in Lima.[68]

Some allegations were contrived, others were exaggerations, and a few were even accurate. More importantly they were the work of Juan de Medina Avila, a political outsider who undoubtedly wanted to gain access to the ruling elite. Like many new treasury officials who purchased their appointments and began taking office in the 1640s, Medina Avila longed to gain his share of the wealth and power monopolized by the political establishment. In all likelihood the purpose of the document was to discredit his colleagues, break up their monopoly of power, and move himself and his cronies into the vacuum.

The document enraged the marqués de Mancera and most of the political elite in Lima, who made a concerted effort to discover the identity of the author and even banished one suspect, a Jesuit named Alonso Messía.[69] One year later, when the identity of the true author became known, authorities in Lima put Juan de Medina Avila in jail, fined him 4,000 ducats, suspended him from office, confiscated his wealth, and finally exiled him to Valdivia for ten years.[70]

The controversy did not end, however, with the imprisonment of Juan de Medina Avila. The contador charged officials in Lima with attempting to cover up their wrongdoing by trying to eliminate him.[71] According to Medina Avila he had served the crown faithfully for all of his sixty-four years, fighting the Dutch in Callao in 1624 and later serving as both the prior and consul of the Lima merchant guild. He had purchased the post on the tribunal for his son and namesake, and had become aware of the corruption of Lima while serving in the agency, until the boy reached the age of majority and took the post himself.[72] For exposing abuses in Lima, he was being persecuted and even feared for his life.[73] Medina's eldest son, Andrés, even carried the case to the Council of the Indies, which agreed to review the matter on July 6, 1646.[74] The councillors agreed that Medina's sentence was excessive, ordered him released from jail, and recommended a modest fine of 400 pesos and the restoration of his wealth and office. The council further called for an investigation into all of the allegations raised by Juan de Medina Avila and his sons.[75]

Outraged by the entire affair, the marqués de Mancera wrote several strongly worded letters to Madrid, denying the charges. He characterized Medina Avila as a senile, "low-born" incompetent, who could neither read, write, nor count accurately; charges that must have sounded preposterous in Madrid, considering Medina Avila's past as a successful merchant and a high official of the consulado.[76] After these shrill denunciations, however, the marqués de Mancera went on to say that all of Medina Avila's charges had been investigated and given a fair hearing before both the tribunal of accounts and the audiencia. The agencies found all of them groundless.[77] Moreover the viceroy declared that Medina Avila was a notorious malcontent, who had also harassed his predecessor, the conde de Chinchón.[78] Finally Mancera labeled the accusations a libelous attempt to discredit the imperial system in Peru and to undermine the foundations of royal power in the viceroyalty.[79]

In the end the residencia of the marqués de Mancera absolved him of any guilt in the case, but the matter was never satisfactorily resolved. The judge of the residencia, Pedro Vásquez de Velasco, came under enormous pressure when investigating the affair, and he found it difficult to recruit officials to aid in the inquiry. As he stated to his superiors in Madrid: "I confess sirs that I feared very much entering into this matter, recognizing the difficulties of performing it and the great risk that it puts me under."[80] The viceroy received the wholehearted support of most members of the Lima government during the investigations, and members of the Lima treasury office even wrote a strong letter defending the marqués de Mancera. Medina Avila and his sons both testified before Vásquez de Velasco, but the weight of the evidence and the strong sentiment within the government against the contador finally led the judge to absolve the viceroy of all charges. Velasco also released Medina Avila and his son from custody, overturned all past sentences against them, and imposed a fine of 2,000 pesos on the contador.[81] The aftershocks from the affair did not end even with the residencia. In a letter dated September 15, 1651, an apparent ally of Medina Avila charged that the seventy-year-old contador had died of natural causes shortly after his release, but his son was never allowed to succeed his father at the tribunal of accounts. The younger Juan de Medina Avila had apparently died "in the flower of his youth" of a sudden and painful stomach ailment.[82]

The controversy surrounding Juan de Medina Avila was not the only scandal to disturb the Lima government. Less than a decade later, the tribunal of accounts uncovered a shocking case of bureaucratic corruption and inefficiency in the Lima treasury caja. For many years treasury officials in Lima had failed to collect conscientiously all of the debts (alcances) owed the royal caja, which had reached considerable sums by the second half of the century. Finally, in 1650, members of the perpetually backlogged tribunal of accounts began investigating the problem, uncovering a debt of 45,409 pesos on the Lima accounts for 1647 alone.[83] The shortage was too large to ignore, and a special investigation, once again headed by Pedro Vásquez de Velasco, began. The treasury officials held responsible for the debt, Bartolomé Astete de Ulloa and Juan de Quesada y Sotomayor, protested their innocence and blamed their deceased colleague, Baltásar de Becerra. The embarrassed officials reported that in recent years they had met the immediate expenses of the caja by borrowing from the personal savings of Becerra, a retired merchant of considerable wealth. When the yearly remissions of silver arrived from the subtreasuries, Becerra simply took crown revenues as repayment. They reasoned that in 1647, when Quesada was absent in Callao and the elderly Astete was ill, Becerra, who was serving as supernumerary of the office, must have taken funds in excess of the original loans.[84]

Quesada and Astete blamed the entire incident on the crown's policy of selling future appointments to the caja. Becerra had been the first to purchase a future, in 1636; by 1650 three other men were in line behind him, waiting for a vacancy in the office.[85] Astete and Quesada alleged that these three men—Sebastián de Navarrete, Francisco de Guerra, and Bartolomé Torres Cavallón—had conspired with Becerra to create the scandal in 1647, in order to replace them. Furthermore the two treasury officials charged that the royal inspector, Pedro Vásquez de Velasco, was in league with Navarrete, Guerra, and Torres Cavallón. According to Astete and Quesada, the investigator had obtained most of his incriminating evidence from the three future holders, while he was their guest in Callao.[86]

The case was a complicated and confusing one, but ultimately the Council of the Indies chose to punish Astete and Quesada. The law held all three treasury officials responsible for any uncollected debts. Their excuses, moreover, did not account for an additional sum of 58,361 pesos that the tribunal and the investigator had found missing for the period 1648–50. Becerra, who died early in 1649, could not be blamed for this shortage.[87] In the end the investigators in Lima finally collected 25,000 pesos from the estate of Baltásar de Becerra and found another 46,600 pesos in a chest carelessly pushed aside in a corner of the treasury office itself. The two treasury officers had no explanation for these hidden or mislaid funds, and continued to blame everything on Becerra. The final verdict held Quesada, Astete, and their fiadores responsible for all additional missing funds. The two treasury officials were also fined 2,500 pesos each and suspended from office for four years.[88]

The scandals surrounding Juan de Medina Avila and the missing funds in Lima are clear evidence of the corruption and confusion in the capital by midcentury. It is no wonder that the officials of the viceregal treasury proved incapable of arresting the fiscal crisis. The sale of treasury appointments was not the sole cause for these scandals and the financial problems in the viceroyalty, but it was a contributing factor. The inept and corrupt venal officeholders who gained control of the treasury office and the tribunal of accounts made the policy decisions that eventually doomed efforts to expand the tax base and reverse the fiscal crisis. Royal authority and the entire imperial system had entered a long period of decline.

Conclusion

During the first three decades of the seventeenth century, colonial treasury officials played a key role in formulating and implementing fiscal policies in the Viceroyalty of Peru. On the whole they performed their duties well. Revenues remained substantial and remissions of silver to the metropolis were kept at high levels. In the long run, however, the decline of the mining industry and the transatlantic trade and the hostility of local magnates to new tax levies posed serious financial problems for the Lima government. Officials attached to the treasury now played the decisive role in the viceroyalty, mediating between the demands of Madrid and the stubborn resistance of colonial taxpayers. These officials had to maintain a political balance of power in order to hold the empire together. The sale of these important positions, at this crucial juncture in the seventeenth century, eventually tipped the balance of power in favor of local partisan interests. The sales allowed purchasers with strong local connections to dominate the key institutions of the treasury. Not surprisingly they were more subject to influence peddling and cooptation. As a result the bureaucracy became divided and riddled with corruption, and royal authority in the viceroyalty declined. These administrative and financial problems proved long lasting. As two royal inspectors, Jorge Juan and Antonio de Ulloa, wrote in 1749: "Those governing Peru are presented with the pleasant prospect of absolute authority growing ever larger and more ostentatious, of precious metals to satisfy their lust and greed, and of people who ingratiate, enrich, and shower praise on the least deserving. These three factors are the poison which chokes and destroys good government in these kingdoms."[89]

As the case of Juan de Medina Avila indicates, the rise to power of these corrupt and venal officeholders was not always a smooth process. Officials in Spain tried hard to maintain control over the viceregal bureaucracy and to reform the tax system in Peru. Indeed the controversies surrounding the financial pressure exerted from Madrid and the opposition of magnates in the viceroyalty to any higher tax levies formed the central political issue for most of the seventeenth century. It took a change of dynasty and a commitment to bureaucratic reform in Madrid before the sale of fiscal offices was ended, in 1750.

PART THREE

Reform, Resistance, and Imperial Decline

6 *The Failure of Arbitrismo, 1607–1664*

During the first half of the seventeenth century, the need to reform the political and financial relationship between Spain and the Viceroyalty of Peru became apparent to royal officials on both sides of the Atlantic Ocean. King Philip III (1598–1621) made few changes in the imperial relationship, for during his reign there was peace in Europe and tax remissions from the Indies remained substantial. This policy of neglect ended in 1621, with the accession of Philip IV (1621–65), who pursued a more active and militant foreign policy in Europe, leading to a series of expensive foreign conflicts. These wars strained the heavily burdened Spanish treasury and forced the crown to embark on a ruinous financial policy of borrowing from foreign and domestic bankers, debasing the royal currencies, and selling public offices throughout the empire. By 1654 the financial position of the crown so deteriorated that the king had to spend over half of the 25,000,000 pesos in revenues collected in that year merely to service the national debt of 165,000,000 pesos.[1] This military and financial crisis in Spain caused administrators in Madrid to intensify their demands for revenue from the Indies, particularly from the silver-producing provinces of the Viceroyalty of Peru.

Shortly after taking the throne, Philip IV and his advisors began framing a reform package for the royal treasury in the Viceroyalty of Peru. The goal of these innovations was to increase royal control over the bureaucracy, bolster income levels in Lima, and thus increase remissions of colonial silver for the Spanish treasury. This effort involved redressing the political balance of power maintained by the Lima bureaucracy between the crown and local elites, tipping it in favor of the crown. To achieve this end the crown first dispatched a visita general to Peru in 1622 and then levied a series of new revenue-producing measures, including new taxes, forced loans and donations, and the sale of juros, public offices, and land titles.

Unlike the Bourbon kings in the eighteenth century, Philip IV and his advisors limited their reform effort to shoring up the fiscal structure of the empire and failed to undertake any important bureaucratic and commercial innovations. Indeed the Madrid government did not even attempt to attack the fundamental "norms, symbols, and levels of political activity" in Peru.[2] As a result the reforming impulse ultimately failed to achieve many of its objectives. The new tax levies imposed by Madrid did lead to a temporary increase in total income levels in Lima from 1630 to 1650, but remissions of money to Spain did not rise accordingly. In addition the crown's reliance on temporary expedients such as the sale of juros instead of permanent imposts, along with the decline in mining taxes, led to the precipitous drop in income levels at the Lima office by the 1660s.[3] The success of the crown's fiscal reforms depended on the support of two powerful groups in Peru—the venal officeholders who staffed the viceregal treasury and wealthy local taxpayers. Ultimately both proved uncooperative.

The Impending Fiscal Crisis in Peru

By the early seventeenth century, officials in Madrid began to view higher taxes in the rich provinces of the Viceroyalty of Peru as a necessity. Although the viceroyalty already sent nearly 1,500,000 pesos each year to the metropolis, the most substantial sums generated in the Indies, Peru had traditionally enjoyed relatively light taxation. As one peninsular observer complained, "in all the world there is no nation that pays less in taxes to its king, since all are limited to the sales tax [alcabala] on the Spaniards that is not even two percent, and on the

Amerindians a personal head tax [tribute], that for the entire year, in all goods, services, and vassalage, does not exceed six pesos."[4]

Despite recent declines in productivity at the mines of Potosí and Oruro, the silver-mining industry appeared vigorous early in the century, and other sectors of the viceregal economy showed signs of growth. Mining still dominated these other activities, but the development of wine, textile, shipbuilding, and artisan industries and the production of agricultural goods such as wheat, olives, sugar, grapes, and cacao gave the viceroyalty a highly diversified economic base. In addition lively trade links in both legal and contraband goods extended to the South American coast, Central America, Mexico, and the Far East. The total productivity of this viceregal economy could not compare with that of Castile, but neither did its tax burden. After 1600 the Spanish crown clearly felt justified in expecting that Peru could make more sizable contributions to the metropolis.

After the near financial and economic collapse of Castile in the 1590s, the new monarch, Philip III, pursued a policy of peace and financial consolidation. Still the financial difficulties of his father continued to haunt the king, and in 1607 the burden of these old debts forced his government to declare bankruptcy.[5] The next year these financial difficulties prompted the chief minister of the crown, Francisco de Sandoval y Rojas, the duque de Lerma, to advocate raising money in the Indies. The duque de Lerma was neither a reformer nor a financial innovator, however, and his suggestion merely involved extending to America a proven financial expedient, the sale of juros.[6] Lerma and his supporters overcame the objections of opponents in the Council of the Indies, who feared overburdening the cajas of the Indies with interest payments on the annuities, and on September 6, 1608, Philip III issued a royal edict (*cédula*) ordering the sales in both New Spain and Peru.[7]

The edict of 1608 assigned to the viceregal treasuries in Peru half of the total levy for the Indies, or 1,000,000 ducats (1,375,000 pesos de ocho). Viceregal treasury offices had to pledge a portion of their revenues as security and agree to make yearly interest payments of 5 percent to any purchasers in their district. The procedures for the sales were relatively uncomplicated. As in Spain the juro became the personal property of the buyer, who could sell it or pass it on to his heirs. The treasury had to pay interest on the annuities three times each year, and theoretically government officials could not suspend, revoke, or liquidate the juro agreement under any circumstances. Furthermore the buyer could redeem the principal at any time, requiring the treasury to repay the sum in the same currency supplied at the sale in no more than two equal installments. The crown further ordered that the 1,000,000 ducats be sold promptly with all of the proceeds remitted in full directly to Spain.[8]

Although officials in Peru complied with the edict of 1608 and raised the funds, the sales evoked strong opposition in both Lima and Madrid. The viceroy, the marqués de Montesclaros (1608–15), led the protest in Peru. He feared that unrestrained juro sales would mortgage the future revenues of the treasury and drain investment capital from productive economic activities such as mining, commerce, farming, and ranching. The viceroy warned that if these sectors languished, remissions of tax revenue to the metropolis would diminish.[9] Opposition to the sales also arose in the Council of the Indies. The councillors expressed concern that such long-range economic problems were already appearing after the sales in 1608; in the end they would far outweigh any immediate gains accruing from the program. In addition the council predicted that a dangerously idle, restive, and unproductive class would form in the Indies, capable of disrupting the harmony of the empire.[10] Dissenters in Spain and the viceroyalty convinced the king to halt plans for any future juro sales, and in 1615 he issued an edict stating that: "We command that no juros be imposed on our royal treasury offices and that the viceroys, presidents, and governors not permit it."[11] For the remainder of his reign Philip III followed this edict. Indeed the sales were the last major effort by his governments to impose any additional financial levies on the Viceroyalty of Peru.

Despite the success of the juro program and the large remissions of tax revenue sent from Lima to Seville, the ominous decline of the silver industry by the 1620s boded ill for the viceregal treasury. Since mining was the core of the colonial economy, any failure in this key industry could have disastrous consequences. Most disturbing were reports about the erosion of the most productive of the silver mines at Potosí. According to the príncipe de Esquilache, viceroy from 1615 to 1621, the situation at Potosí had reached a crisis:

> Potosí has decayed for some years in this way, with notorious and well lamented diminution, because the standard quality of the metal has declined, the mineshafts are of greater depth, the azogueros poor and indebted; the mita, either on account of the corregidores or the lack of Amerindians, has suffered some considerable breakdowns; on account of these matters the royal fifth (quinto) has had a known diminution.[12]

Since remissions from the mining districts, such as Potosí, contributed as much as 70 percent of the treasury's total income, a drastic fall in mining taxes could ruin the viceregal government.[13] In addition if this sector declined, commercial levies and loans or forced donations would also diminish, since miners and merchants involved in the silver trade largely supported these lucrative ramos.

By the second decade of the seventeenth century, the administration of royal finance in the Viceroyalty of Peru was at a crucial juncture. Without the discovery of new silver lodes to offset the declining productivity of the older mining centers, the financial future of the Lima treasury looked grim. The only way to maintain total income levels in Lima would be to raise taxes for the clergy, merchants, and farmers, but this was bound to provoke stiff resistance in Peru. On the other hand the Spanish treasury relied on remissions of silver from Peru to pay its bills, and could not tolerate any declines in these shipments. Indeed the dilemma of a declining tax base in Peru and continual pressure from Madrid to maintain the high level of remissions to Spain provoked the príncipe de Esquilache to remark in 1621 that:

> All of the difficulties that are presented to the government of

> these provinces can be improved upon in part with industry and care, except the administration of the royal treasury, because the chief ministers of Spain do not wish to understand the fact that the breakdown and diminution of the ancient riches have reached a miserable state, and at last it is tremendous work to administer the treasury from which is expected heavy aid for the needs of your Majesty, and at a time when the expenses here are fixed and permanent, and the royal income less and more doubtful.[14]

Should mining in Peru decline more drastically or the crown pass to a more warlike monarch with an expensive expansionist foreign policy, pressures from within and without would necessitate an extensive reform of the royal treasury system. This was the financial situation in Lima in 1621 at the accession of the new king, Philip IV.

Philip IV and the Reforming Impulse

King Philip IV and his enthusiastic advisors intended to extend Spanish influence in Europe and return to the more active imperialism of the late sixteenth century. By 1628 this ambitious foreign policy had led to the outbreak of hostilities on three separate fronts: Germany, Flanders, and Italy. These foreign wars naturally placed a burden on the overextended resources of the Spanish treasury and forced the crown to consider a thoroughgoing reform of the entire imperial treasury system. Crucial to the success of this program was an attempt to raise revenue from the Indies. In the Viceroyalty of Peru, of course, this involved expanding the tax base of the treasury to compensate for the decline in mining taxes. The preoccupations of the crown in Europe did not produce an attitude of "benign neglect" toward the Viceroyalty of Peru, but instead induced an intense level of government activity in Madrid to force greater contributions from the colony to the beleaguered metropolis.[15]

The efforts of King Philip IV to alter the political and financial relationship between Spain and Peru were hardly new. The impulse to reform the imperial bureaucracy on both sides of the Atlantic Ocean grew gradually out of the theories of a group of innovators and specialists called *arbitristas,* who for decades had advocated diverse projects to cure the political, social, and economic ills of the Spanish Empire. These arbitristas were a mixed lot. They included serious economic and political thinkers, inventors of useless gadgets, and even a few charlatans like the alchemists.[16] The best among the arbitristas, however, displayed a strong sense of realism and a stubborn dedication to finding useful solutions for pressing imperial problems. They worked doggedly on compiling a wealth of detailed information on each problem and then directed their energies toward devising a practical solution.[17] The quality of these plans, or *arbitrios,* naturally varied, but most were attempts to apply simple common sense to the task of governmental reform. In general the arbitristas had no unifying ideology or radical programs. Their brand of reformism usually favored specific, ad hoc policies to renovate or repair existing political institutions. Faced with the renewal of hostilities in Europe and a nearly exhausted national treasury, Philip IV had to heed the voices of the arbitristas in Spain and Peru, whose views called for fiscal improvisations to stave off bankruptcy and defeat.

A young Andalusian aristocrat, Gaspar de Guzmán, later the conde duque de Olivares, emerged as the leader of the effort to reform the imperial finances. Olivares had quickly risen to become the king's chief minister in 1622, and until his fall from power in 1643, he dominated the highest echelons of political life in Madrid. Honest, restless, energetic, but inconsistent and brash, Olivares was well suited to grapple with the financial problems of the empire. Under the indolent governments of Philip III, fiscal policy had been allowed to drift. Olivares meant to end this policy and initiate a series of specific, long-range measures to reform the imperial finances. First the conde duque and his allies proposed a full-scale visita general of the Viceroyalty of Peru to gather information and also root out corruption and inefficiency in the local bureaucracy. The second step involved imposing new tax levies, aimed at increasing remissions of silver to the metropolis.

The conde duque first proposed his plan for a visita general of the four audiencias in the Viceroyalty of Peru in 1621.[18] At first the Council of the Indies urged caution, citing the shortcomings of past inspections, but Olivares would not be deterred.[19] For him the visita was the only way to reassert royal control over the viceregal bureaucracy. A centralized and loyal Peruvian treasury was a prerequisite for a successful effort to expand the tax base of the viceroyalty. It would be more responsive to the wishes of the crown and more likely to see that the additional revenues needed in Spain would be forthcoming. As usual the conde duque de Olivares got his way with the king. The visita general of Peru began in 1625, under the direction of Juan Gutiérrez Flores, the candidate favored for the job by Olivares himself.[20]

Gutiérrez Flores arrived in Lima later in 1625, with detailed royal instructions (*autos*) outlining his duties, responsibilities, and goals. The crown ordered the visitador general to make a detailed study of the major mining regions, particularly Potosí and Huancavelica, and to evaluate the performance of the most important treasury offices. The bulk of his inquiries, however, centered on the key administrative agencies in Lima, particularly the audiencia, the tribunal of accounts, and the central treasury office. Gutiérrez Flores had the power to subpoena all pertinent records and to press charges against officials suspected of malfeasance. In short, the scope of the visita was considerably more extensive than the more perfunctory and limited inspections ordered by a viceroy. Furthermore the visitador had the power to collect evidence, to make criminal and civil charges, and to send these findings back to Spain for a final verdict by the king and the Council of the Indies.[21]

The principal barriers before Gutiérrez Flores were the sad state of local records and the hostility of colonial officials. When the visitador general dispatched investigators to Huancavelica, for example, they had serious difficulties examining the treasury accounts, which had not been compiled in any systematic fashion for nearly thirty years. Signs of mismanagement and dishonesty also abounded in the administration of the yearly subsidy from Lima to the mercury mines, but the primitive state of the public records made it difficult to determine who was responsible and where the missing funds had gone.[22]

Similar conditions prevailed at Potosí. The inspector, Alonso Martínez Pastrana, an experienced contador mayor of the tribunal of accounts, took five full years to sort out the evidence of mismanagement and dishonesty from the shoddy records of the treasury office.[23] In the end the frustrated Martínez Pastrana recommended levying fines of 30,000 pesos against local treasury employees.[24] Local officials in both Potosí and Huancavelica contested these findings, using their political leverage to appeal the cases and undermine the visitadores.

Problems also arose in Lima. In his investigations of corruption and inefficiency in the viceregal capital, Gutiérrez Flores found evidence to indicate that at least one member of the audiencia, Dr. Alberto de Acuña, had abused his authority for personal gain.[25] In addition the visitador challenged the accounting practices and competency of the officials serving in the Lima treasury.[26] By the time of his death, in 1631, Gutiérrez Flores had accumulated considerable evidence of malfeasance and in general had thrown the audiencia district into an uproar.[27]

Dr. Pedro de Villagómez, an able and puritanical member of the secular clergy from Spain, succeeded Gutiérrez Flores as visitador general, in 1632, and continued the inspection with renewed vigor.[28] Villagómez strongly criticized the fiscal bureaucracy, particularly the tribunal of accounts. By 1632 the tribunal had accumulated a backlog of 381 unaudited treasury accounts from the twenty-three cajas of the viceroyalty, many of which had not even been sent to the tribunal. When the accountants did receive the records, they lacked the staff to make a careful audit. Accounts for Cuzco had not been examined since 1609, those for Potosí not since 1617, and for Huancavelica at least 36 accounts dating back to the previous century had gone unaudited.[29]

Apart from understaffing Villagómez also blamed the contadores' incompetency for the backlog of accounts. By 1634 he wrote to Madrid that Alonso Martínez Pastrana, recently returned from his inspection of Potosí, was too old and sickly to perform his job; another accountant, Francisco López de Caravantes, was nearly blind, and Francisco Marcos de Morales simply did not understand the normal accounting procedures of the tribunal. That left only José de Suárez to handle most of the agency's workload.[30] With this breakdown in efficiency at the principal auditing agency in the realm, authorities in Madrid or even Lima found it impossible to keep pace with the yearly activities of the widely scattered treasury offices.

Despite his persistence and dedication, Pedro de Villagómez encountered many difficulties in completing the visita general. He uncovered much evidence of mismanagement and corruption and even secured the suspension of several officials, including Alonso Martínez Pastrana and Gaspar de Ochoa, accountant for the *juzgado de bienes de difuntos* (depository for intestate goods).[31] Still, many of his tasks remained unfinished when he took up his post as archbishop of Arequipa, in 1635.[32] Even when the visitador general and his staff secured the unqualified cooperation of local officials in Lima, the task of sorting out testimonies and evidence proved overwhelming. On April 30, 1635, Villagómez wrote that over thirty separate testimonies had been heard about the tribunal of accounts and twenty more concerning the Lima caja.[33] Detailed information about far-away Huancavelica and other, more remote treasuries was still incomplete, even though the visita had begun in 1625. Furthermore when proof of corruption did exist, it was frequently impossible to prosecute officials because of their political prominence or even because they had died or moved away from the region. Collecting old debts posed similar problems when the debtors were unwilling or unable to pay their back taxes.[34] In addition, when the investigation lasted for extensive periods, the visitador himself could unwittingly disrupt the normal administration of the government and thus hinder efficiency and make his own task all the more difficult.[35] For their part local officials could work to undermine the visita, bide their time, and wait for the inspection to end.

Despite its shortcomings the visita general of 1625 at least provided authorities in Madrid with much information on the Peruvian treasury. The most concrete reform to emerge from the visita involved enlarging the tribunal of accounts from four contadores to eight. With the added personnel the visitadores and authorities in Spain believed that the backlog of unaudited accounts could be eliminated and the treasury cajas more closely supervised. Moreover the visita undoubtedly exposed some corrupt and inefficient bureaucrats and helped to consolidate and centralize the viceregal government. With this improved bureaucracy and new information on the operation of the treasury system in Peru, the conde duque de Olivares and his allies at court could frame more effective, practical, and specific policies to raise money in the Viceroyalty of Peru.

While the visita general was still in progress, Olivares and his allies among the arbitristas began working on the second phase of the reform program, the imposition of new tax levies. By 1626 these reformers had decided to make the union of arms the keystone of the financial reform effort in Peru. The union of arms called for contributions from all areas of the empire, including the provinces of Peru, to support a common army. This army was to have 140,000 men, recruited and paid for by the various kingdoms in the following proportions: Catalonia, 16,000 men; Aragon, 10,000; Valencia, 6,000; Portugal, 16,000; Naples, 16,000; Sicily, 6,000; Milan, 8,000; Flanders, 12,000; the Mediterranean and Atlantic Islands, 6,000; and Castile and the Indies, 44,000.[36] The crown assessed the Viceroyalty of Peru a yearly levy of 350,000 ducats (481,250 pesos de ocho) to meet its obligations under the terms of the union of arms.[37] Olivares hoped that having each kingdom contribute to imperial defense according to its resources and needs would impose a greater sense of unity in the Spanish Empire. He expected this military cooperation to be the first step in solving not only the defense problems of the empire, but also in uniting and integrating the treasuries of the whole empire.[38]

Despite predictions that the union of arms would be unpopular in the Viceroyalty of Peru, Olivares felt the levy was modest enough to prove successful. In fact he was much more concerned with the reception of the plan within the kingdoms of the Iberian peninsula. Catalonia, Portugal, and Aragon were separate kingdoms within the empire, and each had preserved its own laws and privileges (*fueros*).[39] The king had to ask the *cortes* of each of these kingdoms to appropriate money for the union of arms voluntarily. The Viceroyalty of Peru, however, had no such elevated legal status. According to the eminent jurist Juan de Solórzano y Pereyra, the Indies were "appendages" of Castile.[40] As a result King Philip could, in theory, simply impose the union of arms and demand compliance for the allotted fifteen years. As events proved the success of the union had little to do with the law. Instead it depended on political realities such as the crown's ability to gain the active support of the colonial bureaucracy and the acquiescence of local taxpayers.

The support of the viceregal government and the local citizenry in Peru proved difficult to attain. The plan called for Peruvians to pay new taxes for a government program not intended for their direct benefit. In an edict of April 9, 1627, King Philip IV explained to his viceroy in Peru, the marqués de Guadalcázar (1621–28), that the 350,000 ducats assigned to the viceroyalty would pay to build and maintain a fleet of twelve ships of the line (*galeones*) and thirteen sloops of war (*pataches*). Of these only four galleons and a sloop would serve in the Indies, to guard the Caribbean area. The remainder of the fleet would patrol in European waters, from the English Channel to the Strait of Gibraltar.[41] The crown did not intend any of these ships for duty in the Pacific Ocean, which meant that they contributed nothing toward the defense needs of the viceroyalty. With the renewal of hostilities with the Netherlands and the likelihood of new Dutch incursions into the Pacific, the proposals outraged many Peruvians. Viceregal taxpayers, who tended to look unfavorably on any new levies during the recession in the mining industry anyway, resisted the union of arms. The king may have been justified in expecting additional help from his South American dominions, but in so doing he clearly risked incurring both the anger and opposition of his subjects.

In spite of the Madrid government's demand that the union of arms begin in 1628 and the presence in Lima of the visitador Juan Gutiérrez Flores, the viceroy delayed enacting the new measures. The crown suggested in a letter of March 27, 1627, that the viceroy use forced donations and new taxes on playing cards, sugar, cacao, honey, wines, and imported slaves and increases in the avería and the cruzada to meet the new levy.[42] All were doomed to be extremely unpopular in the viceroyalty. As a result the marqués de Guadalcázar chose discretely to ignore these orders and leave the responsibility for their implementation to his successor, the conde de Chinchón, named viceroy on February 22, 1627.[43] Meanwhile authorities in Spain ordered the conde de Chinchón to initiate the union of arms immediately after his arrival in Lima. Both the Council of the Indies and Olivares himself informed the viceroy-designate of the necessity of imposing the union of arms immediately.[44]

Despite these clear instructions, the conde de Chinchón realized that unless his treasury officials and local elites accepted the program, it would be doomed. Also the new viceroy hoped to obtain certain patronage concessions from the Council of the Indies, to aid him in getting adequate local support for the new taxes, including the power to distribute more knighthoods, new bureaucratic offices, and several honorific titles.[45] The council, however, denied these requests and reiterated its demand that he implement a tax package capable of supplying the yearly allotment of 350,000 ducats.[46] With rumors of a Dutch attack circulating, the viceroy conferred with the archbishop of Lima and several key bureaucrats, who agreed to delay taking any action on the union of arms.[47]

While the viceroy and the treasury officials in Peru procrastinated, authorities in Madrid formulated a new series of measures to raise the 350,000 ducats assigned to the viceroyalty. The Council of the Indies consulted a group of distinguished public servants with experience in the Indies, including the marqués de Gélves, the príncipe de Esquilache, Juan de Villela, the marqués de Cadereita, Rodrigo de Aguiar, and the marqués de Oropesa. They became responsible for devising a workable tax plan for Peru.[48] This junta and the Council of the Indies also sought the advice of numerous arbitristas and several additional veteran bureaucrats who had served in Peru, such as Juan de Solórzano y Pereyra, before formulating their proposal.[49]

On April 20, 1630, the council finally agreed to send a list of twenty-four arbitrios to the Viceroy of Peru, to raise the money required for the union of arms.[50] The arbitrios may be divided into the following categories: donativos; new taxes on all new food and wine stores (pulperías) in each city or town, a tax on all land or land titles sold in the viceroyalty, a 10 percent surcharge on all jewels and silver jewelry sold, a tax on local vineyards or locally produced wines, an assessment of one or two pesos on mine owners for each Amerindian mitayo working in their operations; the sale of encomiendas, feudal privileges, and new bureaucratic offices such as the *escribano de repartimientos* in Potosí, the *alcalde de la santa hermandad,* the *escribano de cámara* in the tribunal of accounts, the *administrador* and *escribano de censos de indios;* the establishment of royal monopolies on consumer goods such as salt and pepper; temporary imposts (*sisas*) on sugar, cacao, and wool; exemptions from tribute for any Amerindians discovering new mines; and finally a rule demanding the remission of all gold mined in the Indies directly to Spain, instead of sending the equivalent in silver.[51] With these arbitrios the council provided the viceroy and the treasury officers with enough suggestions to create a tax plan capable of supplying the yearly assignment of 350,000 ducats. The challenge of implementing and enforcing these provisions belonged with the conde de Chinchón and the treasury.

The outbreak of the Mantuan War, in 1627, and the loss of the treasury fleet from New Spain, in 1628, added to the financial woes in Madrid and undoubtedly encouraged the crown to push for action on the union of arms in Peru. Along with the arbitrios of 1630, the crown sent a special commissioner, Hernando de Valencia, to aid in their immediate implementation. Valencia had served as the accountant of the royal pensions (*contador de mercedes*) and viewed the position in Peru as a means to gain a post on the Council of the Indies.[52] His personal career rested on the successful enforcement of the arbitrios of 1630, and he worked doggedly to secure their acceptance in Lima. Unfortunately for Valencia, the Council of the Indies never defined his exact powers and responsibilities, except that he was to cooperate with the viceroy and the treasury officers to implement the arbitrios and the union of arms.

The chief obstacle facing Hernando de Valencia in Lima was

the opposition of Luis Gerónimo Fernández de Cabrera y Bobadilla, the fourth conde de Chinchón, Viceroy of Peru and titular head of the viceregal treasury. Before coming to Peru Chinchón had served as a gentleman of the royal household, Treasurer General of Aragon, and a member of the Councils of Aragon, Italy, State, and War.[53] Like many experienced Spanish officials of the day, the conde had little respect for reformers or their proposals. In May of 1630, for example, he stated that: "I am not much inclined towards arbitrios."[54] Stiffer collection procedures and a tighter hold on the mercury-and silver-mining industries seemed more viable sources of revenue than arbitrios formulated in Madrid. Furthermore he distrusted the arbitristas, whom he considered unqualified by birth or experience to make policy decisions.[55] These feelings intensified when Hernando de Valencia, a special commissioner appointed without the viceroy's consent, appeared in Lima in 1632 to secure the imposition of twenty-four separate arbitrios, destined to be most unpopular in the realm.[56] After all the conde de Chinchón already had to share his viceregal powers with the visitador general Juan Gutiérrez Flores, whose investigations had divided and disrupted the bureaucracy. With his government in turmoil, the viceroy saw Valencia and his arbitrios as simply another source of annoyance and problems. As a result Hernando de Valencia had to face the prospect of imposing a set of unpopular reform measures at a time when the viceroy was hostile to the idea and the local bureaucracy was still disrupted by the visita general.

Friction between Valencia and the Lima political establishment began shortly after his arrival, on February 26, 1632.[57] After several long consultations with the viceroy and the audiencia, Valencia still could not secure the adoption of most of the arbitrios. The conde de Chinchón agreed only to support new levies on paper, pulperías, and wine. Even the sale of the alcalde de la santa hermandad provoked discord with the cabildo, which had traditionally viewed the post as its own patronage appointment. As a consequence of this local resistance and his own impatience to see the arbitrios enacted, the commissioner found himself increasingly alienated from most of the Lima establishment.[58] On August 8, 1633, Valencia wrote a stinging letter to the viceroy, admonishing him for failing in his duty to impose the arbitrios and the union of arms. In addition he chided Chinchón for making derogatory remarks in private about both the arbitrios and the royal commissioner.[59] The commissioner then wrote the Council of the Indies, denouncing the obscurantism of the viceroy and the Lima bureaucracy in 1634. Valencia accused local officials in Peru, particularly Chinchón, of placing the interests of merchants in the consulado, vineyard owners, and wheat farmers above the pressing needs of the crown.[60]

When his protests failed to move either the viceroy or Madrid to take any drastic measures, Valencia began to scheme in Lima to gain support for the arbitrios. In July 1633 the commissioner broached the subject of leading an armed uprising of the viceregal guard against Chinchón with the local militia leader, Sebastián Hurtado de Corcuera.[61] A former criado of the viceroy, who also served in the Lima caja, Corcuera displayed no enthusiasm for this bizarre maneuver or the union of arms.[62] For his part the viceroy mustered support for his position in Lima and defended his actions vigorously and effectively to his superiors in Madrid. According to the conde de Chinchón, his delay in imposing the arbitrios resulted from his desire to avoid confrontations with local taxpayers currently suffering from a temporary economic downturn.[63] The conde de Chinchón also denounced the commissioner's lack of tact and modesty in his personal and political dealings in Lima. The net result of the confrontation was to postpone indefinitely any concrete action on the union of arms.

Not all of Hernando de Valencia's problems in Lima grew out of his political machinations over the arbitrios and the union of arms. For the first year and a half of his stay, the commissioner carried on a scandalous liaison with a married woman of an important family. The bad feelings caused by this affair undermined Valencia's support and credibility among the local elite, who complained to the viceroy about the matter. Ultimately the conde de Chinchón had to ask an oidor of the local audiencia, Juan Galdós de Valencia, to intercede with his cousin and houseguest, Hernando, to end the relationship. The viceroy even ordered the commissioner to stay away from the lady's house, and Valencia wound up taking sanctuary in the monastery of San Francisco.[64]

Even more disruptive and dangerous, however, was a confrontation in the same monastery between Valencia and a member of the Lima cabildo, Luis de Mendoza, on July 14, 1633, over seating protocol at mass. In fact the two men both drew their swords, and bedlam ensued.[65] According to Valencia, Chinchón and his allies in the audiencia and the cabildo arranged the incident to discredit him and defeat the arbitrios.[66] Valencia was particularly fearful of facing trial before the Lima Audiencia, since the case was given to Fernando de Saavedra, a man the commissioner described as his enemy and a Dutch agent. In the end Hernando de Valencia withdrew secretly from the city, on August 17, 1633, to seek justice in Spain.[67] Shortly after his flight from Lima, Valencia described himself to authorities in Spain as: "a fugitive, abandoned by all, without reputation, waiting for the aid of your Majesty; for this purpose I beg humbly on my knees."[68] His mission in Lima had been an utter failure.

After Hernando de Valencia's unceremonious departure from Lima, his few supporters were leaderless and, in some cases, subject to harrassment. One young ally of the commissioner, for example, the mercurial Diego de Ayala y Contreras, suffered repeated arrests and abuse. His problems began when he became one of the first to make a bid to purchase the post of alcalde de la santa hermandad. This outraged the aldermen, who still bridled over this loss of patronage, and for six months they managed to block the sale of the post. When the viceroy reluctantly agreed to implement this arbitrio, the cabildo members then transferred their anger to the purchaser, Ayala.

Although he was the son of a former oidor of the audiencia, Gaspar de Ayala, Diego had estranged himself from the political establishment by his outspoken support for Valencia and his attempt to buy this alcaldeship.[69] When the royal commissioner was nearly maneuvered into a duel in the monastery of San Francisco, Diego de Ayala sprang to his friend's side, shouting:

"here I am who owe nothing to aldermen."[70] After Valencia left Lima, Ayala quarreled violently and publicly with an alderman, Juan de Lorca, over the affections of an actress.[71] Members of the cabildo supposedly staged this incident too, in order to discredit Ayala further and block his taking possession of the alcaldeship. Despite serving a short jail sentence as punishment for the quarrel, Ayala demanded to take possession of his office. The cabildo, however, tried unsuccessfully to place a former head of the consulado, Juan de Medina Avila, in the post instead. It took Diego de Ayala a full four years to assume his duties as alcalde, despite offering over 50,000 pesos for the honor.[72] His problems in the capital were still not over. In 1637 Ayala wrote a pathetic letter to Madrid, complaining that local authorities still bothered him, impeded him from carrying out his duties, and tried to limit his jurisdiction.[73] Apparently it did not pay to oppose the viceroy and the political establishment in Lima.

With the meddlesome commissioner gone and his allies in Lima neutralized, the conde de Chinchón was free to devise his own way of imposing the union of arms. Already unrest and violence in Potosí and several other mining towns of Upper Peru had broken out over rumored increases in the alcabala and taxes on wine. As a result the viceroy felt he had good reason to fear that any blatant imposition of the union of arms, without securing the active support of some members of the bureaucracy and local magnates, would result in chaos. Moreover the recent failure of Juan de la Cueva's bank and the commercial downturn that followed meant that little support would be forthcoming from the hard-pressed merchant community in the capital. The riots in Mexico City a decade earlier, leading to the expulsion of Viceroy Gélves during a grain shortage, must also have weighed heavily on Chinchón's mind. Once again the new tax package had to wait.[74]

The conde de Chinchón and the junta de hacienda in Lima finally worked out a two-fold plan to raise the 350,000 ducats for the crown, while still retaining the support of influential local citizens. First the viceroy petitioned his superiors in Spain for the power to sell juros at 5 percent interest, using the port taxes as collateral—the alcabala, almojarifazgo, and avería. He also proposed selling more encomiendas and public offices, making them hereditary, and selling *mayorazgos* (the right to entail a landed estate) to creoles.[75] The second part of the plan involved granting special favors to wealthy, influential citizens, to gain support for the tax package. Specifically he asked to appoint four special Peruvian *procuradores* (commissioners) to sit in the cortes of Castile and to represent Peru at the *juramiento* (swearing in) of the next monarch. Next he requested that the crown name creoles as well as Spaniards to all ecclesiastical and government offices, except those of viceroy and archbishop. The third request involved permission to name creoles to at least one-half or one-third of all available audiencia posts. Fourth he asked that one or two posts on the Council of the Indies be set aside for creoles. Finally the viceroy asked for the power to grant pensions only to those born and residing in the viceroyalty.[76]

If enacted these reforms would have raised most of the necessary tax revenue for the crown, but more importantly they would have signaled an important rise in the legal participation and political power of local elites in Peru. Although the conde de Chinchón probably did not expect all of these measures to be accepted in Madrid, his recommendations clearly demonstrate his awareness and defense of vested interests in Peru. The union of arms signaled a dramatic expansion of the tax base in the viceroyalty, and the conde de Chinchón knew that only royal concessions to local citizens would win their support for the policy. In essence the viceroy proposed opening the ranks of the bureaucracy at unprecedented levels to creoles and native sons, in return for their active support for the union of arms.

Authorities in Madrid adamantly refused to allow the implementation of the bold reforms proposed by the conde de Chinchón. Some provisions, such as like the admission of four Peruvians as procuradores to the cortes of Castile, received careful consideration, but were finally rejected as impractical. The council also rejected other, more radical measures, such as the alternation of creole and peninsular appointees to major bureaucratic and clerical offices. The crown would not concede such important discretionary power over the composition of its own imperial bureaucracy. Finally Philip IV issued a cédula, on March 26, 1636, again calling for the immediate implementation of the union of arms.[77] With nine long years gone since the first call for the 350,000 ducats, and the entry of France into the Thirty Years War on the side of the Protestants, authorities in Spain demanded immediate action.

One of the most crucial problems faced by the viceroy and the treasury was the annual share each audiencia district should contribute toward the 350,000 ducats assigned to the viceroyalty. The conde de Chinchón and the junta de hacienda carefully studied the estimates of the population, mineral production, and agricultural and commercial wealth of the areas before making the assessments. Finally, on August 30, 1638, they agreed that the contributions would be as follows: Lima 140,000 ducats (192,500 pesos de ocho), Charcas 80,000 ducats (110,000 pesos de ocho), Quito 30,000 ducats (41,250 pesos de ocho), Santa Fe 60,000 ducats (82,500 pesos de ocho), Panama 20,000 ducats (27,500 pesos de ocho), and Chile 20,000 ducats (27,500 pesos de ocho).[78] Still to be determined, however, was the thorny question of how to raise this revenue.

On December 22, 1638, the viceroy and the Lima Audiencia finally proposed a tax plan supporting the union of arms, a compromise meant to evoke as little opposition as possible. In the audiencias directly under viceregal control—Lima, Charcas, and Quito—the treasury was to collect the necessary revenue by increasing the sales tax from 2 to 4 percent, by increasing the avería from 1 to 2 percent, and by establishing a new tax of two reales on each bottle of domestic wine imported into any city in the viceroyalty.[79] The viceroy also ordered the presidents of Chile, Santa Fe, and Panama to impose a similar tax plan in their jurisdictions.[80] Both the arbitrios of 1630 and the previous plan of the conde de Chinchón were discarded. Offering no special favors or patronage to local citizens to gain their support, the viceroy expected some protest. Local citizens and the bureaucracy had united behind Chinchón in his struggle with Hernando de Valencia, but now the imposition of these new taxes was bound to evoke dissent.

The new imposts affected merchants and farmers most directly, and the focal point for their unrest was the cabildo of Lima. Merchants opposed the levies because they came at a time when the transatlantic trade had been in a decade-long recession. Likewise the owners of wine-producing haciendas and chacras on the south coast stood opposed to any tax on their lucrative businesses, even though this last levy had been rumored for many years. Since Spanish authorities had long opposed the development of a native wine industry in Peru, this unwelcome tax was not unexpected.[81] Still merchants and farmers alike protested to the city aldermen, who carried these grievances to the treasury officials, the viceroy, and the crown. The aldermen requested a lowering of the imposts, petitioning the crown to grant pensions, encomiendas, and offices in order to placate the community.[82] When these petitions failed to change the government's actions, the cabildo dispatched Pedro de Azaña to Madrid, in 1641, to carry their protests directly to the Council of the Indies and the king.[83] This maneuver also failed.

Discontent over the union of arms was by no means confined to Lima or even to coastal Peru. When word of the tax increases reached Cuzco, an alderman named Andrés Pérez de Castro offered to pay the crown 50,000 pesos of his own money on March 31, 1639, as a substitute for the tax package.[84] The local treasury officers and the cabildo of Cuzco supported the offer and even postponed the collection of the new levies while authorities in Lima drafted a reply. Eventually the Lima government refused the offer, and the union of arms became law in Cuzco and the rest of the viceroyalty.

Although crown revenues from the union of arms were substantial, they never approached the 350,000 ducats demanded by Madrid. Some towns, such as Pisco, in the Lima treasury district, simply ignored the new levies and continued to remit the same amount of money as before the imposition of the union of arms. In other areas, such as Lima, the consulado administered the levies and collected the taxes more conscientiously. Nevertheless the returns from the consulado to the

Table 10. Income from New Taxes in District of Lima, 1631–60 (in pesos de ocho reales)

Tax	1631–40	1641–50	1651–60
Pulperías	44,935	70,495	48,550
Unión de armas	271,706	1,221,498	1,030,198
Media anata	526,855	626,479	540,100
Estanco de nieve	27,179	20,699	10,949
Mesada	83,284	37,805	31,329
Venta y composición de tierras	73,282	585,950	113,010
Papel sellado	36,855	185,933	185,247
Total	1,064,096	2,748,859	1,959,383

Lima treasury averaged over 100,000 pesos each year, well under the 192,500 pesos assigned under the terms of the union of arms (see table 10). Indeed when the *visitador* Francisco Antonio de Manzolo studied the yearly returns in the Audiencias of Lima and Charcas from 1638 to 1664, he found that even in peak years, such as 1641, the treasury collected only 250,184 pesos of the 302,500 pesos demanded by Madrid. In lean years, such as 1648, that figure dropped to under 100,000 pesos.[85] In all likelihood, even if the local elite and treasury officials had cooperated fully, the tax plan in its final form was probably incapable of providing the funds demanded by the crown. Although it did raise some revenue, the union of arms did not expand the tax base of the viceroyalty in any dramatic fashion.

Permanent Taxes and Temporary Fiscal Expedients

The union of arms was the keystone of the reform effort in Peru, but it was certainly not the only attempt to tap new sources of tax revenue in the viceroyalty during the reign of Philip IV. The crown ordered the introduction of two permanent taxes, the mesada in 1625, and the media anata in 1632 and established new royal monopolies on snow in 1634 and stamped paper in 1638. Like the union of arms, however, receipts from these levies provided no dramatic increases in the total income of the viceregal treasury. The media anata and the monopoly on stamped paper provided stable but modest yearly increases, while others, such as the snow monopoly, fell far short of the crown's expectations. As a result the crown began relying on a series of lucrative but temporary fiscal expedients—forced donations, and the sale of additional land and land titles, public offices, and juros. All of these levies were a response to the decline in the mining industry in Peru, the disappointing returns from permanent tax imposts, and the expanding warfare in Europe.

The mesada and the media anata were levies on government and clerical officials. After 1625 all bureaucratic appointees had to pay the equivalent of one month's salary when they took possession of their post, to meet the requirements of the mesada. In 1629 the crown extended the tax to clerical appointees. Three years later the media anata replaced the mesada for all government officials. This heavier tax required half of the officeholder's first year's salary and one-third of any yearly benefits accruing to the post. In the district of Lima the mesada produced only modest sums each decade, ranging from 83,284 pesos in the 1630s to a low of 31,329 pesos in the 1650 (see table 10). The media anata was a more lucrative levy in Lima, averaging over 50,000 pesos each year. Neither tax, however, provided the treasury with sums approaching those collected from the union of arms. Nevertheless these two levies constituted the first major attempt by the crown to raise money by direct levies on the bureaucracy and the clergy. Both groups were directly under royal control, and the taxes were easy to enforce and provoked little active opposition in the viceroyalty. The levies only raised the initial cost of gaining an office or clerical post; they did not constitute a threat to economic sectors such as commerce or agriculture.

Like the mesada and the media anata, the royal monopolies on snow and stamped paper prompted little opposition in Peru. They also yielded only modest financial returns to the treasury. Together they provided the Lima government with an average of under 25,000 pesos each year, which did little to expand the tax base of the Lima office and never counterbalanced the decline in mining taxes.

While the permanent tax levies imposed by the crown produced only modest returns, a temporary expedient, the donativo, or servicio gracioso, proved quite successful in raising considerable sums. The donativo was hardly a new measure, but under Philip IV it became a common tool in both Spain and the Indies to draw money from privileged groups such as the clergy, merchants, farmers, ranchers, and others enjoying relatively light taxes. The first major donativo during the reign of Philip IV came in 1625, when the viceroy was ordered to obtain contributions from prominent private citizens, government officials, and the clergy. This first effort was successful in raising 670,000 pesos. Other donativos in 1631, 1641, 1654, 1657, and 1664 were less lucrative than the original levy, but they still raised substantial sums for the treasury.[86] In 1641, for example, the viceroy, the marqués de Mancera, obtained forced donations worth 350,000 pesos to pay for the expenses of suppressing the Portuguese and Catalan revolts.[87] This levy also helped to fund defenses against the Dutch in the Pacific. The principal problem with the donativo was its uncertainty. The viceroy and the treasury could never predict with any exactitude the amounts which would be raised with each levy. As a result it failed to serve the long-term needs of the crown in Peru as a substitute for declining mining taxes.

Another successful temporary fiscal expedient was the sale of juros. Although the Council of the Indies had pursuaded Philip III to halt the sale of annuities after 1615, the urgent needs of the crown led his successor to ignore the edict. Military setbacks in Europe, such as the loss of Breda in 1637, Breisach in 1638, and the disastrous naval defeat in the Battle of the Downs in 1639, along with the revolt of Portugal and Catalonia in 1640, required the immediate remissions of funds.[88] Philip IV issued his first cédula authorizing the sale of juros in Peru on September 17, 1639, and followed it with additional sales in 1640 and 1641.[89] The king reinstated the policy only reluctantly, writing in 1640 that, "although I know the importance of not overburdening my treasuries in the Indies, the present needs are so great, that what we have in these kingdoms (Spain) is not enough, nor is the ordinary help given to me by my vassals enough to assist us with the speed that is necessary to sustain my armies."[90] The disappointing nature of other reform measures, such as the union of arms, and the pressing defense needs of the crown forced Madrid to rely on this proven fiscal expedient.

These three juro sales between 1639 and 1641 met the crown's expectations, raising over 2,000,000 ducats (2,750,000 pesos de ocho). The key to the success of this policy was its quick acceptance by local elites in the viceroyalty. Unlike the sales of 1608, when many businessmen invested surplus capital in annuities, these juro sales attracted little attention from this group. In fact after 1642 the Lima treasury paid almost all its interest to clerical organizations and the remainder to Amerindian community chests.[91] Clerical organizations had accumulated wealth from dowries, bequests, indulgences, and lucrative investments in commerce and land. Government-supported annuities provided clerical purchasers, in particular, with a secure outlet for their capital that also paid sizable interest returns. The five percent returns paid by the viceregal treasury equaled the rate that borrowers commonly paid on censos funded by the church, and they were backed by the local treasuries, which had remained solvent since their foundation in Peru. In addition buyers could invest as much or as little as they chose in annuities.[92]

Although the government exerted some pressure on local elites to meet royal quotas, the degree of compulsion used was less than that for donativos.[93] In addition, unlike the union of arms, juros did not levy permanent imposts on vocal interest groups, nor did they extend the coercive power of the state farther into the economic and political life of the viceroyalty. Indeed the treasury's reliance on juros and other forms of borrowing may even have made government officials more responsive to the needs of the local citizenry. Consequently the sales proved the most successful fiscal expedient imposed by the crown during the century, provoking virtually no opposition from local interest groups.[94]

Despite the large sums raised from juros, the long-term results of the sales proved mixed. Apart from making the treasury more dependent on local purchasers, the sales also saddled the Lima treasury alone with interest payments of nearly 100,000 pesos each year.[95] Although these payments were not crippling and never exceeded more than 3 percent of the Lima treasury's yearly budget, they still imposed an ongoing burden on the office at a time of rising expenditures and declining income levels, especially from mining taxes. On the other hand the sales were easy to administer and imposed no undue burdens on the manpower of the treasury office. And juro sales gave the Lima government access to the largely tax-exempt holdings of the Catholic Church, without provoking the opposition of clerical authorities.[96] These transfusions of clerical money aided the treasury in meeting the urgent demands of the crown, all without provoking opposition among local taxpayers.

Another temporary financial policy that produced large sums for the crown was the sale of land and land titles (venta y composición de tierras), begun in 1631.[97] With the decline of the mining industry and the Atlantic trade, Peruvians were eager to invest in a secure venture like agriculture or ranching, a trend facilitated by the decline in the Amerindian population, particularly along the Peruvian coast. Since Spaniards had already begun occupying or even usurping land, the crown decided to survey all lands and sell legal titles for those plots vacant for six years or more. If the land had been taken illegally or if the owner had no formal title, the crown instructed its inspectors to sell legal titles to it or return it to the rightful owner.

On May 27, 1631, the crown ordered the Viceroy of Peru, the conde de Chinchón, to begin a full-scale visitation of the realm in order to carry out this potentially lucrative policy.[98] No serious action took place on the proposal until Chinchón's successor, the marqués de Mancera, dispatched a series of highly paid special commissioners, under the supervision of the nearest audiencia, to accomplish the task. The enterprise proved very profitable; in the Lima district alone the program netted nearly 586,000 pesos in the 1640s (see table 10), and the total revenue garnered by the crown from the sales throughout the viceroyalty probably exceeded 2,000,000 pesos.[99] After reaching a peak in the 1640s, returns to the viceregal treasuries declined dramatically, as most of the available land was alienated and taxed. This program was clearly successful in gaining widespread support, but it too provided only temporary relief from the fiscal problems facing bureaucrats in the Viceroyalty of Peru.

Another problem before local officials that resulted from the sale of land and land titles was political curruption. Unlike the sale of juros, which proved relatively easy and inexpensive to administer, the sale of land and land titles was riddled with abuses. Land commissioners often proved susceptible to bribery and too often sold land already occupied by Amerindians. Other officials, traveling in regions unknown to them, had to settle the many confusing and conflicting testimonies of those who struggled to control the land. Abuses, mistakes, and confusion were commonplace.

To help eliminate these problems, the crown issued a cédula on August 20, 1656, ordering clerics to accompany the commissioners and oversee their actions.[100] This too proved inadequate, and the Viceroy of Peru, the conde de Salvatierra, established a special land court, headed by two oidores of the Lima Audiencia, García Francisco de Carillo y Alderete and Bernardo de Iturrizarra y Mansilla, which met every Tuesday and Friday from 11:00 A.M. to 12:00 noon to sort out the many cases of fraud.[101] Still reports of scandals from provinces throughout Peru continued. One of the most notable cases involved a prominent Amerindian of Cajamarca, Lázaro Juloguamán, and one of the commissioners of the province, Juan de Meneses, whose brother Pedro was an oidor of the Lima Audiencia. Juloguamán accused Meneses of selling Amerindian lands without compensation, giving all lands with water to Spaniards (thus making Amerindian holders dependent on the Spanish farmers for their water allotments), and finally of selling too much land in the region without leaving the common pasturelands required by law. The supervisors of the sales, Dr. Antonio de Calatayud, Baltásar de Alarcón, Juan González de Peñafiel, and Pedro de Quesada, were also implicated in the charges for ignoring Meneses's wrongdoing in their reports.[102] For his part Meneses denied the charges, arguing that he had made numerous trips to the area, damaging his frail health. He also claimed to have netted over 250,000 pesos for the crown, despite having to sell land that was often inferior for farming. Furthermore he denied having sold any unoccupied Amerindian lands and stated that he had allocated over 600,000 *fanegas* (1 fanega = 3.5 acres) of grazing land, as the crown had stipulated.

Little came of the case.[103] Like most of the commissioners, Meneses could mount a convincing defense, and his stature in Lima made any conviction unlikely. After all the land sales in Cajamarca and elsewhere benefited the crown, the treasury, and local elites. The king was reluctant to return any funds obtained illegally from the transactions, the bureaucrats were unwilling to risk displacing any Spanish landowners, and the local citizenry often threatened extensive litigation or even violence to protect their holdings. Only the Amerindians suffered, and they had little political influence. Whether legal or illegal, most land sales remained in force.

Like the union of arms, the other levies imposed during the reign of Philip IV proved incapable, in the long run, of offsetting the decline in mining taxes. The principal reason for this failure was the crown's reliance on temporary fiscal expedients such as the sale of land or *juros*. The marqués de Mancera (viceroy, 1639–48), for example, raised nearly 3,000,000 pesos from these sources. His successor, the conde de Salvatierra, on the other hand, collected only 500,000 pesos from these same levies during his six years in office.[104] With the fall of the conde duque de Olivares, in 1643, the reforming impulse lost much of its force, and the viceregal treasury simply failed to impose any new financial levies to substitute for these earlier measures. Neither the beleagured government in Madrid nor the viceregal treasury was able to assess lucrative new taxes on the Church, agriculture, commerce, and industry, which might have averted an eventual fiscal crisis in Lima.

The Onset of Financial Decline

Disturbing signs of financial decline began to appear in the Viceroyalty of Peru by the 1650s. For a time the new tax levies, the discovery of silver deposits in areas such as Cailloma, and tighter collection procedures all combined to bolster treasury receipts to their peak of over 4,000,000 pesos during the height of the reform period.[105] But as mining taxes continued to decline, and the influence of temporary expedients such as the sale of land and land titles began to diminish, total income levels at the Lima treasury office began to drop at an alarming rate. As a consequence officials in the viceregal capital began retaining a larger share of the royal income within the realm just to meet local expenses for defense, the subsidy to Huancavelica, and the repayment of loans and interest on juros. Despite crown pressure to force greater contributions, remissions to the metropolis became very irregular and declined overall. These contributions, for example, fluctuated from a low of 446,421 pesos in 1653 to a high of 1,222,738 pesos in 1656.[106] Obviously the underlying goal of the reformers, to force the colonies to bear a greater share of the expenses of the war effort in Europe, had failed. Officials in Spain began demanding an explanation.

Under this pressure from Madrid, the conde de Santisteban began an extensive investigation of the royal treasury after he assumed his post as viceroy, in 1661. His initial findings showed that the viceregal treasury was reaching a crisis. The gradual fall in total income in Lima from the traditional tax structure had forced his predecessors to borrow in order to meet the spiraling expenses of the treasury and the demands of the metropolis. As the treasury used up its credit and the reform program failed, royal treasury officials began meeting their commitments by withholding funds normally remitted to Spain or by failing to pay their yearly expenses in Peru. This meant only partial payments for the subsidies to Chile and Huancavelica and the postponement of loan repayments.

By the 1650s this policy of deficit spending led to a mass of unpaid bills. When the conde de Salvatierra stepped down as viceroy, in 1655, public debts at the Lima treasury were 416,376 pesos. The conde de Alba de Liste, however, continued the policy; when he resigned, in 1660, the debt figure had risen to 2,418,528 pesos.[107] Since income levels had already dropped considerably, the conde de Santisteban complained that he had less money to pay the normal bills of the government, let alone meet the debts of his predecessors. Indeed by 1662 he gloomily projected that the debt could even reach 3,572,529 pesos.[108] Over 50 percent of these debts were owed to the miners of Huancavelica and the military establishment; the failure to meet these obligations could have disastrous consequences for the defense of the realm and the supply of mercury, which could cripple silver mining.[109]

As a result the conde de Santisteban explained that remissions of silver to Spain would decline still farther, until the debts were repaid and the crisis averted. The viceroy was particularly bitter about the policies of his predecessor, the conde de Alba de Liste. Santisteban charged that Alba had even borrowed 638,414 pesos in future tax revenues for 1661 from the treasury to bolster artifically his final shipment of revenue to Spain.[110] This not only increased the debt in Lima but also made Santisteban's government critically short of operating funds during his first year in office. The treasurer of the Lima caja, Juan de Quesada y Sotomayor, supported his superior, acknowledging that the treasury coffers had literally been emptied by the conde de Alba de Liste before he left office.[111]

The conde de Alba de Liste vigorously defended himself against Santisteban's allegations in a letter to the crown on February 22, 1662.[112] Alba denied having allowed the public debt to top 2,000,000 pesos, and also declared that he had not borrowed tax revenue from 1661 to meet the obligations of his last armada.[113] Indeed the former viceroy boasted of sending yearly shipments averaging over 1,000,000 pesos to Spain. The conde de Alba de Liste did not deny, however, the financial problems outlined by Santisteban. In fact Alba accused his successor of understating these difficulties. According to the former viceroy, when he came to Lima in 1654, the public debt was not 416,376 pesos but 1,306,592 pesos. Alba wrote that he had to repay these debts in the face of declining or stagnant revenues and still meet the rising costs for defense, the mercury mines, and repairs to public buildings following a damaging earthquake.[114] According to Alba, the problems outlined by the conde de Santisteban had developed long before 1662.

Regardless of who was correct, the problems of fiscal irresponsibility, declining revenues, rising expenses, and the accumulation of public debts proved alarming. Further declines in the remissions of revenue from Lima to Seville seemed inevitable. In addition news of a violent uprising of miners in the rich province of Laicocota and the apparent reverses suffered in the Araucanian wars in Chile indicated that the financially hard-pressed Lima government was losing control over the interior provinces. The reforming impulse seemed spent, and the entire imperial system in Peru appeared threatened.

Conclusion

The reign of King Philip IV was a time of financial reform within the Spanish Empire. The high cost of supporting the war effort in Europe forced the monarch and the conde duque de Olivares to impose a series of tax levies and temporary fiscal expedients, aimed at expanding the tax base of the Peruvian treasury and increasing remissions of money from Lima to Seville. At the same time the demands of the Madrid government came at a difficult moment in the economic life of the viceroyalty. The decline of the silver-mining industry had undermined the solvency of the treasury and made local elites sensitive to any new financial imposts on the nonmining sectors of the viceregal economy. These opponents of the reform program and their allies in the bureaucracy worked hard to defeat the new levies and did succeed in delaying or limiting the successful imposition of the most objectionable taxes.

In the end the only really successful elements of the reform program were those taxes that met the needs of both the crown and local taxpayers such as the sale of land titles and juros. Nevertheless the reforms still succeeded in raising total income levels temporarily, by the 1640s. There were no outbreaks of the violence that plagued Mexico City during these years, and it appeared that the crown had achieved its basic objectives. The weaknesses of the reforms began to appear, however, by the middle of the century. By that time the reforming impulse had lost its drive in both Lima and Madrid. Olivares fell from power in 1643, and the crown was too preoccupied with revolts in Catalonia and Portugal to maintain a high level of fiscal pressure on the viceregal treasury. Income levels in Lima declined, as returns from permanent taxes such as the union of arms proved inadequate to substitute for the decline in mining taxes.

The financial measures imposed between 1625 and 1643 were not the cause for the political and financial problems in Lima. Indeed some measures, such as the union of arms, were imaginative efforts to expand the tax base of the viceregal treasury and tap new sources of commercial and agricultural wealth. It was the timing of these measures and the groundswell of popular opposition that undercut the effort. The only recourse open to viceroys by the 1650s was to borrow against future revenues in order to meet local expenses and still make sizable shipments of money to Seville. By the time the conde de Santisteban took office, in 1661, these policies had put the government deeply in debt, which threatened to undermine both the defense of realm and the mining industry. The reform program was clearly spent, and a fiscal crisis was imminent. Officials in Madrid recognized these problems and turned to a traditional political solution, the visita general.

7 *The Visita General, 1664–1690*

Attempts to end the deepening fiscal crisis in the Viceroyalty of Peru occupied the attention of imperial policy makers throughout the second half of the seventeenth century. The financial levies favored by the conde duque de Olivares and the arbitristas had clearly failed to reverse the decline in Peruvian revenues, and the Madrid government abandoned these policies in favor of a proven administrative tool, the visita general. Indeed the political and financial history of Peru during this period was dominated by the visita, initiated in 1664. Officials in Madrid blamed the dismal financial condition of the viceregal treasury on an administrative and political breakdown of the colonial bureaucracy and felt the visita was the best way to correct the problem. As a consequence the goals of the visita were to reassert royal control over the viceregal government and to secure the vigorous enforcement of all royal financial policies. The royal inspectors were commanded to ensure that all existing taxes were collected more efficiently, to root out corruption within the bureaucracy, to put an end to all contraband trade, and finally to take all steps necessary to reinvigorate the mining industry. Efforts to reform the viceregal treasury and to end the fiscal crisis did not stop with the fall of Olivares in 1643, they simply shifted in focus.[1]

Despite its reputation for decadence, the government of Charles II pursued the visita general of Peru with persistence and vigor. In 1664 the crown appointed two well-connected Spaniards,

Juan de Cornejo and Francisco Antonio de Manzolo, to head the inspection. The visita uncovered a host of abuses, but the hostility of local magnates and friction between the two inspectors culminated in Cornejo's recall, in 1666. The visita then progressed at a sluggish pace until 1669, when Madrid appointed a distinguished native son of Lima, Álvaro de Ibarra, to lead the investigation. Along with his viceroy and patron, the conde de Lemos, Ibarra proceeded to prosecute offenders vigorously, particularly those who opposed the conde de Lemos and himself. With the premature death of the viceroy, in 1672, followed three years later by the death of Ibarra himself, the visita general virtually ceased. In 1677, however, the crown again revived the inspection, appointing an oidor of the Lima Audiencia, Agustín Mauricio de Villavicencio, as visitador general; after his death the task fell to another oidor of the Lima tribunal, Juan de Peñalosa, to finish the assignment.

Although the visita general dominated political life in the viceregal capital after 1664, it did little to reverse the financial decline of the viceregal treasury. In fact the investigations proved a divisive force in local politics, hindered the smooth operation of the government, and made it more difficult to respond to disturbances in the interior provinces, such as the uprising at Laicocota. In the end these divisions in the capital, the gradual impoverishment of the viceregal treasury, and the disastrous consequences of the earthquake of 1687 combined to undermine the imperial system in Peru. Like the reforming efforts of Olivares and the arbitristas, the visita general failed to stem the imperial decline of the seventeenth century.

First Stage of the Visita General

By 1660 officials in Madrid had begun to see the need for a full-scale reform of the viceregal treasury system in Peru. Tax records from Lima indicated that income had dropped alarmingly and that remissions of revenue to the metropolis had suffered accordingly. In addition the crown learned that much of the problem was caused by the political and administrative disarray of the viceregal treasury. An anonymous memorial from Lima, dated November 12, 1660, for example, described this administrative breakdown in detail.[2] In twenty-eight separate points, the memorial provided an informed catalog of the rise in corruption, inefficiency, and public debts, echoing reports sent two decades earlier by Juan de Medina Avila and also confirming recent evidence sent from the new viceroy in Peru, the conde de Santisteban, who was conducting his own investigation of the problem.[3] Furthermore reports from important mining centers, particularly Huancavelica, indicated that the breakdown extended beyond the viceregal capital.[4] The aging King Philip IV undoubtedly hoped to rejuvenate the reforming impulse, correct the problems in Peru, and use colonial revenues to put the metropolitan treasury in order before turning the crown over to his young and infirm son.

In October 1662 the Council of the Indies met in a special session (*junta particular*) to discuss the Peruvian problems.[5] Information before the council indicated that the root causes of the fiscal crisis in Peru were political and administrative breakdowns, rather than any economic collapse in the colony. Apart from a slow decline in the mining sector, the viceregal economy appeared buoyant, in sharp contrast to the precipitous drop in royal tax revenues. Apparently treasury officials were ineffective in collecting royal taxes, and they insisted on retaining a larger percentage of what they did collect in Peru, rather than sending it to Seville. The councillors agreed that the best way to reverse this situation was to tighten administrative controls in Peru and to dispatch a full-scale visita general, to aid the reforming efforts of the conde de Santisteban.[6]

The crown usually favored experienced, Spanish-born bureaucrats and members of the Holy Office of the Inquisition to head such important investigations. The stern inquisitors or experienced bureaucrats were more likely to weather local opposition and to resist the many temptations offered by wealthy magnates, anxious to coopt or discredit the visitadores. As a result the council offered the post in Lima to Francisco Enríquez de Oblitas, an alcalde in Navarre.[7] When he declined the council decided to divide the responsibilities of the visita between two well-connected and tested Spanish officers, Juan de Cornejo and Francisco Antonio de Manzolo. Cornejo was completing a similar investigation of the audiencia in Santa Fe at the time, while Manzolo, a protégé of the powerful conde de Castrillo, was serving in the contaduría of the Council of the Indies.[8] Cornejo was to examine the records of the audiencia, the juzgado de bienes de difuntos, the tribunal of the holy crusade, the consulado, and the *correo mayor* (mail service) in Lima; Manzolo was to investigate the tribunal of accounts and the treasury cajas.[9]

The Council of the Indies gave broad powers to the two visitadores, providing them with a specific but wide-ranging set of guidelines (autos), which outlined the duties, responsibilities, and goals of the investigation. The autos required the inspectors to study the collection of the royal fifth (quinto) at the mining regions, and to give special attention to the treasury office and the mercury mines at Huancavelica. At the same time the council wanted detailed investigations of the major subtreasuries of the viceroyalty, particularly Cuzco, Guayaquil, Loja, Potosí, and Panama. The visita's primary focus, however, was to be the chief governmental agencies in the capital city. Along with the viceroy, these agencies had the most extensive powers over the administration of the royal revenues, and the crown needed their unqualified loyalty and honesty to reverse the fiscal crisis. Specifically authorities in Madrid wanted a thorough examination of several key tax ramos such as the avería, the cruzada, and the sale of offices. The council also demanded an explanation for the rising cost of local defense and administration in Peru, especially the subsidies for the *presidio* (fortress and garrison) at Callao, the armada, Chile, and Valdivia. Once cases of wrongdoing were uncovered, the visitadores would have the power to suspend accused officials from office and send them for trial to Madrid.[10]

From the outset Juan de Cornejo became the dominant figure in the visita general of Peru. Cornejo's experience conducting the visita in Bogotá and his appointment to a future post either as an oidor in the chancellery of Valladolid or as a fiscal in the Council of the Indies gave him immense status in Lima, even before his arrival.[11] Meanwhile his colleague, Francisco Antonio de Manzolo, had alienated the viceroy, the conde de Santisteban, by contracting a controversial marriage with a daughter of Fernando Bravo de Lagunas, a retired accountant of the tribunal of accounts. Bravo de Lagunas was not only a former official of one of the agencies Manzolo had to investigate, but he was also a politically powerful native son of Lima.[12] When Cornejo entered Lima, on September 8, 1664, he snubbed Manzolo. After coming into the city secretly, Cornejo went directly to the viceregal palace, to confer with Santisteban.[13] Apparently Cornejo emerged from the meeting with the complete confidence and support of the viceroy.

Friction soon developed between the two visitadores, as Cornejo began ignoring Manzolo and usurping his powers. Manzolo complained bitterly of his colleague's pretensions in a long letter to Madrid on November 20, 1665.[14] He maintained that Cornejo simply overturned decisions in numerous cases that fell under his own jurisdiction as visitador of the financial agencies in Lima. When Manzolo recommended ending the consulado of Lima's control over the port and sales taxes in Lima, for example, Cornejo simply overruled him. Likewise when Manzolo denied a request by the miners of San Antonio de Esquilache to lower the mining tax from 20 to 10 percent, Cornejo again reversed the decision. In fact Juan de Cornejo even took advantage of Manzolo's temporary illness to settle a dispute with members of the tribunal of accounts and also rescinded fines levied against several wrongdoers. The only way to resolve the impasse, according to Manzolo, was through the intervention of the viceroy, the conde de Santisteban.[15]

The conde de Santisteban, who served as viceroy during this early phase of the visita, was ill-suited to mediate between the quarreling officials. He was a pious and almost timid man, who avoided controversies whenever possible. Unskilled at political maneuvering, particularly in Lima, he viewed Peruvian politicians as excessively self-serving and difficult. Instead he relied on strong advisors, such as the Inquisitor General of Peru, Álvaro de Ibarra, and later Juan de Cornejo.[16] The viceroy trusted Cornejo because he believed that a visita general was imperative. The conde de Santisteban was a hard worker, with a particular interest and ability in financial matters. Indeed he had been conducting his own study of the viceregal finances before Cornejo arrived, and he apparently saw the visitador as an ally in his quest to reform the treasury system. The puritanical viceroy also mistrusted Manzolo, whom he feared had already been coopted by local elites. As he wrote to the crown in 1664, "Mr. Dr. Juan de Cornejo has much diligence, in that he seems an honest and well-intentioned minister. Some aloofness was shown by the accountant Francisco Antonio de Manzolo upon his arrival; it might be induced by others against his nature and the favorable opinion that I have of him. Recently he was married to a daughter of another accountant who used to be a member of this tribunal."[17]

Under the viceroy's patronage Juan de Cornejo grew bolder and more pretentious in Lima. In 1666, for example, members of the audiencia complained that Cornejo tried to overshadow the viceroy himself at public functions. He freely used his title as fiscal of the Council of the Indies, even though it was only a future appointment, and assumed the prerogatives of a noble, such as sitting only on a velvet-cushioned chair in a place of honor in front of the viceroy. In addition he had the temerity to address the audiencia while seated, dressed informally, and wearing his hat.[18] Such breaches of protocol were serious matters in highly status-conscious Lima.

Although Cornejo's haughty behavior and the conflicts with his colleague Manzolo provoked anger in Lima, the political establishment did not turn completely against him until he began his investigations. The initial focus of this local opposition was the erratic comptroller of the Lima treasury, Francisco de Colmenares. Like many in Lima Colmenares resented the vain visitador general and openly referred to him as Juan de Cuernejo.[19] The principal cause of this hostility was Cornejo's investigation of a suit worth 80,000 pesos, pending against Colmenares's wealthy wife, Silberia Hermosa de Chillón. When Cornejo asked for a detailed accounting of the couple's wealth, a bitter dispute erupted between the two men in the audiencia chambers. In retaliation for the incident, Cornejo suspended the obstreperous comptroller, threw him in a jail cell with common criminals, and then exiled him to Pisco.[20] This harsh sentence was undoubtedly meant as a warning to anyone else who dared to oppose the visita.

After disposing of Colmenares, Juan de Cornejo tried to discredit his principal enemy in Lima, Francisco Sarmiento de Mendoza, senior oidor of the audiencia. In letters to his superiors in Madrid, Cornejo referred to Mendoza as ambitious, vain, greedy, and seditious. The visitador general even resurrected rumors of Mendoza's alleged dishonesty as corregidor of Potosí and of his complicity in the mysterious death a decade earlier of a visitador from the Audiencia of Charcas, Francisco Nestares Marín. According to Cornejo, Mendoza had also continued his corrupt practices in Lima, becoming a millionaire in the process, with numerous illicit business connections in the capital and powerful political allies in Madrid.[21] Hostility between Cornejo and Mendoza became even more intense after the viceroy fell ill and died. Cornejo assured himself of ultimate success in this power struggle after he secured the aid of Bernardo de Iturrizarra y Mansilla, the man next in line to succeed Mendoza as senior oidor of the audiencia.[22] Together these two outmaneuvered Mendoza by getting a royal edict to suspend their rival for malfeasance in office.[23] On March 17, 1666, the very morning of the conde de Santisteban's death, Cornejo arrived at the house of the *oidor decano* with the royal order suspending Mendoza from office and placing him under house arrest. Several months later, on September 14, 1666, Francisco Sarmiento de Mendoza was formally exiled to Pachacamac, pending his return to Spain for trial.[24]

With his chief rival in Lima neutralized, Juan de Cornejo turned his attention to his other enemies on the audiencia. In letters to Madrid he declared that some justices were corrupt and incompetent.[25] He described the oidor Bartolomé de Salazar, for example, as a dangerous and greedy man, who used his position to build a personal fortune of over 10,000,000 pesos. Cornejo considered another oidor, Francisco de Velasco y Gamboa, to be an unlettered judge with little native intelligence. The oidor Diego Cristóbal de Messía, on the other hand, was too closely connected to the Lima political establishment to suit the visitador.[26] The other major offender was the fiscal and *protector de indios,* Diego Leon Pinelo. Despite his strong academic and government credentials, Cornejo considered Leon Pinelo a dangerous man because of his large family and numerous debts, which made him too subject to bribes and other forms of graft.[27] Among the other judges Cornejo found only Juan de Padilla y Pastrana, Bernardo de Figueroa, Andrés de la Rocha, Tomás Berjón de Caviedes, and Iturrizarra capable and honest men. The remaining members received only an ambivalent evaluation.[28]

Meanwhile, with less fanfare, Francisco Antonio de Manzolo uncovered a host of financial irregularities in the administration of the royal revenues. He found that the tribunal of accounts was staffed by a number of lax and incompetent accountants, who had allowed the agency to fall hopelessly behind in its duties. By 1664 Manzolo established that the tribunal had either failed to receive or audit over four hundred separate treasury accounts. Accounts for the major cajas such as Potosí, Cuzco, and Huancavelica, remained unfinished for over twenty years; not surprisingly, administrative procedures throughout the realm suffered accordingly. At Huancavelica inspectors found that debts totalled 115,000 pesos, while miners at Potosí had accumulated mercury debts of nearly 1,000,000 pesos.[29] The most consistent form of corruption, however, concerned the corregidores de indios. According to Manzolo's aide, Nicolás Polanco de Santillán, tribute debts from these officials had reached nearly 2,500,000 pesos by 1664.[30] Clearly officials throughout the viceroyalty had used the opportunity presented by the breakdown in supervisory procedures in the tribunal to lie, cheat, and otherwise abuse their authority. The result was staggering losses for the treasury.

While Manzolo was in the midst of his investigations, Juan de Cornejo continued to widen his political base in Lima. The most obvious example of this political maneuvering was his attempt to forge an alliance with Sebastián de Navarrete, a young and well-connected official serving in the Lima treasury office. The choice of Navarrete as an ally surprised many in the capital. After his father had purchased the post, Navarrete had involved himself in numerous scandals. In 1651 he was one of the future officeholders accused of engineering the suspension of Juan de Quesada and Bartolomé Astete.[31] Eleven years later, after his election as an alcalde ordinario of the Lima cabildo, Navarrete was excommunicated by the Inquisition for his numerous breaches of morality. Authorities in the city delayed giving the controversial alderman his staff of office for two months and later forced him to pay a fine of 1,000 pesos.[32]

Undeterred by this setback, in 1664 Navarrete was rumored to have been caught at 10:00 P.M. in a darkened room with the wife of a Basque merchant. Although Navarrete escaped before violence erupted, the merchant later left his wife, which lead to strained relations between the clannish Basques and the rest of the city's Spanish population.

The entire affair so upset the pious conde de Santisteban that he exiled Navarrete from the city to maintain order and ensure the treasury official's protection from the vengeful Basques.[33] Despite his checkered career, however, Navarrete was a knight of Calatrava, a future treasury official, and related through his wife to a retired oidor of the audiencia, Juan de Loayza Calderón, and a justice currently serving on that same body, Bartolomé de Salazar. And as an alderman of the cabildo, Navarrete had strong connections on that prestigious stronghold of creole power. These ties to the political establishment in Lima undoubtedly led Cornejo to favor the erratic young official; after the conde de Santisteban's death, in 1664, the visitador general reversed the sentence of exile imposed on Navarrete.[34]

Even after he returned to Lima and established a close relationship with the visitador general, controversy still followed Navarrete. Under Cornejo's patronage the recently disgraced official received a post in Callao, collecting the port taxes, as well as command of the galleys and the armada of 1666 to Portobelo.[35] Navarrete and Cornejo's opponents complained, however, that the appointment was a political payoff, since only one poorly outfitted galley remained in service. In addition these same critics charged that Navarrete's expenses for outfitting the treasury fleet were too high and that he had wasted both time and money in completing the task.[36] Finally, on the evening of February 6, 1667, an even more striking incident took place when Navarrate was shot outside of the city gates by a mysterious assailant.[37] Still Sebastián de Navarrete continued as a close ally of Juan de Cornejo.

Some of the visitador general's other friends and allies in the capital proved almost as controversial as Navarrete. According to his enemies Cornejo commonly ignored the normal bureaucratic hierarchy to patronize his friends with jobs, particularly members of the family of his mistress, Angela Flores. Earlier Cornejo had scorned his colleague Francisco Antonio de Manzolo for taking a local wife, but gossips in Lima pointed out that one member of the Flores clan in particular, Antonio de Monroy, had received two lucrative corregimientos from the visitador.[38] These charges of nepotism in the cases of Navarrete and Monroy together with Cornejo's increasingly open lust for power clearly undermined his position in Lima.

Another incident that hurt Cornejo's standing in Lima was his open conflict with a popular former viceroy still living in Lima, the conde de Alba de Liste. The two men quarreled when Cornejo attempted to investigate the findings of the former viceroy's residencia and his sons' activities in Lima.[39]

Each of these squabbles divided the political establishment, threw the normal administrative procedures of the government into disarray, and weakened royal authority in the realm, making it extremely difficult to quell the regional disturbances that erupted during the 1660s. Disgruntled Amerindians in Tucumán, Jauja, and even in Lima itself conspired to revolt against Spanish authority.[40] In addition military reverses suffered at the hands of the Araucanian Indians, coupled with the disruptive governorship of Francisco de Meneses (1664–68), brought Chile to the edge of revolt.[41] The most serious unrest, however, occurred in the rich mining province of Laicocota. Here difficulties arose as a result of friction between the Andalusian emigrés and their creole allies, who owned the most lucrative mines in the province, and Basque settlers. The Andalusian and creole faction was led by the two wealthiest miners, the brothers Gaspar and José de Salcedo, while the Basques followed their two leading citizens, Martín de Garayer and Gaspar de la Serna.

When hostilities finally broke out, in June of 1665, government officials in Laicocota and nearby San Antonio de Esquilache became involved. Soon the unrest threatened to embroil the entire mining belt, from Chucuito to Cuzco. Successive governors only fueled the uprising, which continued on its bloody course for six months.[42]

The war in Laicocota served to polarize the political establishment even further, as factions within the capital took sides in the dispute. During his lifetime, for example, the conde de Santisteban had favored the Basque faction and ordered Gaspar de Salcedo to Lima to answer charges. For his part Salcedo delayed and told his political allies in the capital that the viceroy's two Basque secretaries had prejudiced his case and would deny him a fair hearing.[43] When Santisteban insisted, Salcedo was quoted as remarking, "Why should I go down to Lima? He [Santisteban] is no more a king than I."[44] The death of the viceroy ended this squabble, and Gaspar de Salcedo never appeared before him.

At this point Salcedo also managed to gain the support of Juan de Cornejo and his chief ally, Bernardo de Iturrizarra. According to unconfirmed reports, Cornejo's enthusiasm for the Salcedos resulted from a bribe of 50,000 pesos sent directly to the visitador general in Lima, along with the promise of an additional 50,000 pesos if either brother received the local corregimiento.[45] In three separate letters in 1666, Juan de Cornejo promised the Salcedos his help with the audiencia and called them good and loyal vassals of the crown. Later in that year Cornejo secured the appointment of José de Salcedo as corregidor of Lampa and governor of Laicocota.[46] Meanwhile Cornejo's ally Bernardo de Iturrizarra wrote a scandalous private letter to Gaspar de Salcedo, asking for a large gift to a Lima convent, where his daughter coincidentally was cloistered.[47] The close association of the conde de Santisteban with the Basque faction in Laicocota and later the ties established among the Salcedos, Cornejo, and Iturrizarra tainted all parties involved. The visita had been launched just two years before to repair the administrative breakdown in Lima, but instead it became enmeshed in a host of murky and divisive local issues.

The deteriorating political situation in Lima and the spread of disorder in the interior gave Juan de Cornejo's enemies in Lima the opportunity to derail the visita general. On November 29, 1665, several members of the Lima Audiencia signed a long list of grievances against the visitador general, which they sent to Madrid. The letter underscored Cornejo's arrogance, ambition, and constant feuding with local authorities.[48] Along with the near paralysis of the viceregal government, such complaints undoubtedly contributed to his recall. The crown ordered Cornejo to leave Lima and take up his post as an oidor in the chancellery at Valladolid. After turning over the materials he had subpoenaed from the institutions of government in Lima, Juan de Cornejo left the city on December 10, 1666, his mission a failure.[49] He had been defeated by a combination of his own arrogance and the weakened position of the crown in Peru.

After Cornejo's withdrawl from Lima, the visita lost its strength. Francisco Antonio de Manzolo continued his fiscal investigations, but no important convictions resulted. Manzolo apparently confined most of his actions to improving the administrative procedures of the tribunal of accounts and collecting debts. Before returning to Spain, in 1670, Manzolo had become virtually indistinguishable from the other auditors on the tribunal. The fiscal crisis deepened during the 1660s, and the administrative and financial problems that had given rise to the *visita general* worsened.

The Conde de Lemos and the Revival of the Visita

While the political and financial situation in Peru deteriorated, officials in Madrid remained undecided on a candidate to fill the vacant viceregal throne in Lima. The two most influential members of the Council of the Indies, the conde de Castrillo and the conde de Peñaranda, favored an experienced nobleman, the marqués de Fresno.[50] On the other hand the confessor and personal advisor of Queen Mariana, Juan Everardo Nithard, lobbied for his young protégé, Pedro Antonio Fernández de Castro, the conde de Lemos.[51] Shortly before the recall of Juan de Cornejo, the full council met and named the conde de Lemos to fill the post.[52]

At thirty-four the young grandee was relatively inexperienced, and his appointment clearly disappointed certain members of the Madrid government, particularly the conde de Castrillo and the conde de Peñaranda. Nevertheless the conde de Lemos was a decisive, vigorous, and confident young man, who promised to provide the strong leadership so desperately needed in Peru. Before his departure the conde de Peñaranda informed the viceroy-designate of the difficult problems facing him in Peru. In particular Peñaranda warned of the recent dissention caused by the visita; the growth of factions opposed to reform in the audiencia, the tribunal of accounts, and the treasury office in Lima; and the disruptions of the interior provinces.[53] Forewarned, the conde de Lemos left Spain, determined to reverse both the fiscal crisis and the decline of royal authority in the viceroyalty.

Even before his arrival in Lima, the conde de Lemos demonstrated his ability for bold and even ruthless action. Shortly after he landed in Panama, the new viceroy intervened in a dispute between the local audiencia and the president of that body, Juan Pérez de Guzmán. Despite Guzmán's excellent record and his strong connections in Madrid, the conde de Lemos deposed and imprisoned him for improprieties in office.[54] Rumors of this affair preceded the viceroy to Lima, and when he arrived in Callao, on November 17, 1667, local magnates undoubtedly greeted him with some apprehension. It surely came as little surprise when the viceroy immediately began exercising his authority firmly and decisively. While reviewing the troops in Callao, just one week after his arrival, the conde de Lemos challenged local authorities to explain the failure of the royal galleys to tow his ship into the port. The commander of the galleys, Sebastián de Navarrete, was not present at the inspection, and no one else ventured an answer to the angry viceroy. In disgust the conde de Lemos abolished the post of commander of the galleys, stripped Navarrete of his title of general, and terminated his salary.[55] Although the viceroy alienated the irascible Navarrete, he sent a clear signal to local elites of his intention to reestablish royal control in the realm.[56]

Upon his arrival in Lima, on November 21, 1667, the conde de Lemos immediately turned his attention to the unrest in Chile and Laicocota. Within ten weeks he had dispatched his friend and advisor, the marqués de Navamorquende, along with four hundred soldiers, to remove the corrupt Francisco de Meneses in Chile. Meneses tried to flee before the soldiers arrived, but the new governor quickly had him apprehended, tried, convicted, and imprisoned.[57] With the Chilean matter settled, the viceroy next turned to the delicate task of ending the hostilities in Laicocota. After a quick review of the matter, he decided personally to lead a military force to the region and punish the guilty parties.

Even before leaving for Puno, the viceroy determined to his own satisfaction that the Salcedo brothers bore most of the blame. He then summoned Gaspar de Salcedo to Lima, where he was immediately imprisoned.[58] With one of the brothers in jail, the viceroy was free to take action against the rest of the Andalusian and creole faction, after arriving in Laicocota in August. He ordered the arrest of José de Salcedo, whom he later condemned to be beheaded and quartered. The grisly sentence was carried out in Laicocota, on October 11, 1668.[59] Gaspar de Salcedo was not convicted until the following March; he was sentenced to the more moderate punishment of imprisonment and the loss of his wealth.[60] Finally the viceroy ordered all persons who had business dealings with the brothers to turn over all assets advanced by the Salcedos within four days or face the death penalty.[61] In all the viceroy and the audiencia convicted and sentenced forty-two men to death in the affair.[62]

The divisions among Lima politicians caused by the Laicocota affair only deepened when the brash young viceroy undertook a serious overhaul of the viceregal bureaucracy. With his customary bluntness the conde de Lemos reported in 1668 that many high-ranking officials in Lima, particularly on the audiencia, were corrupt, inefficient, or incompetent.[63] The viceroy described the senior oidor, Bernardo de Iturrizarra, as a profane swearer, a drunkard, a swindler, and thoroughly corrupt. Another justice, Fernando de Velasco y Gamboa, was reviled for his dishonesty and lack of knowledge and tact. The conde de Lemos not only criticized the oidor Pedro González García Güemes for his poor judgment and abrasive personality, but also alluded to a rumor about the justice's apparent attempt to force his attentions on a well-bred woman of virtue. The viceroy also had harsh words for the justices Sebastián de Alarcón, Andrés de Villela, Francisco Sarmiento de Mendoza, and Bartolomé de Salazar.[64] The viceroy did not direct all of his venom, however, against the audiencia. He declared three members of the tribunal of accounts, Bartolomé de Solórzano, Andrés de Mieses, and Álvaro de Alarcón incompetent; and recommended that another, Juan de San Miguel y Solier, be replaced by the more capable José de Bolívar.[65] Furthermore he judged the officials serving in the Lima treasury to be an equally dismal lot. Juan de Quesada was competent but too old to perform his duties properly, while Cristóbal de Llanos Jaraba had good intentions but little native intelligence.[66] The conde de Lemos described Sebastián de Navarrete as a man of "foul conduct" and listed numerous scandals involving the treasury official since the 1650s.[67]

The viceroy's frank and too often unflattering appraisal of many in the Lima political establishment, along with his authoritarian style of government, added to his list of enemies in the city. These opponents of the viceroy bided their time and worked to undermine the powerful ruler in both Lima and Madrid. Men like Sebastián de Navarrete, Bartolomé de Salazar, Bernardo de Iturrizarra, Tomás Berjón de Caviedes, and Pedro González García Güemes had accumulated considerable political power, particularly after the death of the conde de Santisteban.[68] Several had been active in working for the recall of Juan de Cornejo, and they deeply resented the tough, activist policies of the conde de Lemos.

The viceroy was not without his own allies. He chose as his chief councilor (privado) the preeminent politician of his day, Álvaro de Ibarra. The son of a Basque merchant, Ibarra had entered the clergy, had served on the faculty of the University of San Marcos, as a canon of the cathedral in Lima, and as the Inquisitor General of Peru. Despite his oft-repeated claims to favor clerical and academic duties over politics, Ibarra was a veteran political infighter, who held posts as protector de naturales of the Lima Audiencia, Visitador General of Chile and Huancavelica, and was a valued advisor to both the conde de Santisteban and the conde de Alba de Liste.[69] Ibarra's chief ally in supporting the viceroy was the current fiscal and protector de naturales in Lima, Diego Leon Pinelo. Both men had strong academic and bureaucratic credentials, were past opponents of Juan de Cornejo, and had always remained social outsiders in Lima.[70] Ibarra was a Basque, from a merchant family perennially short of cash, and also a clergyman. His enemies in Lima derisively referred to him as the son of a dyer and most likely a mestizo.[71] Leon Pinelo, on the other hand, was descended from a Portuguese *converso* (convert) family; his grandparents had been burned as Judaizers by the Inquisition, in Lisbon.[72] Along with three justices of the audiencia, Diego de Baeza, Lucas de Segura y Lara, and Pedro García de Ovalle, they formed the core of a political faction that the conde de Lemos hoped to exploit in his governmental reforms.[73]

Under the conde de Lemos the visita general again assumed a central political role in Peru. Francisco Antonio de Manzolo continued his investigations, and in a report to Madrid of March 22, 1669, he claimed to have made considerable progress.[74] Manzolo and others in the tribunal of accounts had audited most of the back treasury accounts through the 1650s, and in Lima alone they had uncovered debts of nearly 85,000 pesos.[75] These results did not satisfy the impatient viceroy, however, who wanted to eliminate corruption at all levels and undertake a major reform of the administration of finance and justice, not just uncover and collect debts. As a result he engineered the appointment of his privado, Álvaro de Ibarra, as senior oidor of the Lima Audiencia and Visitador General of Peru. Now the viceroy and his faction had the added power and prestige of the revived visita with which to overwhelm their opponents.[76]

The newly appointed visitador general quickly began his investigations in Lima and made numerous findings and charges against his political enemies in the city. According to his instructions Álvaro de Ibarra had the authority to examine the records of high officials, levy any necessary fines, and make recommendations about punishment to the Council of the Indies.[77] Despite the strong sentiment in Lima against the visita, Ibarra repeated Cornejo's condemnation of Francisco Sarmiento de Mendoza for crimes in Lima and Potosí, and also found Tomás Berjón de Caviedes guilty of incompetency in his handling of the royal monies while governor of Huancavelica. Indeed Ibarra was rumored to have told intimates that he only regretted not having the power to garrote louts like Berjón de Caviedes.[78] The visitador general also recommended heavy fines for other political enemies, such as Bernardo de Iturrizarra, Diego de Messía, Bartolomé de Salazar, Fernando de Velasco, and Pedro González García Güemes.[79] Ironically Ibarra had no power to suspend the officials or convict them himself, and all survived the visitador's condemnations with only minimal discomfort.

The conde de Lemos and Álvaro de Ibarra did not confine their reforming activities to Lima. Both recognized the need to revive the mining industry, and they gave considerable attention to the cajas of Huancavelica and Potosí. The viceroy dispatched Francisco Antonio de Manzolo to investigate the office at Huancavelica and wrote personally to the treasury officials, demanding that they redouble efforts to collect debts.[80]

The visitador general and the viceroy expended even more energy, however, on attempting to reform the mita system, particularly at Potosí. Ibarra first recommended that clerical officials conduct a new census of the sixteen mita provinces, in order to stop the Amerindians from shirking their responsibilities. Ibarra felt that once an accurate count had been taken, there would be enough mitayos to run the mines, if these forced laborers were assigned to the miners on a prorated basis. If any shortfalls occurred, the number of mitayos could easily be supplemented by recruiting *yanaconas.* (Amerindian serfs)[81] When the corregidor of Potosí, Luis Antonio de Oviedo balked at these and other reform measures, the frustrated viceroy threatened, in 1670, to end the mita entirely. According to the viceroy's letter of July 4, 1670, the mita was in complete disarray, the Amerindians were abused, and silver production continued to decline.[82] Before the conde de Lemos and his superiors in Madrid could take any action in the matter, however, the viceroy fell ill and then died, on December 6, 1672.[83]

With the death of the viceroy, his enemies tried to undermine the position of his strong-willed wife and the visitador general, Ibarra. The chief agitator for the opposition faction was Sebastián de Navarrete. Navarrete spoke openly against the condesa de Lemos and the visitador, and tried to turn public opinion against them. On January 23, 1673, Navarrete and his brother-in-law, an alcalde of the Lima cabildo, Francisco de la Cueva Guzmán, appeared before the city council with a letter ostensibly written by the deceased viceroy. Although probably a forgery, the letter condemned the citizens of Lima as traitors. Navarrete and Guzmán used the letter to enflame the cabildo and the city at large.[84] The members of the city council and thirty-three influential citizens signed a petition condemning the conde de Lemos and Álvaro de Ibarra. According to the condesa de Lemos, the city tottered on the verge of insurrection, and she petitioned the audiencia to intervene and calm matters.[85] Led by the viceroy's old nemesis, Bernardo de Iturrizarra, the oidores ignored her request and even tried to subpoena the viceregal letters to determine if any had slandered the audiencia.[86]

Not content with this mischief, Navarrete urged a former member of the viceregal faction, Diego de Baeza, to blame the conde de Lemos's effort to reform the mita system for the declining productivity of the Potosí mines.[87] Navarrete was also apparently behind several of the charges brought against the viceroy during his residencia. Among the more serious of these allegations was a charge that the viceroy had bribed the marqués de Navamorquende with 12,000 pesos from the Lima treasury to replace Francisco de Meneses in Chile. A further charge declared that the viceroy had failed to send the situado to Chile punctually.[88]

Another antagonist of the conde de Lemos and Álvaro de Ibarra was Francisco de Colmenares, an official of the Lima treasury office. At the outset of his administration the conde de Lemos treated Colmenares well, even recalling him from his exile in Pisco, imposed by Juan de Cornejo. Within a short time, however, relations between the two men became strained.[89] Rumormongers in Lima claimed that the puritanical conde de Lemos sent Colmenares to investigate the treasury offices of Chile to rid the government of the contentious official. In fact there is some evidence to indicate that the viceroy intended the Chilean investigation as another exile for Colmenares; assignments to strife-torn Chile were seldom popular among Lima officials, and the viceroy provided an armed escort of six soldiers to ensure that Colmenares left as commanded.[90]

During Lemos's residencia, Francisco de Colmenares apparently attempted to exact his revenge on the viceroy. Colmenares's wife, Silberia Hermosa de Chillón, allegedly wrote a letter to the judge of the residencia, declaring that the conde de Lemos had smuggled 180 bars of untaxed silver to Acapulco as part of a routine mercury shipment. She also charged that on two other occasions the viceroy had shipped over 150,000 pesos in smuggled merchandise from Callao. Her husband's Chilean post, according to Chillón, had been merely a pretext to exile him for unmasking the viceroy's corruption. The outraged condesa de Lemos demanded proof of these allegations, forcing Colmenares and his wife to back down, and even to deny that they had written the controversial letters.[91]

In the end the viceroy's enemies failed and the residencia absolved the conde de Lemos of all serious charges. Álvaro de Ibarra also survived with his power intact, remaining as head of the ruling audiencia and visitador general of Peru. Without the support of his patron, however, Ibarra had neither the time nor the political power to pursue the visita vigorously. In addition members of the Council of the Indies had never viewed the conde de Lemos's appointment enthusiastically, and they remained skeptical of the policies of the former viceroy and Ibarra in Lima. Eventually they overturned the convictions of Juan Pérez de Guzmán and Gaspar de Salcedo, for example, and restored both men to their former wealth, power, and influence.[92] Moreover the members of the audiencia indicted by the visitador, received only light punishments, despite the evidence compiled by both Cornejo and Ibarra. Since the visitador had no power to suspend the officials, the Audiencia of Lima rendered judgment on these cases involving its own members. Not surprisingly the audiencia demonstrated more leniency towards the indiscretions of its members than the viceroy and his faction had. Once again the visita general had accomplished little permanent change in the administration of royal finance in Lima.

The Final Phase of the Visita General

The arrival of the new viceroy, Baltásar de la Cueva Enríquez, the conde de Castellar, promised to tip the unstable balance of political power in Lima in favor of the visitador general, Ibarra, and the reformers. Unlike his impetuous predecessor, the conde de Castellar was a seasoned bureaucrat, who expressed his determination to reverse the financial decline in Peru. Although many high-level government appointments during the reign of Charles II resulted from political or family connections, the new viceroy had made his reputation on the basis of his knowledge and skill as a financial expert, precisely the qualities he would need in Lima. In fact he had only gained his title of nobility by contracting a favorable marriage. Before his arrival in Lima the viceroy had served in a variety of important positions. He took his bachelor's and licentiate degrees at the University of Salamanca and later held positions as oidor in the Granada chancellery, fiscal in the Consejo de Órdenes, counsellor on the Council of the Indies, and member of the royal cámara.[93] This wide experience made the conde de Castellar appear the ideal choice to revive the visita general and restore administrative and financial order to the Viceroyalty of Peru when he arrived in Lima in August of 1674. A scant five months later, however, the viceroy and the reformers received an unexpected setback, when Álvaro de Ibarra died, on January 19, 1675.[94]

Although the crown delayed appointing a successor to Ibarra, the conde de Castellar resolved to revive the reforming impulse in Peru and eliminate corruption, inefficiency, and the accumulation of debts from the subtreasuries. These problems contributed to a decline in remissions from the subordinate treasuries to an average of only 1,440,931 pesos each year between 1672 and 1678, a low for the century (see table 11). The conde de Castellar attacked this with his customary energy, ordering that no more mercury be distributed to the silver miners until all quicksilver debts had been paid. Furthermore he prohibited debtors from holding public office and even demanded the resignation of several members of the Arequipa cabildo who owed money to the local caja.[95] He also sent a member of the tribunal of accounts, Sebastián de Collado, to audit the key treasuries of Potosí and Oruro and ordered detailed accountings from the rest of the subordinate treasuries. These efforts led to the collection of 535,503 pesos in back taxes, including 353,788 pesos from the treasury at Potosí alone.[96]

The conde de Castellar's gains from his investigation were impressive, but his most spectacular victory came in rooting out corruption in La Paz. Mismanagement and fraud at the La Paz treasury were notorious throughout the realm, and the viceroy wanted to set a clear example. He ordered the corregidor of the region, Pedro Luis Enríquez, to conduct a pesquisa of the local treasury, giving him the power to deal with any offenders on the spot. Informants in La Paz told Enríquez that the treasurer, Luis de Toledo, and his aide, Gonzalo de Monzón, frequently entered the caja at night and stole royal funds. Both men also hired unruly elements of the mestizo population as a private bodyguard, to protect their position and to intimidate other local authorities. The corregidor secretly raised a force of his own, ostensibly to fight in Valdivia, and captured both Toledo and Monzón. Enríquez then reviewed their books, confiscated all evidence of malfeasance, and emprisoned both men. By the time the corregidor had completed his investigation, he had uncovered 414,169 pesos in debts and ordered the property of both men confiscated. As punishment Enríquez had both Toledo and Monzón garroted, leaving their bodies to rot on a stake in the public square as an example to others.[97]

The viceroy also directed his energy toward meeting the financial emergency in Lima. By the 1670s he found that the

Table 11. Average Annual Income and Expenses for Each Tax Category in Lima Treasury by Viceregal Administration, 1660–90 (in pesos de ocho reales)

Category	Conde de Santisteban 1661–65	Audiencia–Conde de Lemos 1665–72	Audiencia–Conde de Castellar 1672–78	Viceroy-Archbishop 1678–81	Duque de la Pala 1681–89
Income					
Commerce and Production	278,730	308,365	516,852	318,316	371,569
	9%	10.2%	17.7%	12%	13.4%
Tribute	12,095	9,647	28,028	17,474	26,781
	.4%	.3%	.9%	.6%	1%
Bureaucratic	102,957	73,938	69,670	64,740	71,943
	3.3%	2.5%	2.5%	2.5%	2.6%
Mining	1,615	4,176	1,123	1,942	3,711
	.05%	.1%	.03%	.07%	.1%
Monopolies	36,031	16,159	17,323	24,881	12,800
	1.2%	.5%	.6%	.9%	.5%
Clerical	50,655	57,728	55,877	57,168	43,073
	1.6%	1.9%	1.9%	2.2%	1.5%

Loans	119,157	179,232	45,473	93,644	88,898
	4%	6%	1.6%	3.5%	3.2%
Miscellaneous	439,537	435,700	750,720	546,991	640,867
	14%	14.5%	25.7%	20.6%	23%
Remissions	2,046,186	1,923,854	1,440,931	1,532,261	1,517,658
	66%	63.9%	49%	57.6%	54.6%
Expenses					
Defense	1,095,829	903,768	651,522	1,080,030	1,149,650
	34.6%	30.8%	29%	38.6%	43%
To Spain	475,434	387,372	506,059	336,377	141,132
	15%	13%	22.7%	12%	5.3%
Huancavelica	210,068	198,664	294,271	286,273	332,602
	6.6%	6.8%	13%	10%	12.4%
Loans	232,835	235,918	113,656	175,266	145,485
	7.4%	8%	5%	6.3%	5.4%
Administrative	407,801	370,690	303,067	352,375	267,186
	12.9%	12.6%	13.6%	12.6%	10%
Miscellaneous	743,545	836,049	363,942	565,516	639,129
	23.5%	28.5%	16.3%	20.2%	24%

yearly deficits at the Lima caja regularly topped 200,000 pesos. This deficit spending had led to the accumulation of a total debt of 3,534,292 pesos.[98] This massive debt and the shrinking yearly remissions of revenue from the interior threatened to bankrupt the viceregal treasury, and the conde de Castellar took immediate steps to rectify the situation. When he found, for example, that the consulado owed the treasury over 300,000 pesos in backpayments on its tax-farming contracts, the viceroy demanded prompt payment.[99] In addition he was shocked to find that the treasury had sent 650,000 pesos in interest payments to the caja de censos de indios over the past eighty years, on an original set of loans that totaled only 249,625 pesos.[100] This overpayment on censos and the debts of the consulado were staggering examples of the administrative chaos that the conde de Castellar sought to end.

The viceroy also found that treasury officials were paying excessive exchange rates on Peruvian silver collected for taxes, which also robbed the treasury of funds. Apart from ending these abuses, he also ordered that taxes be collected more efficiently and even proposed a tax on tobacco to raise further funds. Finally the conde de Castellar demanded the right to approve all payments of royal monies from the Lima caja and repeatedly ignored requests, even those of the archbishop of the city, to expend government funds for repairing the damage to public buildings and churches after the earthquake of 1678.[101] As a result of this austerity, the conde de Castellar sent an average yearly remission of 506,059 pesos to Spain, the largest shipments in the second half of the seventeenth century (see table 11).

The viceroy's meddling in the administration of royal finance made him many enemies in Lima. Some officials tried to undermine his political position, as they had that of other reformers, while others simply ignored his edicts. One functionary of the Lima treasury office, Juan de Villegas, was even found forging the viceroy's signature on authorizations for payments to soldiers in Callao.[102] The conde de Castellar was outraged at this flagrant disregard for his authority and used his influence to have Villegas sentenced to two hundred lashes, a year of hard labor in the galleys, and permanent banishment from Peru. After his public whipping in Lima, on March 18, 1675, Villegas was sent to Tierrafirme. There he managed to escape his jailers and return to the capital, intent on killing the viceroy.[103] Disguised as a priest Villegas stalked the conde de Castellar for several days and finally tried to shoot him in the chapel of El Rosario, in Lima. The pistol failed to fire, however, and the viceroy's bodyguard captured Villegas. Although the conde de Castellar claimed to have asked for clemency, the audiencia convicted Villegas of attempted murder and had him executed in the public square in Lima.[104]

Not all of the conde de Castellar's enemies proved as ineffective as Juan de Villegas. By 1678 the treasury officials, Archbishop Liñan y Cisneros, and the Consulado of Lima were all alienated from the viceroy. The consulado, however, aired its grievances most vehemently. Its members resented the viceroy's demands for the entire 300,000 pesos owed to the treasury in back taxes, and were further enraged when he ordered a temporary suspension of the legal trade ban on commerce between Mexico and Peru.[105] The result of the suspension was a considerable influx of Chinese goods, reexported from Manila to Acapulco. The angry consulado demanded an end to the commerce, which they claimed undermined the Portobelo fairs, causing great hardship to the guild and hindering their ability to repay the 300,000 pesos. The complaints of this powerful constellation of enemies apparently had a strong impact in Madrid, because the crown ordered the removal of the unpopular viceroy in a cédula of July 7, 1678.[106] His ad interim successor was an old enemy, the Archbishop of Lima, Melchor de Liñan y Cisneros.

Although officials in Madrid recalled the controversial conde de Castellar, they still were not willing to abandon the reform effort and the visita general. By 1677 the crown issued a cédula naming two local bureaucrats to head the visita, Agustín Mauricio de Villavicencio and Juan de Saiceta y Cucho.[107] Villavicencio was an oidor of the Lima Audiencia; Saiceta y Cucho had purchased an appointment as contador mayor on the tribunal of accounts in 1652.[108] Both had wide experience, especially

Saiceta y Cucho who had figured in the reform movement in Lima under both the conde de Lemos and the conde de Castellar.[109]

Officials in Madrid instructed the visitadores to focus their investigations specifically on the financial bureaucracy, especially the caja of Lima. The archbishop-viceroy, an outspoken critic of the conde de Castellar, nevertheless recognized the need to reform the administration of royal revenues. Liñan y Cisneros blamed most of the financial problems in Peru on the sale of fiscal offices and suggested that the crown name only "individuals with technical training and conscience."[110] In short the interim viceroy and the crown were both willing to support this more specialized visita general.

Related to the renewal of the visita was a cédula dated December 12, 1680, which ordered the archbishop-viceroy to arrest the controversial Sebastián de Navarrete, citing Navarrete's efforts to undermine the reputation of the conde de Lemos, various forms of malfeasance in office (particularly his shoddy administration of the tax on stamped paper), and his alleged complicity in the murder of a cleric, Fray Juan de Carbonero.[111] After listing these crimes the edict then demanded the confiscation of Navarrete's wealth and his permanent exile to Mexico City.[112]

The harshness of the punishment caused a stir in Lima, and the viceroy delayed in complying with the sentence, explaining that he was waiting for the next mercury ship leaving for Acapulco. For his part the astonished Navarrete wrote a flurry of letters to Madrid, complaining of the injustice of the harsh verdict. He frequently mentioned his advanced age and infirmities, his longing to remain with his family in Lima, and his distinguished service to the crown. According to Navarrete he was a knight of Calatrava, a former alderman in the city cabildo, a descendent of a noble family of Baeza, in Spain, and a loyal servant of the crown over the past thirty years. During this time Navarrete claimed to have supervised the armada, to have served with distinction during the suspension of his colleagues Juan de Quesada and Bartolomé Astete, to have participated actively in negotiating contracts for tax asientos with the consulado, to have aided the visitador general, Juan de Cornejo, and to have saved the crown over 3,000,000 pesos through his vigilance in collecting taxes and cutting expenses. Indeed Sebastián de Navarrete not only requested a reversal of his sentence, but the return of his post in the Lima caja, an encomienda, and a knightly appointment for his son.[113]

Navarrete also received strong endorsements from his colleagues in the Lima treasury office, Cristóbal de Llanos Jaraba and Francisco de Colmenares. Probably recognizing their own peril, since the crown held treasury officials collectively responsible for any wrongdoing, these two officials argued that neither they nor Navarrete had done anything improper. Instead they declared that Juan de Saiceta y Cucho was an enemy and accused him of misinforming the crown for his own selfish purposes. While acknowledging some shortfall in the ramo of stamped paper, they declared that all officials in Lima had worked successfully to collect the funds. In addition Llanos Jaraba and Colmenares claimed that the confiscation of Navarrete's goods posed an extreme hardship on his virtuous wife, Constanza de Loayza y de la Cueva.[114] Despite these protests, however, the crown remained inflexible. Navarete's political position in Lima had apparently deteriorated steadily since the death of his ally and protector, Bartolomé de Salazar, in 1670, and his murky past finally led to his exile, by 1682. He died penniless and in disgrace in Mexico City, two years later.[115]

After October 21, 1681, the controversies surrounding the Navarrete affair and the visita general became the responsibility of the new viceroy, Melchor de Navarra y Rocaful, the duque de la Palata. The new viceroy probably gained the prestigious Peruvian post through his close association with the queen mother, but he also had over thirty years of government experience to prepare him for the post. Among the duque de la Palata's numerous positions were co-visitador of the Audiencia of Barcelona, member of the Council of Naples, fiscal of the Supreme Council of Italy, and vice-chancellor of Aragon.[116] This experience and his natural tact would serve the new viceroy well in Peru, a land beset by deep political divisions and financial distress.

From the outset the duque de la Palata proved prudent and decisive. His first problem was to execute the sentence against Sebastián de Navarrete. His predecessor had not only procrastinated in the matter, but had even allowed Navarrete to draw his full salary from the treasury. The duque de la Palata quickly imprisoned the former official, impounded all of his property, and put him on the first ship bound for Mexico.[117] Another pressing issue left by the archbishop was the selection of a replacement to the recently deceased head of the visita general, Agustín Mauricio de Villavicencio. The crown's selection was another oidor from the Lima tribunal, Juan de Peñalosa, but he proved reluctant to assume his duties. Although Peñalosa had no specific reason for declining the post, he probably feared the traditional rancor shown by the Lima political establishment toward the visita general. In a letter of February 16, 1683, Peñalosa plaintively asked the viceroy to absolve him of the burdens of the office and to await further royal instructions, which he hoped might name another to the post.[118] The duque de la Palata replied promptly and firmly, ordering the oidor to assume his duties as visitador general, without any further delay or excuses.[119]

Once Juan de Peñalosa joined his colleague Juan de Saiceta y Cucho on the visita general, both men prosecuted the investigation with intensity. To their dismay they found a host of treasury accounts still unaudited, despite the efforts of past visitadores. Accounts for the Potosí office, for example, had been audited only sporadically between 1617 and 1673, while Cuzco accounts remained unchecked for the years from 1608 to 1638, 1640 to 1664, and 1669 to 1681. The situation was equally dismal for most of the other major treasuries. Even the accounts for the Lima office had not been checked in the tribunal of accounts since 1675.[120] Under the watchful eye of the viceroy, the visitadores approached the task systematically and assigned accountants from the visita and the tribunal of accounts in pairs to audit all of the outstanding records and determine the debts to the treasury. Although they expected to complete the task by 1683, a report written in November of that year indicated that much remained to be done.[121] In fact the job was still unfinished by the end of the century.

Despite their slowness the investigators did uncover a host of debts owed to the treasury. On June 7, 1687, the visitadores reported that 3,806,623 pesos in debts remained outstanding in the treasuries of Peru. The largest amounts were owed to the wealthier offices in the realm, such as Oruro, which had 300,000 pesos outstanding, and Cuzco, with over 170,000 pesos. In fact the visitadores managed to collect only 325,304 pesos of this massive debt, largely because the debtors had died, moved, or simply lacked the funds to pay the treasury.[122]

The findings of the visita and the controversy surrounding the exile of Sebastián de Navarrete caused considerable unrest in Lima. On November 14, 1683, Juan de Saiceta y Cucho wrote that two treasury officers, Cristóbal de Llanos Jaraba and Francisco de Colmenares, had consciously obstructed the progress of the visita. He further charged that treasury officials and their allies in the audiencia had managed to embezzle over 150,000 pesos from the crown. Furthermore Saiceta y Cucho complained that these royal enemies and their cohorts had threatened his life. The visitador described himself as a sick man; while he was bedridden, these corrupt and seditious bureaucrats had provoked mob demonstrations outside his house to intimidate him.[123] Over time the passions aroused by the visita subsided, however, and the consistent support of the viceroy and his guards ultimately insured that no harm came to Saiceta y Cucho and his colleagues.

One reason for the animosity in Lima against the visitadores was the strong criticism they leveled against treasury officials in the city. Peñalosa and Saiceta y Cucho wrote often of the shoddy records of the Lima office and of the officials' sloth, approval of illegal payments, and fraud in the ramos of papel sellado and the media anata. In fact Saiceta y Cucho declared that the administration of royal revenues under Navarrete, Colmenares, and Llanos Jaraba had been "the most blind and careless that has been seen in many centuries."[124] The visitadores recommended that virtually all of the officials serving in Lima be "stripped of their offices, putting in their place capable and intelligent people."[125] In all the visitadores made twelve serious charges against treasury officials in Lima.[126]

The treasury officials vigorously defended their actions against the onslaught of the visitadores. On December 9, 1682, they empowered two men at court in Madrid, Diego de Villatoro and Sebastián de Colmenares, to defend their interests against the charges of the investigators.[127] In addition they wrote the crown denying the allegations of Peñalosa and Saiceta y Cucho, whom they charged with being their political enemies, interested only in using their offices for partisan political ends.[128] The Lima treasury officials also declared that the visita had cost the government over 100,000 pesos in salaries alone and had failed to present any solid evidence against them.[129] Moreover they pointed out that Juan de Saiceta y Cucho had not yet paid a fine levied on him in 1645, when he was the treasurer of Oruro.[130] Finally they attacked Saiceta y Cucho for his nepotism in securing the appointment of his inept nephew, Juan de Esquiluz Corcuera, to the tribunal of accounts and the staff of the visita. The visitador general, Peñalosa, knew of these abuses, according to Colmenares and Llanos Jaraba, but simply chose to ignore them.[131]

While the controversies aroused by the visita continued, the duque de la Palata persisted in his efforts to reform the political and financial system in Peru. He recognized the need to strengthen auditing procedures and authorized the appointment of four additional accountants to the tribunal of accounts in Lima.[132] He also gave Peñalosa his support in collecting debts owed to the treasury. In addition the viceroy addressed the perpetual shortage of currency in Peru by establishing a mint in Lima to share the responsibility for coining gold and silver and to curtail the fraud often associated with the isolated Potosí mint.[133] The duque de la Palata realized, however, that such administrative reforms could not affect the declining productivity of the two pillars of the mining economy, Potosí and Huancavelica. To ease the burden on miners at these two locations, the viceroy initiated a new census of Amerindians subject to the mita, including forasteros and yanaconas in the tribute and mita quotas for the first time, which promised to increase the supply of cheaper forced laborers and bolster tribute revenues.[134]

Another important problem facing the viceroyalty was the rising intensity of pirate attacks. To meet this challenge the viceroy increased local defense expenditures to shore up the wall in Callao and authorized the construction of defensive fortifications in both Lima and Trujillo.[135] The fall in royal income from the treasuries of the interior proved a major handicap in financing these projects (see table 11). The viceroy himself complained of the rising trend toward regional autonomy in Peru, which made it difficult to force revenues from the distant subtreasuries. He circumvented this problem to some extent by raising miscellaneous sources of income from temporary taxes to a yearly average of nearly 650,000 pesos, and also by withholding funds from Spain (see table 11).

When these sources of income proved inadequate to pay the bill of over 1,600,000 pesos for the new defense measures, he turned to private and corporate contributions and the sale of noble titles.[136] His long-range efforts to raise the tax base of the viceroyalty were thwarted, in 1687, by the great earthquakes that devastated Lima and the entire central-coastal region of Peru. The destruction hindered commerce, and the agricultural lands of the coast suffered severe damage to their irrigation system; this damage, along with soil erosion, severely curtailed the productivity of the area. The viceroy spent most of his remaining two years in office trying to rebuild Lima and Callao and recovering from the economic consequences of the quake. Questions of financial and administrative reform no longer occupied the preeminent position of concern.

The earthquake of 1687 and the recall of the duque de la Palata did not put an end to the visita general, but the investigations did become both less important and less controversial. The new viceroy, Melchor Portocarrero Laso de la Vega, the conde de Monclova, was a military man who displayed little enthusiasm for reform. Instead he concentrated on ending past political squabbles and moderating some of the more controversial recommendations of the visitadores. When Peñalosa demanded heavy fines and suspensions for four functionaries of the Lima caja, for example, the conde de Monclova substituted more modest fines of 1,000 pesos and let the officials remain in office. The senior treasury officials, Francisco de Colmenares, Cristóbal de Llanos Jaraba, and Francisco Antonio de los Santos, stayed in office and unpunished.[137]

On September 15, 1696, the visitador general informed the crown of the investigation's progress. He claimed to have raised over 30,000 pesos from the sale of an hacienda formerly owned by Sebastián de Navarrete and told of his efforts to collect 47,000 pesos owed by the Consulado of Lima and an additional 148,000 pesos in miscellaneous back taxes. Finally he boasted that his investigators had collected 250,000 pesos in debts owed to the Lima treasury.[138] In short the main work of the visita was almost completed; what remained was simply to collect old debts. The investigation had uncovered much corruption and inefficiency, but in the end achieved no dramatic reform of the treasury system. Among the senior treasury officials in Lima, only Sebastián de Navarrete was convicted of any serious crimes. Furthermore the conde de Monclova and the visitador general made no real progress toward reversing the nearly fifty-year decline in royal revenues.

In any case the economic dislocation caused by the earthquake of 1687 and lesser quakes in 1694, 1697, and 1699 probably made any such efforts to raise taxes futile. When the crown ordered a new juro sale in 1695, for example, the conde de Monclova failed to implement it, claiming that local magnates were then too poor to support the policy. For their part authorities in Madrid were more preoccupied with the illness of the childless Charles II and the brewing succession crisis in Europe than with events in Peru. The net result was a weakened government in Lima, a nearly bankrupt viceregal treasury, and a visita general whose energy was spent.

Conclusion

The ultimate failure of the visita general is not really surprising. Bureaucrats in Lima had little interest in imposing controversial tax levies, increasing remissions of revenue to Seville, or reforming the administration of royal finance. While the fiscal crisis and the many flaws in the accounting system in Peru alarmed and annoyed administrators in Madrid, officials at the local level actually benefited. By failing to give their support to the tax levies imposed by the crown, treasury officials eased tensions with local elites. In addition, without making up-to-date yearly audits of the returns from each treasury caja, the viceroy, the visitador general, and their superiors in Spain could not keep tight control over the administration of royal finance. Treasury officials could hide administrative short-comings, the accumulation of debts, use tax revenue for their own purposes, and exercise greater independence in implementing royal policies.

In Lima, and in all likelihood in other areas of the realm, ties of family, kinship, ethnic origin, and economic or political self-interest often exercised a stronger influence on treasury officials than their loyalty to the crown. The status and power of the bureaucrats made them acceptable to local elites. The sale of treasury appointments, of course, abetted this process of local cooptation and even allowed creoles, native sons, and radicados to gain access to these important positions themselves. Indeed several of the key officials cited for malfeasance by the visita, such as Sebastián de Navarrete, were corrupt office-holders. Corruption and inefficiency were simply the tools used by these bureaucrats to advance their own interests and respond to the needs of elites in the colony. What the crown viewed as corruption or graft, treasury officials and elites in Peru saw as merely the means to achieve their own legitimate needs, frequently at the expense of the weakened Spanish crown. Reformers in Spain and Peru could alter this system and temporarily eliminate some of these weaknesses in the imperial system, but corruption, inefficiency, and the accumulation of treasury debts continued throughout the period and became an increasingly important element in the administrative procedures of the royal treasury during the seventeenth century.

8 *Conclusion*

Peru was not the only kingdom in the Spanish Empire that experienced political and financial problems during the seventeenth century. To support its military commitments in Europe, Madrid framed a series of controversial new taxes aimed at raising additional revenue in Peru and elsewhere in the empire. What these new levies signaled was a shift in the traditional allocation of economic resources and political power in the Spanish Empire; this was bound to provoke discontent, particularly in the more lightly taxed royal possessions outside of Castile. Increased fiscal pressure contributed to the outbreak of armed revolts by 1640 in both Catalonia and Portugal, followed in 1647 and 1648 by popular uprisings in Sicily and Naples.[1] Even Mexico suffered periodic political instability between 1621 and 1660.[2] Royal demands did not provoke similar unrest in Peru, in large part because viceregal treasury officials were successful in maintaining a workable political balance of power that preserved imperial unity. Unlike their counterparts in Catalonia, Portugal, Sicily, Naples, and even Mexico, these bureaucrats were able to diffuse tensions by enacting measures that temporarily produced the desired funds but did not strike at the vital economic interests of Peruvian elites. When these fiscal policies no longer compensated for the fall in mining taxes, by the 1660s, however, a fiscal crisis developed that undermined the imperial system on both sides of the Atlantic.

Economic Change and Fiscal Crisis

Economic changes in Peru during the seventeenth century reinforced the normal antipathy of local elites to the higher taxes and rigid trade regulations demanded by Madrid during the reign of Philip IV. During the first half of the century, the viceregal economy was undergoing a process of evolutionary change from a dependence on silver mining and the transatlantic trade to a more diversified base. Mining still retained an important position, but increasingly regional agricultural systems, local industrial enterprises, and intercolonial trade networks became the principal engines of economic development.

The growth of the Spanish population, particularly in urban centers like Lima; the gradual integration of the Amerindian population into the market economy; greater investments by the church, merchant bankers, and the viceregal government; and the rise of the Pacific trade all combined to stimulate aggregate demand and promote economic development. There is no evidence of a sustained depression or even that elites lived any less well, at least until the earthquakes of 1687, which devastated much of central Peru and altered economic patterns in the viceroyalty. In this period of transition from a largely export-oriented economy to a more integrated series of regional economies, local elites were unwilling to accept any royal financial policies capable of draining Peru of investment capital and stunting the process of economic change. In short the reforming impulse of Philip IV and the conde duque de Olivares put the crown on a collision course with powerful viceregal interest groups. A bitter political struggle over taxation policy loomed, and Peru seemed destined for the strife that enveloped Mexico, Italy, and the Iberian peninsula.

The treasury officials entrusted to implement the fiscal policies imposed by Madrid, however, failed to fulfill their responsibilities to the crown. An examination of the treasury accounts for the period reveals that both total income levels and remissions to Spain remained relatively stable until the 1660s, when a serious downward trend began. Although these declines in royal revenues in Peru did not become acute until

Table 12. Average Annual Income by Period and Category for Lima Treasury, 1607–90 (in pesos de ocho reales)

Tax Category	1607–22	1622–59	1660–90*
Commerce and Production	172,286 (5%)	283,526 (7.7%)	355,238 (12.6%)
Tribute	16,911 (.6%)	24,929 (.7%)	19,421 (.7%)
Bureaucratic	38,784 (1%)	101,051 (2.7%)	73,931 (2.6%)
Mining	9,298 (.3%)	14,814 (.4%)	2,564 (.1%)
Monopolies	17,525 (.5%)	24,278 (.7%)	18,242 (.6%)
Clerical	55,402 (1.6%)	55,254 (1.5%)	49,901 (1.8%)
Borrowing	229,050 (6%)	335,210 (9%)	116,656 (4.1%)
Miscellaneous	621,193 (16.7%)	380,840 (10%)	560,985 (20%)
Remissions from Subtreasuries	2,016,674 (69%)	2,500,707 (68%)	1,609,866 (57.5%)

*Complete accounts for the years 1662–64 are missing from the AGI (Seville) and the AGN (Lima)

the 1660s, the roots of the problem may be traced to the 1620s, when the mining decline became pronounced.

Between 1607 and 1622 nearly 70 percent of the viceregal income came from provinces outside of Lima, particularly the mining centers (see table 12). Declining productivity of the silver lodes at Potosí and elsewhere threatened to undermine the fiscal solvency of the treasury at precisely the time Madrid began demanding more money from Peru. The royal treasury in Mexico was able to maintain its income levels in large part because new silver strikes at Guanajuato and Pachuca offset declines at older mining zones, such as San Luis Potosí.[3] To be successful in Peru, royal tax reforms had to expand the tax base of the Lima government, so that it could increase remissions of silver to the metropolis. During the reform period from 1625 to 1643, these fiscal measures did succeed in raising annual income from commerce, production, borrowing, and remissions from the subtreasuries to the highest levels of the century (see table 12). Most of these increases, however, did not come from permanent new taxes, but from temporary expedients such as the sale of juros and land titles. Although such policies temporarily appeased the crown and met the immediate needs of the viceregal government, they provided no long-term solutions. When these sources of money became scarce and mining taxes dropped still further, government income levels fell and a fiscal crisis developed (see table 12). In fact this fiscal decline in Lima allowed Mexico to surpass the southern viceroyalty by 1680, to become the most important revenue producer in the Indies.[4]

Administrative Barriers to Reform

A major reason for the treasury's failure to impose the new taxes demanded by Madrid and to avoid the fiscal crisis was the weak administrative apparatus of the colonial bureaucracy. Administrative power in the Peruvian treasury was dispersed among a series of private and public organizations. The viceroy, the audiencia, the tribunal of accounts, the treasury officers, and tax farmers all administered the public revenues that financed the viceroyalty. This collection of officials lacked a clearly defined set of duties, and relations between superiors and subordinates were poorly defined by the law. Furthermore Spanish colonial legislation often embodied lofty, abstract, or contradictory principles that could only be applied selectively in dealing with concrete financial problems. As a result jurisdictional conflicts, inefficiency, and corruption abounded. This decentralization of political power severely handicapped efforts to implement vigorous new fiscal policies, especially when local elites objected.

Treasury officials also acted as barriers to reforming the tax system in Peru. The decentralization of the bureaucracy allowed individual bureaucrats much discretionary power over the implementation of crown policies, which they used to balance the needs of both the crown and the local community. Ties of loyalty bound royal officials to traditional metropolitan interests, while social and economic connections in Peru helped them carry out their duties effectively. During the reform period, however, powerful vested interests in the viceroyalty used their influence to drive a wedge between the crown and the colonial bureaucracy. At the same time the crown undercut its position in Peru and tipped the political balance of power in favor of local elites, when it began selling appointments to the royal treasury offices and the tribunal of accounts, in 1633. The sale of these appointments allowed Peruvian elites to buy high office and thus gain considerable political power. The officeholders who came to power by the 1650s were also inefficient, poorly trained, and often dishonest. In short the sales meant a loss of royal authority over the bureaucracy as local family, business, and political ties in the viceroyalty proved stronger than any allegiance to far-away Madrid. While the colonial bureaucracy in New Spain became parasitic and isolated from the needs of Mexican elites, its counterpart in Peru became ever more responsive to the demands of the local citizenry, even at the expense of Madrid.[5] As a result the Viceroyalty of Peru remained politically stable, but the price for this harmony was the fiscal crisis of the 1660s.

Reform and Resistance

During most of the reign of Philip IV, financial reform was a dominant political issue in the Spanish Empire. Like the Bourbon reformers a century later, the king and the conde duque de Olivares had to frame a coherent program of levies capable of tapping more effectively the economic wealth of the empire. The keystone of this program in Peru was the union of arms, a project favored by the conde duque himself to support the common defense of the empire. As in Catalonia, however, the crown underestimated the strength of the opposition in the viceroyalty and its influence over the colonial bureaucracy.[6] As a result, despite dispatching a visita general in 1625 and sending a special commissioner in 1630, the union of arms and the other tax levies imposed from Madrid failed to meet metropolitan expectations. The only successful measures were temporary imposts, such as the sale of juros, which found wider acceptance among the local citizenry. Although such expedients did push income levels to new heights during the 1640s, the rise was only temporary. By the next decade the failure of the reformers was all too apparent. As mining taxes declined and returns from temporary levies fell off, successive viceroys and treasury officials began borrowing to meet local expenses and maintain silver shipments to Seville.[7] By the 1660s these policies had left the government deeply in debt.

From the 1660s policy makers in Madrid and Lima shifted their attention to regaining control over the viceregal bureaucracy and enforcing the levies imposed during the reform period. To achieve this end the crown dispatched a full-scale visita general of the viceroyalty in 1664 and later sent several vigorous reformist viceroys. As these crown agents tried to regain political and financial power in Peru, however, they encountered the bitter hostility of the wealthy, influential citizenry and their allies in the political establishment. Lima was the focal point for this confrontation. These political enemies of the visita proved well entrenched. They secured the recall of troublesome officials such as Juan de Cornejo and the conde de Castellar and continually blocked the progress of the investigations. Even when powerful limeños such as Álvaro de Ibarra controlled the visita, they often used it to punish their political enemies as well as to secure needed reforms.

In the end the visita general exposed some abuses and collected debts, but it also became mired in a host of petty local squabbles and never secured any lasting improvements in the administration of Peruvian finances. Moreover the fiscal crisis continued to worsen, and by the end of the century the treasury was nearly bankrupt. The crown had failed in its century-long effort to overcome the resistance of privileged elites to higher taxes, to control the colonial bureaucracy, and to turn more of Peru's economic wealth to the metropolis. A century later the Bourbon reformers had greater success in achieving these goals, in large part because they coupled tax reform with a comprehensive set of commercial and administrative changes.

Imperial Decline

The overall decline of Spain in Europe during the seventeenth century was due largely to the crown's inability to increase its control over the economic resources of the monarchy. Even the halting efforts of Olivares to establish "one king, one law, and one coinage," provoked widespread opposition in the Spanish kingdoms.[8] Although the disruptions in Catalonia, Portugal, Sicily, Naples, and Mexico had their own distinct causes, a common factor in each was the increased fiscal pressure from Madrid.[9] In the Viceroyalty of Peru these royal demands led to political unrest but no serious disturbance of the peace. Such actions were simply not necessary; Peruvian elites and their allies in the royal bureaucracy defeated the reforming impulse of the crown without resorting to such extreme measures. The failure of the new taxes and the resulting fiscal crisis, however, led to the crown's loss of control over much of the viceroyalty's resources. The declining income levels in the Lima caja encouraged officials to curtail remissions of silver to Seville from an annual average of 1,483,849 pesos in the 1630s to a low of 127,189 pesos by the 1680s (see table 7). This drastic decline occurred at a time when the crown was struggling for hegemony in Europe; along with the loss of money from rebellious provinces in Italy and the Iberian peninsula, it undoubtedly contributed to the eventual military and political decline of Spain.

The fiscal crisis also had a profound political and economic impact in the Viceroyalty of Peru. The loss of treasury income left the viceregal government weakened and impoverished by 1700. This overall decline of the imperial system also undermined the economic centrality of Lima. Elites in the capital had finally defeated the crown's reform program, but it was a Pyrrhic victory. The city needed a vigorous central government to enforce the trade monopolies that insured its economic primacy in the viceroyalty. As a result the financial and political decline of the royal government, the diminishing productivity of the mines, the recession in the Atlantic trade, the diversification of the colonial economy, and the catastrophic consequences of the 1687 earthquake all combined to erode the power of limeño elites in the viceroyalty. The net result was to create a more cantonal viceroyalty by 1700, made up of regions less dependent on either Lima or Madrid. It took a new dynasty and another major reform program in the eighteenth century for the imperial system in Peru to recover from the damage done by the fiscal crisis.

Appendixes

I Ramos of Accounts in Caja of Lima, 1607–1690

Cargo (Income)

Alcabala (sales tax)
Alcances de cuentas (collected debts)
Almojarifazgos (port taxes)
Avería de armada (fleet taxes)
Avería de negros y bozales (import tax on black slaves)
Bulas de la santa cruzada (indulgences)
Censos y juros (long-term loans, or annuities)
Comisos (confiscated contraband goods)
Composiciones de pulperías (licensing tax on stores selling wine and provisions)
Composiciones de tierras (sale of land and land titles)
Depósitos (deposits)
Donativos, or Servicios graciosos (forced contributions)
Emprestidos, or Emprestitos (loans)
Estranjeros (tax on foreign immigrants)
Expolios (goods belonging to recently deceased clergymen)
Extraordinarios (extraordinary)
Lanzas (tribute revenues set aside to pay the salaries of the viceregal guard)
Limosnas (charitable donations)
Media anata (tax on bureaucratic offices)
Mesada (tax on clerical offices)

Multas (fines)
Naipes (tax on playing cards)
Nieve (tax on snow and ice)
Novenos (tithe)
Oficios vendibles y renunciables (salable and transferable offices)
Papel Sellado (stamped paper)
Quintos y cobos (mining taxes)
Real del ducado (bureaucratic tax)
Sal (tax on salt)
Sala de Armas (tax to support military)
Salarios (salaries held on deposit)
Situaciones y mercedes (pensions, payments, and donations held on deposit)
Situado de Chile (payments from Chile and military deferments purchased)
Solimán (tax on sale of bichloride of mercury, used as an antiseptic and in certain cosmetics)
Tercias de encomiendas (royal share of the tribute from Amerindians under the jurisdiction of an encomienda grant)
Tributos reales (tribute from Amerindians under royal control)
Tributos vacos (tribute from vacant encomiendas)
Trueques de barras (precious metals held on deposit for smelting)
Unión de armas (commerce and production taxes)
Vacantes de obispados (income from vacant episcopal sees)
Venido de fuera (remissions from subtreasuries)
Visitas (income from visitas)

Data (Expenditures)

(Ramos translated in income section—*)
Alcances de cuentas*
Avería de armada*
Bulas de la santa cruzada*
Censos y juros*

Comisos*
Composiciones de pulperías*
Composiciones de tierras*
Condenaciones (money taken from fines)
Depósitos*
Donativos*
Emprestidos*
Espolios*
Extraordinarios*
Gastos de minas de Huancavelica (subsidy to the Huancavelica mercury mines)
Guerra (war expenses)
Lanzas*
Limosnas*
Media anata*
Mesada*
Novenos*
Oficios vendidos y renunciables*
Remitido a España (remissions to Spain)
Sal*
Salarios (bureaucratic salaries)
Situaciones y mercedes*
Situado de la armada (subsidy to the Pacific fleet)
Situado de Chile (subsidy to Chile)
Situado de Guayaquil (subsidy to Guayaquil)
Situado de Panama (subsidy to Panama)
Situado de Valdivia (subsidy to the garrison at Valdivia, in Chile)
Tributos reales*
Tributos vacos*
Unión de armas*
Vacantes*
Visitas*

II Lima Treasury Accounts for the Seventeenth Century

Any examination of the political and financial life of the Viceroyalty of Peru in the seventeenth century must depend on the accounts of the royal treasury. These records list all the income and outgo of the various treasuries of the viceroyalty and provide the most detailed picture of the financial position of the colonial government. In this study I have relied fundamentally on the accounts of the central treasury in Lima because of its crucial importance as a clearing house for funds from Peru and Upper Peru, its location in the administrative capital of the viceroyalty, and the availability of documentation for this office; only fragmentary records exist for all other treasuries except Potosí for the seventeenth century. It is my contention that the Lima accounts reveal the financial parameters of the viceregal government and provide insights into the strengths and weaknesses of the colonial system over time. Indeed, when related to a wide variety of other, more traditional sources, the accounts can help to provide a more precise political chronology for the viceroyalty and also identify some of the basic continuities and changes in the political and financial relationship between the metropolis and the colony.

Methodological Pitfalls

Despite the potential usefulness of the accounts, any historian interested in working with them must overcome a number of difficulties. Changes in accounting procedures, the varied quality and availability of the records, and questions about their accuracy all pose problems for the modern historian. In addition the treasury officers in Lima only closed out their books when the Armada left Callao, which happened at very irregular intervals during the seventeenth century. As a result the time periods covered by each account can vary from several years to a few months, depending on the frequency of the fleet sailings. Also seventeenth-century treasury officials did not formulate any type of modern budget to regulate their financial dealings. Instead they only set general priorities, or goals, which they frequently altered to meet new circumstances. Keeping track of these changes can be a frustrating and difficult task.

At the same time many of these problems are less important to the historian interested in examining broad, general trends over long time periods; convenient summaries at the middle or end of the accounts usually provide enough specific information. In addition the summaries for smaller subtreasuries also provide an accurate portrayal of the financial activities of these offices. The exhaustive study by John J. TePaske and Herbert S. Klein, for example, uses material gathered from these summaries to provide an index of the general state of the economy in the various treasury districts of the empire between 1580 and 1820. My own more limited study of short-range changes in the political and financial life of the viceroyalty, however, had to correct for many of the problems inherent in working with the accounts. I found that the best way to overcome these methodological problems was to read each page of the accounts, which for Lima varied in length from five hundred to over one thousand folios, and whenever possible to check the entries against the existing workbooks (*libros manuales*) of the individual bureacurats.

The income (cargo) section of the Lima accounts had forty-two basic entries (ramos); each presented its own separate problems. Several *ramos*, such as Amerindian tribute or the novenos were collected by tax farmers or other government officials, and they commonly sent the money owed to the Lima office in a haphazard fashion. These quasi-independent tax collectors often withheld funds for several years, apparently to use the money free of interest for their own purposes. The corregidores de indios, who collected Amerindian tribute, for example, usually sent the bulk of the money owed to the treasury when they left office, every three or five years. As a result the amounts listed in the account summaries for tribute actually represent income that had been collected several years earlier. The historian must be wary, then, of making sweeping generalizations about tax collection on the basis of yearly fluctuations in income from certain ramos.

Another set of problems involved funds remitted from the subtreasuries. First these monies do not represent the total income of the subordinate offices, but only the surplus income remaining after the local treasury officials had paid their operating expenses. Second most but not all of the funds from the subtreasuries were recorded in the Lima accounts under the ramo of venido de fuera. The rest, which in some cases reached as high as 20 percent of the total remissions, was recorded in other ramos. Funds paid for the cruzada in the Potosí district and later remitted to Lima, for example, were commonly recorded in that ramo of the Lima accounts, rather than in venido de fuera. Consequently the summaries for many years of the Lima accounts understate the amounts coming from the subtreasuries, by listing only a portion of the total remissions in venido de fuera. On the other hand the totals from entries such as the cruzada can be inflated in some years with money from both Lima and the subtreasuries. To complicate matters even further, this practice of moving money from one ramo to another seldom followed any consistent pattern during the seventeenth century. As a consequence, to monitor short-term political or financial changes in the viceroyalty, I had to read the entire account in order to separate the amounts collected in the Lima district from the funds sent from the subtreasuries.

The thirty-five ramos that comprised the expenditure, or data, portion of the accounts posed equally complicated problems. Bureaucratic salaries, for example, were paid not only from the ramo of salarios, but also from a variety of other unlikely entries like alcances de cuentas (collected debts). Likewise the amount of money remitted to Spain was listed not only in the ramo of remitido a España, but also in oficios vendibles y renunciables, vacantes de obispados, the cruzada, the media anata, and the mesada. In most years the sums sent to Spain from these other ramos were small, but in other years they represented at least 40 or 50 percent of the total remission. The only way to determine with any precision the amounts spent on salaries or remitted to Spain was to read each ramo of the data section of the accounts. Another common problem involved extraordinary expenditures. For most years the ramo of extraordinarios represented a wide variety of miscellaneous expenses, as the name implies. In certain periods of military crisis, however, money from this entry went almost exclusively to meet the defense needs of the viceregal government. Any effort to determine defense expenditures of the viceroyalty, therefore, involved a thorough check of the ramo of extraordinarios. Finally in some years of the seventeenth century treasury officials combined two ramos, for instance, emprestidos and trueques de barras. For these years I had to read each page of the entry to separate the loan repayments from the silver and gold held on deposit for smelting.

Coding and Computer Analysis

After gathering the needed information from both the cargo and data, I began coding the material and analyzing it with the aid of a computer. Using the SPSS package, I coded each entry of cargo and data as separate cases and created the following seven variables: (1) month and year of the beginning of the account period; (2) month and year of the end of the account period; (3) total number of months in the accounting period; (4) assigned tax or expenditure category; (5) specific type of tax or expenditure; (6) amounts collected in pesos de ocho; and (7) amounts collected in *pesos ensayados* (12½ reales). Then I converted all of the money into pesos de ocho and calculated the total income and total expenditures for each accounting period.

The next step involved plotting this total of the treasury's income for each year on a graph, in order to examine visually the general trends for the century. Since the accounts were not kept on a yearly basis, this necessitated combining income totals for accounting periods that were less than twelve months in length and dividing those which were longer than one year. For example the accounting period from 1678 to 1681 was thirty-six months, so I divided the total income in pesos de ocho by three, to arrive at an approximate twelve-month total for each of the three years. This inevitably involved some distortion of the data set, but I compensated for this problem, in part, by using the convention of a three-year moving average in plotting the graph. The final version of the graph provided a basic picture of the income flowing into the Lima treasury for each year during the century and clearly demonstrated the dramatic fall in tax receipts that occurred from the 1660s (see graph).

To analyze the reasons for this rise and fall in treasury income levels, I examined the changing contribution of each source of income to this total revenue flowing into the Lima caja, and how this fluctuation influenced patterns of expenditures. Since there were forty-two basic ramos of cargo and thirty-five data entries, I grouped ramos of income and expenditures into the categories outlined in chapter 2 in order to simplify the task of analyzing changes in the tax base and expenditure patterns during the century. The problem of unequal accounting periods still complicated any effort to make such comparative judgments about the income and outgo of the Lima office. I circumvented this problem, however, by grouping the materials into longer time periods, equal and nonoverlapping, such as decades or viceregal tenures (see tables 2, 4, 5, 7, 8, 10, 11 and 12). When the chronological periods were unequal in length, as were the various viceregal tenures, I simply took the yearly averages of the income and expenditures for the various time periods, in order to facilitate comparative judgments (see tables 11 and 12).

Notes

Introduction

1. Woodrow Borah, *New Spain's Century of Depression*, Ibero-Americana, 35 (Berkeley and Los Angeles, 1951).

2. François Chevalier, *Land and Society in Colonial Mexico: The Great Hacienda*, trans. by Alvin Eustis (Berkeley and Los Angeles, 1963, 1952). Pierre Chaunu, *Séville et l'Atlantique (1504–1650): La Conjoncture (1504–1592), vol. 7, 2,2 (Paris, 1959); Séville et l'Atlantique (1504–1650): La Conjoncture (1593–1650)*, vol. 8, 2,2 (Paris, 1959). Murdo J. MacLeod, *Spanish Central America: A Socioeconomic History, 1520–1720* (Berkeley and Los Angeles, 1973).

3. J. I. Israel, "Mexico and the General Crisis of the Seventeenth Century," *Past and Present* 63 (May 1974), 33–57; and *Race, Class, and Politics in Colonial Mexico, 1610–1670* (Oxford, 1975).

4. Andre Gunder Frank, *Latin America: Underdevelopment or Revolution* (London and New York, 1969), pp. 3–30; John Lynch, *Spain Under the Habsburgs*, vol. 2, *Spain and America 1598–1700* (Oxford, 1969), pp. 160–228. Lawrence A. Clayton, "Local Initiative and Finance in Defense of the Viceroyalty of Peru: The Development of Self-Reliance," *Hispanic American Historical Review* 54 (May 1974), 284–304.

5. P. J. Bakewell, *Silver Mining and Society in Colonial Mexico, Zacatecas, 1546–1700* (Cambridge, Eng., 1971); Lawrence A. Clayton, *Caulkers and Carpenters in a New World: The Shipyards of Colonial Guayaquil* (Athens, Ohio, 1980).

6. Lynch, *Spain Under the Habsburgs*, 2:195. In the second edition of this work, published in 1981, even John Lynch supports the notion that the impact of seventeenth-century trends varied in different regions of the empire.

7. Louisa S. Hoberman, "Elites and the Commercial Crisis in Seventeenth-Century New Spain" (Unpublished paper delivered at the American Historical Association Meeting, 1980), pp. 1, 14.

8. For a preliminary presentation of this argument for the Viceroyalty of Peru in the seventeenth century, see Kenneth J. Andrien, "Reform, Resistance, and Imperial Decline in Seventeenth-Century Lima" (Unpublished paper delivered at the American Historical Association Meeting, 1982).

9. John J. TePaske and Herbert S. Klein, "The Seventeenth-Century Crisis in New Spain: Myth or Reality," *Past and Present* 90 (February 1981), 134.

10. Ibid.

11. John C. Super, "Querétaro: Society and Economy in Early Provincial Mexico, 1590–1630," (Ph.D. diss., University of California, Los Angeles, 1973); William B. Taylor, *Landlord and Peasant in Colonial Oaxaca* (Stanford, 1972); Richard Boyer, "Mexico in the Seventeenth Century: Transition of a Colonial Society," *Hispanic American Historical Review* 57 (August 1977), 455–78; Miles Wortman, *Government and Society in Central America, 1680–1840* (New York, 1982); Carlos Sempat Assadourián, "Sobre un elemento de la economía colonial: Producción y circulación de mercancías en el interior de un conjunto regional," *EURE* 8 (1973), 135–81; Steve J. Stern, *Peru's Indian Peoples and the Challenge of Spanish Conquest: Huamanga to 1640* (Madison, 1982); Karen Spalding, *De indio a campesino: Cambios en la estructura social del Perú colonial* (Lima, 1974); Louisa Schell Hoberman, "Merchants in Seventeenth-Century Mexico City: A Preliminary Portrait," *Hispanic American Historical Review* 57 (August 1977), 479–503; Nicholas P. Cushner, *Lords of the Land: Sugar, Wine, and Jesuit Estates of Colonial Peru, 1600–1767* (Albany, 1980); Kenneth J. Andrien, "The Sale of Fiscal Offices and the Decline of Royal Authority in the Viceroyalty of Peru, 1633–1700," *Hispanic American Historical Review* 62 (February 1982), 49–71.

12. Fernando de Armas, "Los oficiales de la real hacienda de Indias," *Revista de Historia,* 16 (1963), 11–34; José María Ots Capdequi, "El tributo en la época colonial," *El trimestre económico* 7 (1940–1941), 586–615; Clarence Haring, *The Spanish Empire in America* (New York, 1947); Ismael Sánchez Bella, *La organización financiera de las Indias, siglo XVI* (Sevilla, 1968).

13. John L. Phelan, *The Kingdom of Quito in the Seventeenth Century: Bureaucratic Politics in the Spanish Empire* (Madison, 1968); Mark A. Burkholder and D. S. Chandler, *From Impotence to Authority: The Spanish Crown and the American Audiencias, 1687–1808* (Columbia, 1977) and

Biographical Dictionary of Audiencia Ministers in the Americas, 1687–1821 (Westport, 1982).

14. John J. TePaske, *La real hacienda de Nueva España: La real caja de México, 1576–1818* (Mexico City, 1976); TePaske and Klein, "Seventeenth-Century Crisis"; John J. TePaske and Herbert S. Klein, *The Royal Treasuries of the Spanish Empire in America*, 3 vols. (Durham, 1982). Miles Wortman, "Government Revenue and Economic Trends in Central America, 1787–1819," *Hispanic American Historical Review* 55 (May 1975), 251–86; María Encarnación Rodríguez Vicente, "Los caudales remitidos desde el Perú a España por cuenta de la Real Hacienda: Series estadísticas (1651–1739)," *Anuario de Estudios Americanos* 21 (1964), 1–24.

15. Mario Góngora, *Studies in the Colonial History of Spanish America*, trans. by Richard Southern (Cambridge, Eng., 1975), p. 97. Since Góngora wrote this statement, only one book-length study of the royal treasury has been published: Amy Bushnell, *The King's Coffer: Proprietors of the Spanish Florida Treasury, 1565–1702* (Gainesville, 1981). Although this book provides a fine social and institutional examination of the Florida treasury officials during the seventeenth century, the problems faced by crown officials in that frontier province were not typical of the empire as a whole.

Chapter 2

1. Historians of seventeenth-century Europe have also begun to argue that the vigor of the economy varied in each region of the continent. The most concise description of this theory may be found in Jan De Vries, *The Economy of Europe in an Age of Crisis, 1600–1750* (Cambridge, Eng., 1976). Three recent unpublished essays that explore the applicability of this theory to the Spanish Indies are Andrien, "Reform Resistance"; Miles L. Wortman, "Elites and Habsburg Administration: Adaptations to Economic Fluctuations in Seventeenth-Century Central America" (Unpublished paper delivered at the American Historical Association Meeting, 1980); and Hoberman, "Elites and the Commercial Crisis."

2. The expression Spanish Peru has been taken from James Lockhart, *Spanish Peru, 1532–1560: A Colonial Society* (Madison and London, 1968). The concept that the Audiencias of Lima, Quito, Chile, Charcas, and later the Río de la Plata comprised Spanish Peru is also found in

Assadourián, "Sobre un elemento," pp. 135–38. Assadourián, however, uses *bloque colonial* instead of Spanish Peru.

3. This total was derived from yearly production figures in marks taken from: Peter J. Bakewell, "Registered Silver Production in the Potosí District, 1550–1735," *Jahrbuch für Geschichte von Staat, Wirtschaft, und Gesellschaft Lateinamerikas* 12 (1975), 94–96; Modesto Bargalló, *La minería y la metalurgia en la América española durante la época colonial* (México, 1955), p. 218.

4. TePaske and Klein, "The Seventeenth-Century Crisis," p. 120.

5. Jeffrey Austin Cole, *The Potosí Mita under Habsburg Administration: The Seventeenth Century.* (Ph.D. diss., University of Massachusetts, 1981), pp. 115–16, 274; Lynch, *Spain Under the Habsburgs,* 2:240.

6. Bakewell, "Registered Silver Production," pp. 94–6.

7. Ibid., pp. 88–89.

8. Cole, *Potosí Mita,* p. 104; Bakewell, "Registered Silver Production," p. 89.

9. Lynch, *Spain under the Habsburgs,* 2:241.

10. Arthur P. Whitaker, *The Huancavelica Mercury Mine* (Cambridge, Mass., 1941), p. 12.

11. Guillermo Lohmann Villena, *Las minas de Huancavelica en los siglos XVI y XVII* (Sevilla, 1949), pp. 453–55.

12. *Ibid.,* p. 371.

13. Lawrence Clayton, "Trade and Navigation in the Seventeenth-Century Viceroyalty of Peru," *Journal of Latin American Studies* 7 (May 1975), 2–3.

14. Pierre Chaunu, *Séville et l'Atlantique (1504–1650): La Conjoncture (1593–1650),* vol. 8, 2,2 (Paris, 1959), pp. 916–19; Lynch, *Spain under the Habsburgs,* 2:200–211.

15. Henry Kamen, *Spain in the Later Seventeenth Century, 1665–1700* (London and New York, 1980), pp. 116–19.

16. Clayton, "Trade and Navigation," p. 3.

17. Fray Martín de Murua, *Historia general del Perú,* vol. 2 (Madrid, 1964), p. 161, cited in Assadourián, "Sobre un elemento," p. 138.

18. Bakewell, "Registered Silver Production," pp. 94–96; Bakewell, *Silver Mining and Society,* pp. 241–45.

19. Noble David Cook, *Demographic Collapse: Indian Perú, 1520–1620* (Cambridge, Eng., 1981), p. 94.

20. This general information on the rural economy of Spanish Perú was drawn from a number of printed primary sources and secondary works. The primary sources are the following: Bernabé Cobo, *Historia del nuevo mundo,* Biblioteca de autores españoles, vols. 91–92 (Madrid,

1956); Marcos Jiménez de la Espada, *Relaciones geográficas de Indias,* Biblioteca de autores españoles, vols. 183–85 (Madrid, 1965); and Antonio de Alcedo, *Diccionario geográfico histórico de las Indias occidentales o América,* Biblioteca de autores españoles, vols. 205–8 (Madrid, 1967). Useful secondary works include: Assadourián, "Sobre un elemento"; Kendall W. Brown, *The Economic and Fiscal Structure of Eighteenth-Century Arequipa* (Ph.D. diss., Duke University, 1978); Cole, *Potosí Mita;* Cook, *Demographic Collapse;* Cushner, *Lords of the Land;* Keith Arfon Davies, *The Rural Domain of the City of Arequipa, 1540–1665* (Ph.D. diss., University of Connecticut, 1974); Robert G. Keith, *Conquest and Agrarian Change: The Emergence of the Hacienda System on the Peruvian Coast* (Cambridge, Mass., 1976); Susan Ramirez-Horton, *Land Tenure and the Economics of Power in Colonial Peru* (Ph.D. diss., University of Wisconsin, 1977); Emilio Romero, *Historia económica y financiera del Perú* (Lima, 1937); Stern, *Peru's Indian Peoples;* Robson Brines Tyrer, *The Demographic and Economic History of the Audiencia of Quito: Indian Population and the Textile Industry, 1600–1800* (Ph.D. diss., University of California at Berkeley, 1976).

21. Robert G. Keith ed., *Haciendas and Plantations in Latin American History* (New York and London, 1977), pp. 1–35.

22. Keith, *Conquest and Agrarian Change,* p. 134.

23. Brown, *Economic and Fiscal Structure,* pp. 27, 41; Davies, *Rural Domain,* pp. 102–4.

24. Brown, *Economic and Fiscal Structure,* pp. 27, 41.

25. Brian R. Hamnett, "Church Wealth in Peru: Estates and Loans in the Archdiocese of Lima in the Seventeenth Century," *Jahrbuch für Geschichte von Staat, Wirtschaft und Gessellschaft Lateinamerikas* 10 (1973), 113.

26. Demetrio Ramos Pérez, *Trigo chileno, navieros del Callao y hacendados limeños entre la crisis agrícola del siglo XVII y la comercial de la primera mitad del XVIII* (Madrid, 1967), p. 23.

27. Fray Buenaventura de Salinas y Córdoba, *Memorial de las historias del nuevo mundo Pirú* (Lima, 1957 [1630]), p. 248. Some estimates of grain imports from the central coast to Lima reach as high as 300,000 bushels; Cobo, *Libro primero,* p. 315.

28. Biblioteca Municipal de Lima (hereafter cited as BM), Libros de cabildo, 1639–1644, 1649–1655.

29. Ramos Pérez, *Trigo chileno,* p. 26. For an eighteenth-century analysis of the decline of the estancias de pan llevar of the central coast, see Pedro Bravo de Lagunas y Castilla, *Voto consultivo que ofrece al excelentísimo señor Joseph Antonio Manso de Velasco, Conde de Superunda,*

Cavallero del Orden de Santiago, Gentilhombre de la Cámara de su Magestad, Teniente General de sus reales ejércitos, Virrey Governador, y Capitán general de los reynos del Perú (Lima, 1761).

30. Keith, *Conquest and Agrarian Change*, p. 135.

31. Henri Favre, "Evolución y situación de la hacienda tradicional de la región de Huancavelica," in José Matos Mar, ed., *Hacienda, comunidad, y campesinado en el Perú* (Lima, 1976), pp. 105–10.

32. Ramirez-Horton, *Land Tenure*, p. 244.

33. Ibid., pp. 209, 232, 318–19. For an account of the decline of the rural economy of Lambayeque, see ibid., pp. 398–509.

34. Keith, *Conquest and Agrarian Change*, p. 135.

35. Virgilio Roel, *Historia social y económica de la colonia* (Lima, 1970), pp. 142–44.

36. Fernando Silva Santisteban, *Los obrajes en el virreinato del Perú* (Lima, 1964), p. 118.

37. Tyrer, *Demographic and Economic History*, p. 101.

38. Silva Santisteban, *Los obrajes*, p. 131.

39. Roel, *Historia social*, pp. 142–44.

40. Tyrer, *Demographic and Economic History*, pp. 35–38.

41. Ibid., p. 102.

42. John L. Phelan, *The Kingdom of Quito*, p. 69.

43. Tyrer, *Demographic and Economic History*, pp. 141–42.

44. Ibid., pp. 171, 175.

45. Ibid., pp. 77, 100, 280–81.

46. Ibid., pp. 38, 77.

47. Geoffrey J. Walker, *Spanish Politics and Imperial Trade, 1700–1789* (Bloomington, 1979), p. 2; Haring, *Spanish Empire*, p. 139.

48. This tax was a levy of two reales per bottle of domestic wine sold in the viceroyalty. It was part of the union of arms tax package, imposed in 1638. See Archivo General de Indias de Sevilla (hereafter cited as AGI), Indiferente general, 2690, Acuerdo de hacienda, Lima, June 8, 1638.

49. The definitive work on the shipyards of Guayaquil is Clayton, *Caulkers and Carpenters*.

50. Ibid., pp. 31–35.

51. Ibid., pp. 77–96, 121.

52. Tyrer, *Demographic and Economic History*, pp. 280–83.

53. Clayton, "Trade and Navigation," p. 10.

54. Ramos Pérez, *Trigo chileno*, p. 27.

55. AGI, Lima, 289, conde de Monclova to crown, Lima, February 13, 1693.

56. Biblioteca Nacional de Lima (hereafter cited as BN), Manuscritos, F768, "El resumen de los habitadores de Lima," conde de Monclova to crown, Lima, no date.

57. Ramos Pérez, *Trigo chileno,* p. 27.

58. Ibid.

59. Ibid., pp. 36–53.

60. Bravo de Lagunas, *Voto consultivo,* folio 1.

61. Cushner, *Lords of the Land,* p. 46.

62. Manuel Moreyra y Paz Soldán and Guillermo Céspedes del Castillo, *Virreinato peruano: Documentos para su historia. Colección de cartas de Virreyes, conde de Monclova, 1695–1698,* vol. 2 (Lima, 1954), p. 23.

63. Jonathan C. Brown, *A Socioeconomic History of Argentina* (Cambridge, Eng., 1979), p. 22.

64. AGI, Lima, 43, conde de Chinchón to crown, Lima, February 5, 1632, No. 36, Libro III.

65. Brown, *Socioeconomic History,* p. 23.

66. Angel Rosenblat, *La población indígena y el mestizaje en América,* vol. 1 (Buenos Aires, 1954), p. 59.

67. Lynch, *Spain Under the Habsburgs,* 2:238.

68. Buenaventura de Salinas y Córdoba, *Memorial de las historias,* p. 245.

69. Ramos Pérez, *Trigo chileno,* p. 27.

70. A revisionist account of the population growth of Lima is Fred Bronner, "The Population of Lima, 1593–1647: In Quest of a Statistical Bench Mark," *Ibero-Amerikanisches Archiv* 2 (1979), 107–19; Bronner suggests that Lima's growth rate may have been sluggish during the seventeenth century, never exceeding .51. His figures for the city's population at 1700, however, were taken after the great earthquake of 1687, and he ignores any figures from between 1650 and 1687. These materials may well be less reliable than earlier figures and the accounts at the end of the century, but ignoring them completely is bound to produce a very conservative estimate of the city's population growth during the century.

71. Buenaventura de Salinas y Córdoba, *Memorial de las historias,* p. 248.

72. Cook, *Demographic Collapse,* p. 94.

73. Tyrer, *Demographic and Economic History,* pp. 35–38.

74. Stern, *Peru's Indian Peoples,* p. 139. The principal agents for promoting this integration of the Spanish and Amerindian peoples were the *corregidores de indios* and the clan leaders (*kurakas*). The corregidores regulated all commercial contact between Europeans and Amerindians, and thus had the opportunity to extort funds, plunder local community chests (*cajas de communidad*), sell European goods at inflated prices, and force local laborers to work for Spaniards. These problems often became more acute at the end of the century, when the crown introduced the *repartimiento de comercio,* which allowed the corregidores to distribute an allotment of European goods to the Amerindians in their districts. For a concise description of the role of the corregidor and the repartimiento de comercio, see Javier Tord Nicolini, "El corregidor de indios del Perú: Comercio y tributos," *Historia y cultura* 8 (1974), 173–214; an excellent general description of the corregidor de indios in Peru is Guillermo Lohmann Villena, *El corregidor de indios en el Perú bajo los Austrias* (Madrid, 1957). The kuraka played an intermediary role in contact between Europeans and Amerindians. For an excellent discussion of the changing role of the kuraka in commercial ventures, see Karen Spalding, "Kurakas and Commerce: A Chapter in the Evolution of Andean Society," *Hispanic American Historical Review* 53 (November 1973), 581–99. For a stimulating discussion of these problems on the regional level, see Stern, *Peru's Indian Peoples,* pp. 183–84. The best survey of the tribute system is Ronald Escobedo Mansilla, *El tributo indígena en el Perú: Siglos XVI y XVII* (Pamplona, 1979).

75. Cook, *Demographic Collapse,* pp. 146–50.

76. Frederick Bowser, *The African Slave in Colonial Peru, 1524–1650* (Stanford, 1974), p. 11.

77. AGI, Lima, 43, conde de Chinchón to crown, Lima, April 26, 1636, No. 21, Libro 2, folios 32–34.

78. Cushner, *Lords of the Land,* pp. 50–56.

79. Ibid., p. 139.

80. Ibid.

81. Ibid., p. 116.

82. Hamnett, "Church Wealth," p. 115.

83. Ibid.

84. María Encarnación Rodríguez Vicente, "Una quiebra bancaria en el Perú del siglo XVII," *Anuario de historia del derecho español* 26 (1956):709.

85. Ibid., pp. 725–39.

86. Angel Altoaguirre, *Colección de las memorias o relaciones, que es-*

cribieron los virreyes del Perú acerca del estado en que dejaban las cosas generales del reino (Madrid, 1930), p. 78.

87. AGI, Contaduría, 1702–1759B, Cuentas de la caja de Lima, Lima, 1607–1690.

88. See table 4.

89. Chaunu, *Séville et l'Atlantique,* vol. 8, 2,2, pp. 1330–32; Lynch, *Spain under the Habsburgs,* 2:203–4, 214; Antonio Domínguez Ortiz, *Política y hacienda de Felipe IV* (Madrid, 1960), p. 294.

90. Kamen, *Spain in the Later Seventeenth Century,* pp. 131–40; Albert Girard, *Le commerce français a Séville et Cadiz au temps des Habsbourg* (Paris, 1932), pp. 273–391.

91. Manuel Moreyra y Paz Soldán, *El tráfico marítimo en la época colonial* (Lima, 1944), pp. 13–15.

92. The trade in dyes from Central America for the obrajes of Quito and Peru must have been substantial. Inadequate supplies of indigo existed in Spanish Peru, while substantial reserves of the dye remained in Central America, especially after the decline in the dye trade in Europe. In Quito royal authorities tried to limit the number of paños that could be dyed blue, for example, but obrajeros continued to favor using the blue dye and imports continued. See Tyrer, *Demographic and Economic History,* p. 190; Demetrio Ramos Pérez, *Minería y comercio interprovincial en hispanoamérica* (*Siglos XVI, XVII, XVIII*) (Valladolid, 1970), p. 228. In addition, one recent study shows that the indigo-producing regions in Central America thrived during the seventeenth century, and the city of San Vicente in a new indigo zone was even granted the right to establish a cabildo. See Wortman, "Elites and Habsburg Administration," pp. 2–4. Even the consulado of Lima asked to have the trade legalized, in order to curtail the considerable contraband trade in dyes from Central America for wine and cacao; AGI, Lima, 427, Cédula, Madrid, May 20, 1676.

93. Clayton, "Trade and Navigation," p. 6.

94. John J. TePaske, "New World Silver, Castile, and the Far East (1590–1750)," *Precious Metals in the Later Medieval and Early Modern World,* ed. by John Richards (Durham, 1982), p. 8.

95. Ibid., p. 11.

96. Woodrow Borah, *Early Colonial Trade and Navigation Between Mexico and Peru* (Berkeley, 1954), p. 118.

97. Ibid., p. 123.

98. Lynch, *Spain Under the Habsburgs,* 2:246.

99. William Lytle Schurtz, *The Manila Galleon* (New York, 1939), p. 81.

100. C. R. Boxer, "Plata es sangre: Sidelights on the Drain of Spanish-American Silver to the Far East, 1550–1700," *Journal of Philippine Studies* 18 (July 1970), 461.

101. Clayton, "Trade and Navigation," p. 6; Borah, *Early Colonial Trade*, p. 125.

102. AGI, Lima, 109, Cabildo of Lima to crown, Lima, May 30, 1638.

103. The figures for goods entering the Philippines are taken from: Pierre Chaunu, *Les Philippines et le Pacifique des Ibériques (XVIe, XVIIe, XVIIIe siècles): Introduction méthodologique et indices d'activité, ports-routes-trafics* (Paris, 1960), 12:136–43; 14:200–216. Chaunu's figures provide only a crude approximation of the changes in trade entering Manila. The port taxes, on which his figures are based, were tax-farmed, and the fluctuations show the changes in remissions from the tax farmers, not actual fluctuations in the trade itself. At best they provide an approximation of trade cycles, since tax-farming contracts and remissions from tax farmers usually mirrored general trends in the legal trade.

104. Moreyra y Paz Soldán and Céspedes del Castillo, *Virreinato peruano*, 3:235.

105. Rubén Vargas Ugarte, *Historia del Perú: Virreinato (siglo XVII)* (Lima, 1954), p. 425.

106. Ibid., p. 426.

107. Guillermo Céspedes del Castillo, "Las Indias en el siglo XVII," vol. 3 of *Historia social y económica de España y América*, ed. by Jaime Vicens Vives (Barcelona, 1961), p. 506.

108. Clayton, "Trade and Navigation," p. 3.

109. AGI, Lima, 427, Consulado of Lima to Diego de Villatoro, Lima, no date.

110. Clayton, "Trade and Navigation," pp. 17, 18.

111. Vargas Ugarte, *Historia del Perú*, p. 425.

112. For a concise survey of the French incursion into the Pacific, see Walker, *Spanish Politics*, pp. 19–63.

113. Gwendolin Cobb, "Supply and Transportation for the Potosí Mines, 1545–1640," *Hispanic American Historical Review* 29 (February 1949), 28–31.

114. Peter Mathias, *The First Industrial Nation: An Economic History of Britain, 1700–1914* (London, 1969), pp. 13–14.

115. Murdo J. MacLeod, *Spanish Central America*, p. 389.

Chapter 3

1. For additional information on the status of the colonial treasuries of the Spanish Indies, see TePaske and Klein, "The Seventeenth-Century Crisis," pp. 116–36.

2. Surplus income was that income remaining in the subtreasury after operating expenses had been paid.

3. The Río de la Plata and Chile were more closely dependent for money and supplies on Peru and Upper Peru than were Tierrafirme, Santa Fe, or even Quito.

4. The cajas of Chachapoyas and Huancavelica never remitted any surplus income to Lima during the seventeenth century. The mines at Chachapoyas were minor and quickly became exhausted; the caja produced little revenue. Huancavelica required yearly subsidies from Lima to support the mercury mines of the district.

5. *Recopilación de leyes de los reynos de las Indias* (hereafter cited as *Recopilación*) (Madrid, 1973 [1681]), libro VIII, título VII, ley 2.

6. Biblioteca del Palacio Real (hereafter cited as BP), Madrid, Manuscrito 1278, Francisco López de Caravantes, "Relación de las provincias que tiene el govierno de Perú, los oficios que en el se proveen y la hacienda que allí tiene su Magd., lo que se gasta de ella y le queda libre y otras cosas que se sustenten con la Rl. Hacienda y tocan al govierno superior, y conservación del reino, con el origin que an tenido, y el estado que al presente tienen," 1614, folio 115. From 1613 there were three senior treasury officials in the Lima caja: a comptroller, a treasurer, and a factor. The comptroller was responsible for two workbooks, a *libro de contaduría* and a *libro de pliegos* (suits). The factor kept three workbooks, a *libro de factoría,* a *libro de pliegos,* and a *libro de asientos y fundaciónes,* which dealt with mining taxes and smelting. The treasurer managed a *libro general,* a *libro de pliegos,* and a *libro de entradas y pasos,* which monitored all income and disbursements.

7. Roberto Levillier, ed., *Gobernantes del Perú, cartas y papeles del siglo XVI,* vol. 8 (Madrid, 1938), p. 9. For a list of the *repartimientos* in the Lima district see Escobedo, *El tributo indígena,* pp. 260–61.

8. Ibid.

9. In areas where tribute returns were too meager to pay the salary of the corregidor, either the treasury paid his salary or the audiencia authorized its payment from the *cajas de communidad* (community chests) of the region. The Audiencia of Lima, for example, had the salary of

the corregidor Diego Messía, of the *cercado* (Amerindian quarter) of Lima paid in this manner on August 1, 1631. Archivo General de la Nación (hereafter cited as AGN), Lima, Real hacienda de Lima, 1630–1688.

10. Encomiendas were granted to distinguished Spaniards from the first days of the conquest. They gave the holder the right to enjoy tribute from the Amerindians falling under the jurisdiction of the grant. By the seventeenth century, the encomenderos received only the money remaining after corregidores had deducted the collection expenses and the royal third. Juan de Solórzano y Pereyra, *Política indiana* (Madrid, 1972 [1739]), libro VI, capítulo VII, número 1.

11. The tithe was divided into two equal parts. One part went to the bishop and the cathedral, and the other was divided into ninths: two ninths went to the treasury, four to the local parish clergy, and three to the construction and repair of churches. Haring, *Spanish Empire,* p. 266.

12. Indians were expected to pay tithes on products introduced to them by the Spaniards, such as cattle, wheat, and sheep; but the amount collected was theoretically deducted from their yearly tribute assessment. Haring, *Spanish Empire,* p. 266.

13. Municipal revenues in Lima were meager. All major tax sources accrued to the treasury cajas. Only the sale of some lands, local judicial fines, the income from some local offices, marketplace licenses, and anchorage fees at Callao provided funds to the municipality. Any other taxes and all expenditures by the cabildo had to be approved by the audiencia. In fact the cabildo members wrote to the crown on May 13, 1641, asking for permission to take a portion of the rents from the yearly tribute collections to pay some of the many outstanding censo loans taken out by the city. The contract to collect the tax on pulperías was one of the few sources of revenue open to the financially pressed city council in Lima. *Recopilación,* libro IV, título VIII, ley 12; Haring, *Spanish Empire,* p. 158; BM, Lima, Manuscritos, Libros de cabildo de Lima, 1639–1644.

14. *Recopilación,* libro VIII, título XIII, leyes 1, 14.

15. Ibid., libro VIII, título XIII, leyes 17, 24.

16. Ibid., libro VIII, título XIII, leyes 19, 20, 21, 22, 23.

17. The assessed value of goods for the purposes of taxation was determined by taking the average price collected for the merchandise in the marketplace of Lima for the thirty-day period before the arrival of the fleet. *Recopilación,* libro VIII, título XV, leyes 1, 11; título XVI, ley VIII.

18. Gaspar de Escalona y Agüero, *Gazofilacio real del Perú,* Biblioteca Boliviana, tomo II, serie I (La Paz, 1941 [1647]), libro II, parte II, capítulo VI, números 2, 4.
19. *Recopilación,* libro VIII, título XV, ley 2.
20. Ibid., ley 10.
21. AGI, Contaduría, 1698, Cuenta de la caja de Lima, Lima, 1589.
22. A temporary tax on all black slaves imported into Callao was collected from 1638 until 1648 in Lima. AGI, Contaduría, 1723–1733, Cuentas de la caja de Lima, Lima, 1638–1648. For a full discussion of the legal aspects of the avería in the Spanish Indies, see Guillermo Céspedes del Castillo, *La avería en el comercio de Indias* (Seville, 1945).
23. AGI, Indiferente general, 2690, Acuerdo de hacienda, December 22, 1638.
24. *Recopilación,* libro VIII, título XX, leyes 10, 25; libro IV, título IX, ley 11.
25. Ibid., libro VII, título XX, leyes 1, 11.
26. Ibid., libro VIII, título XIX, ley 4. Until the adoption of the media anata, in 1632, all secular appointees were required to pay the *mesada,* initiated in 1625. It was not until 1629 that the crown required clerical appointees to pay the mesada. Haring, *Spanish Empire,* pp. 273–74; *Recopilación,* libro I, título XVII, ley 1; libro VIII, título XIX, ley 4.
27. The word *cobo* was derived from Francisco de los Cobos, who was granted the exclusive right to smelt silver at Potosí by the king. This grant reverted to the crown after the death of Cobos. These duties usually were performed in each treasury office by an official known as the *ensayador y balancario.* The 1½ percent tax on all smelted silver paid the salary of the ensayador and was called the cobo in the seventeenth century. Escalona Agüero, *Gazofilacio,* libro II, parte II, capítulo I, número 12.
28. In practice the corregidor and the treasury officers often inspected mines to insure that all taxable silver flowed into the royal coffers. In many cases the corregidor, his lieutenants, or the treasury officers actually shipped the royal fifth to the caja. AGN, Lima, Superior Gobierno, 32, Cuaderno 92, Lima, 1643–1649.
29. Haring, *Spanish Empire,* p. 274.
30. *Recopilación,* libro VIII, título XXII, ley 18.
31. Creditors offered capital to the government either at no interest or at very modest rates, such as 5 percent.
32. To redeem a censo, the creditor simply repaid the principal of the loan and canceled the debt. In practice, however, this rarely oc-

curred; most censos were held for long periods. The yearly interest rate was set most commonly at 5 percent. Hamnett, "Church Wealth," p. 115.

33. Kenneth J. Andrien, "The Sale of Juros and the Politics of Reform in the Viceroyalty of Peru, 1608–1695," *Journal of Latin American Studies* 13 (May 1981), 1–19.

34. Ballesteros, *Tomo primero,* libro I, título XXIX, leyes 1, 9, 10, 11; BP, Madrid, Manuscrito 1278, López de Caravantes, "Relación de las provincias," folios 113, 114.

35. BP, Madrid, Manuscrito 1278, López de Caravantes, "Relación de las provincias," folios 113, 114.

36. Ibid.

37. *Recopilación,* libro I, título XVII, ley 1.

38. The study begins in 1607 because the first major attempt to reform the tax system in Peru came one year later, in 1608. The terminal date of 1690 was chosen because that is the last year in the century when reliable accounts were kept. In addition the accounts for 1662–64 and 1690–1700 have not been found in either the AGI (Seville) or the AGN (Lima).

39. TePaske and Klein, *Royal Treasuries,* 2:274–346.

40. For the caja of Cuzco, only the accounts for the years 1607–9, 1639–40, and 1676–90 were found after examining the AGI (Seville), AGN, (Lima), and the Archivo Departamental in Cuzco. TePaske and Klein, *Royal Treasuries,* 1:127–44.

41. TePaske and Klein, *Royal Treasuries,* 2:274–346.

42. The most complete survey of the Amerindian population in Peru is: Noble David Cook, *Demographic Collapse.*

43. When a bishopric became vacant through the death or transfer of the incumbent, the surplus proceeds of the bishopric went to the treasury. *Recopilación,* libro VIII, título XXIV, ley 2.

44. Strictly speaking *depósitos* and *trueques de barras* were not income. Deposits were simply carried over from the credit to the debit side of the ledger, since the goods were only held in escrow. The same was done with trueques, which were merely bars smelted and put into some kind of currency.

45. In small towns of the Lima district, such as Guara, Jauja, and Ica, local individuals frequently received the contracts for these taxes. In other cases the cabildo performed the task. In 1660, for example, the cabildo of Pisco agreed to pay 5,100 pesos each year for a four-year contract to collect the alcabala and the union of arms in the

region. AGN, ex–Archivo Histórico de Ministerio de Hacienda y Comercio (hereafter cited as ex-AHMH) 20, Libro de remates, 1660.

46. AGI, Lima, 281, Conde de Santisteban to crown, Lima, November 22, 1664; Scriptura que otorgo el comercio del Perú sobre la nueva prorogación de las averías del mar del norte, December 6, 1664.

47. The most lucrative of the clerical taxes in Lima, the cruzada, was not collected by the treasury.

48. AGI, Contaduría, 1728A-1735, Cuentas de la Caja de Lima, Lima, 1643–1649.

49. AGI, Contaduría, 1728, 1729, 1734–35, Cuentas de la Caja de Lima, Lima, 1642, 1644, 1649.

50. Loans played a similar role in the financial transactions of the treasury in Mexico City. The viceroys of New Spain all had their own so-called subrosa bankers to extend them private credit for personal business transactions or to help the viceregal treasury. See Louisa S. Hoberman, "Elites and the Commercial Crisis," pp. 7–8.

51. AGI, Contaduría, 1708, Cuentas de la Caja de Lima, Lima, 1619–20.

52. AGI, Contaduría, 1725, 1736, 1737, Cuentas de la Caja de Lima, Lima, 1640, 1650.

53. One major exception to this trend was the caja of Cuzco, whose remissions to Lima declined at a much slower rate. Cuzco, however, became very irregular in its shipments after 1660, declining during that decade, rising again in the 1670s, and falling during the 1680s.

54. AGI, Lima, 182, Conde de Santisteban to crown, Lima, November 22, 1664.

55. Bakewell, "Registered Silver Production," pp. 93–103.

56. AGI, Contaduría, 1735–54, Cuentas de la Caja de Lima, Lima, 1650–70.

57. AGI, Contaduría, 1780A, Conde de Santisteban to crown, Lima, February 12, 1662. "Razón general del estado en que está la real hacienda según los instrumentos que la comprueban como se refiere en los puntos que contiene que corresponde désde el número 1–27 en el indice general désde el número 16 hasta el número 40 los quales se refieren en la carta de hacienda número 75." Part 1, "Relación del estado en que se halla la real hacienda al tiempo que entré a governar estos reynos."

58. Ibid.

59. Ibid.

60. Lawrence A. Clayton, "Local Initiative," pp. 287, 288, 293; Peter

T. Bradley, "Maritime Defence of the Viceroyalty of Peru (1600–1700)," *The Americas* 36 (October 1979), 157, 158, 160, 166.

61. Clayton, "Local Initiative," pp. 294–302; Bradley, "Maritime Defence," p. 169.

62. Bradley, "Maritime Defence," p. 156.

63. Ibid., p. 158.

64. Ibid., p. 161.

65. Clayton, "Local Initiative," pp. 288–91.

66. Ibid., p. 292; Bradley, "Maritime Defence," pp. 163–65.

67. Clayton, "Local Initiative," 293–94; Bradley, "Maritime Defence," pp. 165–67.

68. Guillermo Lohmann Villena, *Las defensas militares de Lima y Callao* (Sevilla, 1964), p. 116.

69. Bradley, "Maritime Defence," pp. 166–67; Clayton, "Local Initiative," pp. 293–94.

70. Clayton, "Local Initiative," pp. 294–302.

71. Ibid., pp. 290–91, 295–302.

72. Ramos Pérez, *Minería y comercio interprovincial,* p. 152.

73. Andrien, "Sale of Juros," pp. 16–17.

74. Ibid.

75. Burkholder and Chandler, *From Impotence to Authority,* p. 18; Andrien, "Sale of Fiscal Offices," pp. 49–72.

Chapter 4

1. The term *traditional,* as it is used here, refers to Max Weber's definition of traditional authority, found in Max Weber, *The Theory of Social and Economic Organization,* trans. by Talcott Parsons (New York, 1964), pp. 341–45.

2. These characteristics are typical of Weber's patrimonial form of authority. For a detailed discussion of this concept, see Weber, *Social and Economic Organization,* pp. 352–58; Magali Sarfatti, *Spanish Bureaucratic-Patrimonialism in America* (Berkeley, 1966), pp. 5–38; Max Weber, *Economy and Society,* vol. 3, trans. by Guenther Roth and Claus Wittich (New York, 1968), pp. 1006–1104.

3. For a precise definition of rational-legal authority, see Weber, *Social and Economic Organization,* pp. 329–41.

4. Ibid.

5. Considering its power the Council of the Indies was not large by modern standards. Its exact size varied, but in the seventeenth

century it was composed of the following officials: a president (*presidente*), a grand chancellor (*gran canciller*), nine or ten councilors (*consejeros*), an attorney (*fiscal*), two solicitors (*procuradores*), three reporters (*relatores*), two secretaries (*escribanos*), a treasurer (*tesorero*), four clerks (*contadores*), a bailiff (*alguacil*), a historian (*cronista mayor*), a cosmographer (*cosmógrapho*), a mathematician (*catedrático de matemáticas*), a chaplain (*capellón*), several notaries (*notarios*), and a group of ushers (*porteros*). Haring, *Spanish Empire*, pp. 95–96.

6. Ibid., p. 98.

7. Ibid., pp. 298–300.

8. In order to coordinate the activities of these councils, the crown established a committee on finance (*junta de hacienda*), composed of councilors from the Council of the Indies and the Council of Finance of Castile in 1600. By 1630, however, the junta de hacienda no longer met on a regular basis. It only convened on an ad hoc basis to discuss matters of extraordinary importance. Sánchez Bella, *La organización financiera*, p. 91, n. 60.

9. Ernesto Shafer, *El consejo real y supremo de las Indias*, vol. 2 (Seville, 1935–47), pp. 221–25.

10. J. H. Elliott, *Imperial Spain, 1469–1716*, (New York, 1977), pp. 331–32.

11. Juan de Solórzano y Pereyra, *Política indiana*, libro VI, capítulo XV, números 1–44.

12. Ibid., libro VI, capítulo XV, números 3–5.

13. Thomas de Ballesteros, *Tomo primero*, libro 1, título 5, ordenanzas 4,6.

14. Ibid., ordenanza 5.

15. *Recopilación*, libro 1, título XX, leyes 1–4; and libro 1, título XXX, ley 5.

16. Although the royal orders that established the tribunal of accounts were issued in 1605, the agency began functioning only in 1607. Before this time the audiencias had audited the fiscal accounts of the treasury offices.

17. *Recopilación*, libro VIII, título 1, ley 5.

18. Ibid., libro VIII, título 1, ley 1.

19. Ibid., libro VIII, título 1, ley 49.

20. AGI, Lima, 573, conde de Salvatierra to crown, Lima, November 3, 1652; September 9, 1651.

21. Manuel de Mendiburu, *Diccionario histórico biográfico del Perú*, vol. 8, p. 73; and AGI, Lima, 288, tribunal of accounts to crown, Lima, December 18, 1682.

22. Ballesteros, *Tomo primero,* libro 1, título 27, ordenanza 28.

23. AGI, Lima, 573, conde de Salvatierra to crown, Lima, November 3, 1652; and AGI, Lima, 55, Conde de Salvatierra to crown, Lima, September 9, 1651.

24. Ballesteros, *Tomo primero,* libro 1, título 27, ordenanzas 32, 33.

25. When the tribunal issued orders, the auditors gave them to the alguacil mayor of Lima for execution. If they involved action against the cabildo, a corregidor, or the treasury officers, either the viceroy or the president of the audiencia had to countersign them. Ballesteros, *Tomo primero,* libro 1, título 28, ordenanza 9.

26. *Recopilación,* libro VIII, título 1, leyes 3,6.

27. Ibid., libro VIII, título 1, ley 41; Ballesteros, *Tomo primero,* libro 1, título 27, ordenanzas 37, 38. The salaries of these judges were paid by the guilty party. The viceroy, an oidor of the audiencia, and a contador of the tribunal agreed on the exact powers and jurisdiction of the judges.

28. AGI, Lima, 36, marqués de Montesclaros to crown, Lima, April 13, 1611.

29. AGI, Lima, 573, tribunal of accounts to crown, Lima, July 15, 1646.

30. *Recopilación,* libro VIII, título 1, ley 42.

31. AGI, Lima, 309, Pedro de Villagómez to crown, Lima, April 29, 1634.

32. Ibid.

33. Altoaguirre, *Memorias,* p. 29.

34. *Recopilación,* libro VIII, título 3, leyes 8, 10.

35. Altoaguirre, *Memorias,* p. 268.

36. Ibid., pp. 273–81.

37. A copy of part of the original ordenanzas for the treasury office at Castrovirreyna may be found in BN, Manuscritos, F472, ordenanzas de la caja de Castrovirreyna, Lima, no date.

38. Sánchez Bella, *La organización financiera,* p. 99; AGI, Lima, 36, marqués de Montesclaros to crown, Lima, March 9, 1616.

39. José de Varallaros, *Historia de Huánuco* (Buenos Aires, 1959), p. 325. During the second half of the seventeenth century, treasury officials also moved the caja of Castrovirreyna to Otoca and the caja of San Antonio de Esquilache to Chucuito. AGI, Lima, 73, conde de Castellar to crown, Lima, March 12, 1675.

40. The jurisdiction of a caja did not conform to the boundaries of any other political or clerical administrative unit such as an audiencia or a bishopric.

41. AGI, Lima, 573, conde de Salvatierra to crown, Lima, August 11, 1652.

42. Ibid.

43. Sánchez Bella, *La organización financiera*, p. 96.

44. The mines at New Potosí in the province of Huarochirí were administered by a separate caja, which had jurisdiction only over the immediate area surrounding the mines. The New Potosí, or Bombón, office was moved to Huarochirí from the neighboring province of Canta, when the mines of Santiago de Guadalcázar in that province became less productive. AGI, Lima, 47, conde de Chinchón to crown, Lima, March 22, 1635. When the junta de hacienda decided to close the caja of Conchucos in 1652, it stipulated that tax-collecting duties in the province should be split evenly between the Lima and Trujillo offices. AGI, Lima, 573, conde de Salvatierra to crown, Lima, December 31, 1653.

45. AGI, Contaduría, 1704–1759B, Cuentas de la caja de Lima, Lima, 1607–90.

46. The crown held each treasury officer responsible for paying one-third of all fines charged against the office or any money missing from the strongbox (*caja fuerte*). In certain extraordinary cases one official might be held culpable, but normally all three officers shared the guilt and the burden of repayment. Escalona Agüero, *Gazofilacio*, libro I, parte II, capítulo I, números 11, 12.

47. Ibid., libro I, parte II, capítulo II, números 8,9.

48. Ibid., libro I, parte II, capítulo III, números 1–6.

49. *Recopilación*, libro VIII, título IV, leyes 6,7.

50. AGI, Lima, 290, Fianzas de los oficiales reales de Lima, Lima, October 18, 1683.

51. Escalona Agüero, *Gazofilacio*, libro I, parte II, capítulo XIII, números 1–6.

52. Royal officials in Lima sold all taxes collected in kind, confiscated materials, and goods received as fines at public auctions, usually held on Fridays in the main plazas of the city. The senior treasury officials conducted the auction with the aid of the recorder of the mines and registers (*escribano de minas y registros*), and an oidor and a fiscal of the audiencia. Each official present signed the agreement of sale. The law permitted no credit transactions. The president of the audiencia sanctioned these sales. The law required treasury officers to give thirty days public notice before each auction, unless it involved goods collected from Amerindian tribute, in which case only nine days notice was demanded. *Recopilación*, libro VIII, título VI, ley

10; Escalona Agüero, *Gazofilacio,* libro I, parte II, capítulo XVI, números 5, 7, 13.

53. *Recopilación,* libro VIII, título III, leyes, 2,3.

54. Escalona Agüero, *Gazofilacio,* libro I, parte II, capítulo VI, número 3. Before 1567 all such cases fell under the jurisdiction of the audiencia.

55. Sanchez Bella, *La organización financiera,* p. 183.

56. Royal treasury officers placed all debts and other collected revenues in a strongbox, stored in their office. They also kept the many seals, marks, and stamps of the office in this same strongbox. The office itself, located in the Plaza de Armas of Lima, was sturdily built, with barred windows and heavy doors, and was well guarded. Only the three senior treasury officials had a key to the strongbox. As an added precaution the law required all three treasury officials to be present each time they opened the box to deposit or remove funds. *Recopilación,* libro VIII, título VI, leyes 8,9.

57. AGN, Lima, ex-AHMH, Sección Colonial, manuscrito 172, folio 69.

58. AGI, Lima, 39, marqués de Guadalcázar to crown, Lima, April 28, 1623. Treasury officials could not demand the accounts or income from another district without the permission of a superior authority. Escalona Agüero, *Gazofilacio,* libro I, parte II, capítulo XVII, número 26.

59. AGI, Contaduría, 1704–1759B, Cuentas de la caja de Lima, Lima, 1607–90.

60. AGI, Lima, 309, Visita of Callao, Lima, April 28, 1634.

61. AGI, Lima, 114, Treasury officials of Lima to crown, Lima, July 21, 1647.

62. Ibid.

63. Ibid.

64. To complicate matters even further, the corregidor of Huarochirí, Diego Moreno de Zárate, was also under the jurisdiction of the Lima office and responsible for collecting tribute for that office. AGN, Lima, Superior gobierno, 32, cuaderno 92.

65. Ibid.

66. AGI, Lima, 8, Consulta, Madrid, September 22, 1653.

67. AGN, Lima, Superior gobierno, 32, Cuaderno 92.

68. AGI, Lima, 8, Consulta, Madrid, September 22, 1653.

69. Sánchez Bella, *La organización financiera,* pp. 283–84.

70. Only the crown, the viceroy, or the audiencia could initiate a visita or a pesquisa. In either case authorities in Madrid or Lima

named a *visitador* to head the investigation. This official had the authority to question any official or citizen of the realm and subpoena any pertinent documents. Everyone was supposed to cooperate. While the investigation continued, the visitador's authority was supreme in everything relating to the inquiry. The guilty were sent to authorities in Spain or Peru for the appropríate punishment, and all appeals went to the Council of the Indies. Sánchez Bella, *La organización financiera,* p. 283.

71. AGI, Lima, 106, tribunal of accounts to crown, Lima, November 15, 1647.

72. Sánchez Bella, *La organización financiera,* p. 284.

73. Ibid., pp. 282–83.

74. AGI, Lima, 309, Pedro de Villagómez to crown, Arequipa, April 2, 1637.

75. Weber, *Social and Economic Organization,* pp. 329–36; 347–58.

Chapter 5

1. John Leddy Phelan has argued forcefully that colonial audiencia officials played an important mediating role between the crown and its subjects in the Indies during the seventeenth century. Phelan's work does not focus on financial or economic matters, and consequently he does not discuss the role that treasury officials played in the political decision-making process in the Spanish Empire. See Phelan, *The Kingdom of Quito,* and "Authority and Flexibility in the Spanish Imperial Bureaucracy," *Administrative Sciences Quarterly,* 5 (June 1960), 47–65.

2. AGI, Indiferente general, 757, Consulta, Madrid, April 27, 1633.

3. Only one of the six men, Juan López de Hernani, served in the Lima caja. The others, Gregorio Pérez Andrade, Juan Bautista de Aramburu, Felipe de Abreu, Pedro de Gordejuela Castro, and Alonso Ibañez Poca, served in the tribunal of accounts. Seventy-five members of the tribunal of accounts and the treasury office were examined for this study, representing the total number of *títulos* found in the AGI, AGS, and the Archivo General de la Nación in Lima (hereafter cited as AGN). Since interim appointments and part-time officials usually did not receive a título, they were not included in the study. For the tribunal the títulos were found from 1605, when the agency was founded, until the end of the century. For the treasury caja títulos were only found for the period from 1613 until the end of the sev-

enteenth century. Of these seventy-five títulos, thirty-one fell before 1633 and forty-four were issued after that date. All but eight of the forty-four títulos issued after the sales began were sold by the crown. Prosopographical information on these bureaucrats came from the following sources: AGI, Lima, 1070, 1123, Títulos de Indias, Madrid; AGI, Lima, 3–13, Consultas, Madrid; AGI, Lima, 33–91, Cartas de los virreyes, Lima; AGI, Lima, 109, 115, 276, 280–90, 573, Visitas, Lima; and AGI Indiferente general, 595, 1692, Lima; Archivo General de Simancas, Simancas, Dirección general del tesoro (hereafter cited as DGT), Inventarios 1, 2, 24, Títulos de Indias, Madrid; BN, Manuscritos, Z-222, B-1107; AGN, 1699, Protocolo, ante Francisco Sánchez Becerra, folio 338; AGN, Superior gobierno, 4, Lima; Burkholder and Chandler, *From Impotence to Authority;* Hanke and Rodríguez, *Los virreyes,* I–VI: Guillermo Lohmann Villena, *Los americanos en las órdenes nobiliarías, 1529–1900,* 2 vols. (Madrid, 1947); Guillermo Lohmann Villena, *El Conde de Lemos, Virrey del Perú* (Madrid, 1946); Manuel de Mendiburu, *Diccionario biográfico,* 14 vols. (Lima, 1874); Joseph Mugaburu and Francisco Mugaburu, *Chronicle of Colonial Lima, 1640–1697,* trans. by Robert R. Miller (Norman, 1975); Pedro Rodríguez Crespo, "Sobre parentescos de los oidores con los grupos superiores de la sociedad limeña (a comienzos del siglo XVII)," *Mercurio peruano* (julio-septiembre, 1964); Juan Antonio Suardo, *Diario de Lima, 1629–1639,* 2 vols. (Lima, 1936); and Luis Varela y Orbegoso, *Apuntes para la historía de la sociedad colonial* (Lima, 1905).

4. The previous government experience of eight men serving in the tribunal of accounts and the treasury office in Lima from the period before 1633 could not be determined.

5. Salinas y Córdoba, *Memorial de las historias,* p. 246.

6. AGI, Lima, 106, Relación de los servicios y méritos de Fernando Bravo de Lagunas, Lima, May 30, 1637.

7. AGI, Lima, 48, conde de Chinchón to king, Lima, May 22, 1638. The conde mentioned sending letters to the cabildos of Lima, Potosí, Oruro, La Paz, Cailloma, Carabaya, Cuzco, Huancavelica, Castrovirreyna, Arica, Arequipa, Huánuco, Trujillo, Piura, Loja, Quito, and Tucumán, asking each to name six nominees to serve in their local treasury offices.

8. Rodríguez Crespo, "Sobre parentescos," p. 52; Lohmann Villena, *Los americanos,* 2:128.

9. Lohmann Villena, *Los americanos,* 1:120; AGI, Lima, 3, Consulta, Madrid, January 16, 1613.

10. Alberto García Carraffa and Arturo García Carraffa, *Enciclopedia*

heráldica y genealógica hispanoamericana (Madrid, 1920), vol. 45, pp. 30–31; Lohmann Villena, *Los americanos,* 1:63, 67, 150, 243 and 2:146, 228.

11. García Carraffa, *Enciclopedia,* 12:174, 17:14.

12. AGI, Lima, 5, Consulta, Madrid, August 22, 1629; AGI, Lima, 4, Consulta, Madrid, December 26, 1619; AGS, DGT, Títulos de Indias, 1–12–123; Suardo, *Diario,* 1:262, 2:190.

13. AGI, Lima, 5, Consulta, Madrid, March 25, 1630.

14. Mugaburu and Mugaburu, *Chronicle,* p. 142.

15. AGI, Lima, 4, Consulta, Madrid, July 1, 1616.

16. *Catálogo XX, Archivo General de Simancas, Títulos de Indias* (Valladolid, 1954), p. 575; AGI, Lima, 1070, Título de Bartolomé Astete de Ulloa, July 14, 1628; AGI, Lima, 5, Consulta, Madrid, April 22, 1628; AGI, Lima, 7, Consulta, Madrid, July 7, 1650.

17. Suardo, *Diario de Lima,* 1:258, *Catálogo XX,* p. 400.

18. AGI, Lima, 5, Consulta, Madrid, April 4, 1628.

19. Suardo, *Diario de Lima,* 1:147, 177.

20. When officials held more than one office, they usually leased the right to serve in the lesser of the two to someone else; *Catálogo XX,* p. 671.

21. AGN, Lima Protocolo 1699, ante Francisco Sánchez Becerra, Lima, 1688, f. 338.

22. AGI, Contaduría, 1715, Cuentas de la Caja de Lima, ramo de salarios, Lima, 1630; Lohmann Villena, *Los americanos,* 1:150; Suardo, *Diario de Lima,* I:75.

23. Sánchez Bella, *La organización financiera,* pp. 145–48; *Recopilación,* libro VIII, título II, ley 13.

24. Sánchez Bella, *La organización financiera,* p. 147; Escalona Agüero, *Gazofilacio,* libro I, parte II, capítulo XVII, número 4; libro II, parte II, capítulo XVI, números 1–3.

25. Sánchez Bella, *La organización financiera,* p. 147.

26. Escalona Agüero, *Gazofilacio,* libro I, parte II, capítulo XVII, números 1, 2; libro II, parte I, capítulo XVI, número 2.

27. *Ibid.,* libro II, parte I, capítulo XVI, número 9.

28. Suardo, *Diario de Lima,* 1:101, 102, 109, 141, 155, 171, 181.

29. Members of the tribunal of accounts did not have to offer a fianza.

30. The complete list of fiadores and their contributions are as follows: B. González, 6,000 ducats; T. Paredes, 6,000 ducats; P. de Melgar, 3,000 ducats; D. Sánchez Badillo, 3,000 ducats; A. Román de Herrere, 3,000 ducats; J. de Tejeda, 3,000 ducats; J. Morales Fartón,

3,000 ducats; P. Sánchez de Aguilar, 3,000 ducats. From Juan Bromley, ed. *Libros de cabildo de Lima* (Lima, 1937), 20:323.

31. Lohmann Villena, *Los americanos,* 1:35, and 2:13.

32. *Ibid.*, 1:120, 150.

33. Suardo, *Diario de Lima,* 1:75.

34. AGI, Indiferente general, 757, Consulta, Madrid, April 27, 1633.

35. Ibid.

36. J. H. Parry, *The Sale of Public Office in the Spanish Indies Under the Habsburgs* (Berkeley, 1953), p. 5.

37. The list of salable offices expanded to include corregimientos in 1678 and audiencia judgeships in 1687. By 1700 even the office of Viceroy of New Spain and Peru was sold. Guillermo Lohmann Villena, *El corregidor de Indios,* p. 130; Alberto Yalí Román, "Sobre alcaldías mayores y corregimientos en Indias," *Jahrbuch für Geschichte von Staat, Wirtschaft, und Gesellschaft Lateinamerikas,* 9 (1974), 1–39; Burkholder and Chandler, *From Impotence to Authority,* p. 19; Antonio Domínguez Ortiz, "Un virreinato en venta, "*Mercurio peruano,*" 49 (enero-febrero 1965), 46–51.

38. The prices for treasury offices in the Viceroyalty of Peru may be found in the following locations: AGI, Lima, 1070, Títulos de oficiales reales, Madrid, 1613–1700; AGS, DGT, Títulos de Indias, Inventarios, 1, 2, 24.

39. The prices for posts on the tribunal of accounts in Lima may be found in the following locations: AGI, Lima, 1123, Títulos del tribunal de cuentas, Madrid, 1605–1700; AGS, DGT, Títulos de Indias Inventarios 1, 2, 24.

40. Ibid.

41. AGI, Lima, 7, Consulta, Madrid, April 13, 1646.

42. AGI, Lima, 1070, Título de Francisco Antonio de los Santos, Madrid, December 4, 1680.

43. Hanke and Rodríguez, *Los virreyes,* 4:243.

44. AGI, Lima, 48, conde de Chinchón to crown, Lima, May 17, 1637.

45. AGS, DGT, Títulos de Indias, Título de Juan de Quesada y Sotomayor, 1–10–144.

46. Hanke and Rodríguez, *Los virreyes,* 7:148; AGI, Lima, 1123, Título de José de Bernal, Madrid, September 9, 1697.

47. AGI, Lima, 1070, Título de Baltásar de Becerra, Madrid, October 17, 1636; AGI, Lima, 57, Bartolomé Astete de Ulloa and Juan de Quesada y Sotomayor to crown, Lima, April 6, 1650; AGI, Lima, 48, conde de Chinchón to crown, May 17, 1637; María Encarnación Rodríguez

Vicente, *El tribunal del consulado de Lima en la primera mitad del siglo XVII* (Madrid, 1960), pp. 383, 390.

48. AGI, Lima, 1070, Título de Cristóbal de Llanos Jaraba, Madrid, August 7, 1655; AGI, Lima, 1070, Título de Francisco Antonio de los Santos, Madrid, April 12, 1680; AGI, Lima, 1070, Título de Francisco de Arnao y Granados, Madrid, December 20, 1680.

49. Llanos Jaraba paid only 5,000 pesos for his post, but he had a distinguished record of government service.

50. AGS, DGT, Títulos de Indias, 24–167–37.

51. The origin of two other purchasers, Juan Iturras Pagoaga and Juan de Saiceta y Cucho, could not be determined.

52. Mendiburu, *Diccionario biográfico,* 3:126.

53. AGI, Lima, 1123, Título de Álvaro de Alarcón, Madrid, March 24, 1653.

54. AGI, Lima, 7, Consulta, Madrid, April 13, 1648; AGI, Lima, 1070, Título de Cristóbal de Llanos Jaraba, Madrid, August 7, 1655.

55. AGI, Lima, 1070, Título de Sebastián Amescua Navarrete, Madrid, March 24, 1641.

56. AGI, Lima, 57, Bartolomé Astete de Ulloa and Juan de Quesada y Sotomayor to crown, Lima, April 6, 1650.

57. Mugaburu and Mugaburu, *Chronicle,* p. 273.

58. Clayton, "Trade and Navigation," p. 5.

59. AGI, Lima, 290, Fianza of Cristóbal de Llanos Jaraba, Lima, September 22, 1683.

60. Varela y Orbegoso, *Apuntes,* p. 182; García Caraffa, *Enciclopedia,* 73:144.

61. Lohmann Villena, *Conde de Lemos,* p. 385–86, n. 24.

62. *Ibid.,* p. 135, n. 27; Suardo, *Diario de Lima,* 1: 190.

63. BN, Manuscritos, Z-222, Inquisition records, Seville, April 13, 1636.

64. Mugaburu and Mugaburu, *Chronicle,* p. 23.

65. The inspectors also found that Juan Bautista de Aramburu was often absent, working at his other job as a professor at the University of San Marcos, while Bartolomé de Solórzano was away serving as corregidor of Chilques y Másques. Although neither had purchased the post, their actions indicate just how poorly the tribunal functioned. AGI, Lima, 280, Francisco Antonio de Manzolo to crown, Lima, 1664.

66. AGI, Lima, 280, Conde de Alba de Liste to crown, Lima, September 10, 1659.

67. AGI, Lima, 288, Juan de Peñalosa to crown, Lima, September 15, 1696.
68. AGI, Lima, 277, Juan de Medina Avila to crown, Lima, July 20, 1644.
69. Mendiburu, *Diccionario biográfico,* 10:367.
70. AGI, Lima, 277, Andrés de Medina Avila to crown, Lima, July 9, 1647; AGI, Lima, 7, Consulta, May 29, 1647.
71. AGI, Lima, 277, Juan de Medina Avila to crown, Lima, July 20, 1647.
72. Ibid; AGI, Lima, 1123, Título de Juan de Medina Avila, Madrid, January 9, 1641.
73. Ibid.
74. AGI, Lima, 7, Consulta, Madrid, July 6, 1646.
75. AGI, Lima, 7, Consulta, Madrid, July 6, 1646; September 9, 1646; May 29, 1647.
76. AGI, Lima, 277, Marqués de Mancera to crown, Lima, July 15, 1647; AGI, Lima, 53, Marqués de Mancera to crown, Lima, July 5, 1646.
77. AGI, Lima, 277, Marqués de Mancera to crown, Lima, July 15, 1647.
78. Hanke and Rodríguez, *Los virreyes,* 3:268.
79. AGI, Lima, 53, Marqués de Mancera to crown, July 15, 1647.
80. Hanke and Rodríguez, *Los virreyes,* 3:196–97.
81. AGI, Lima, 278, tribunal of accounts to crown, Lima, November 29, 1646; Pedro Vásquez de Velasco to crown, Lima, March 18, 1650; AGI, Lima, 53, Audiencia of Lima to crown, Lima, March 14, 1646; July 5, 1646.
82. AGI, Lima, 278, Pedro de Meneses to crown, Lima, September 15, 1651.
83. AGI, Lima, 57, Tribunal of accounts to crown, Lima, April 15, 1651.
84. AGI, Lima, 57, Bartolomé Astete de Ulloa and Juan de Quesada y Sotomayor to crown, Lima, April 6, 1651.
85. Ibid., September 15, 1651.
86. Ibid.
87. AGI, Lima, 57, Tribunal of accounts to crown, Lima, April 15, 1651.
88. Ibid.
89. Jorge Juan and Antonio de Ulloa, *Discourse and Political Reflections on the Kingdom of Peru,* ed. and trans. by John J. TePaske and Besse A. Clement (Norman, Okla., 1978), p. 247.

Chapter 6

1. Juan Reglá, "La época de los dos últimos Austrias," vol. 3 of *Historia social y económica de España y América*, ed. by Jaime Vicens Vives (Barcelona, 1961), p. 287.
2. S. N. Eisenstadt, *The Political Systems of Empires* (New York, 1963), p. 313.
3. For a fuller discussion of the onset of the fiscal crisis see chapter 2; chapter 4 covers the rise of venal officeholders to power in the treasury.
4. Antonio Domínguez Ortiz, "Los caudales de Indias y la política exterior de Felipe IV," *Anuario de Estudios Americanos*, 12 (1956), 313.
5. Elliott, *Imperial Spain*, p. 287.
6. AGI, Lima, 7, Consulta, Madrid, August 14, 1604.
7. AGI, Lima, 1171, Cédula, Madrid, September 6, 1608.
8. Ibid.
9. AGI, Lima, 7, Consulta, Madrid, September 12, 1639.
10. AGI, Lima, 7, Consulta, Madrid, August 14, 1604.
11. *Recopilación*, libro VIII, título VIII, ley 9.
12. Hanke and Rodríguez, *Los virreyes*, 2:159.
13. See table 4.
14. Hanke and Rodríguez, *Los virreyes*, 2:194.
15. Andrien, "Sale of Juros," p. 1.
16. Fred Bronner, "Peruvian Arbitristas under Viceroy Chinchón, 1629–1639," *Scripta Hierosolymitana*, 26 (1974), 35.
17. Ibid., p. 59.
18. The last visita general of the Lima Audiencia had taken place in 1594; Phelan, *The Kingdom of Quito*, p. 221.
19. Ibid., p. 222.
20. Ibid., p. 223.
21. AGI, Lima, 42, Autos de la visita general, Madrid, November 9, 1626.
22. AGI, Lima, 276, Juan Gutiérrez Flores to crown, Lima, May 11, 1629.
23. AGI, Lima, 276, Juan Gutiérrez Flores to crown, Lima, May 21, 1629.
24. AGI, Lima, 276, Juan Gutiérrez Flores to crown, Lima, May 23, 1629.
25. AGI, Lima, 276, Juan Gutiérrez Flores to crown, Lima, February 1, 1630.

26. AGI, Lima, 276, Juan Gutiérrez Flores to crown, Lima, February 26, 1630.

27. Suardo, *Diario de Lima,* 1:185.

28. *Ibid.*, p. 258; Mendiburu, *Diccionario biográfico,* 11:315.

29. AGI, Lima, 309, Pedro de Villagómez to crown, Lima, April 29, 1634. Villagómez began investigating the tribunal of accounts in response to a royal cédula of April 19, 1633. AGI, Lima, 309, José de Suárez to crown, Lima, March 1, 1639.

30. AGI, Lima, 309, José de Suárez to crown, Lima, March l, 1639.

31. Suardo, *Diario de Lima,* 1:283.

32. Mendiburu, *Diccionario biográfico,* 11:316. On July17,1635, Pedro de Villagómez received word that he was to suspend his visita of the audiencia and other tribunals in Lima and turn the inspection over to the new visitador, Juan de Carvajal y Sandi. Since the investigations in Lima were complete, Carvajal y Sandi spent most of his time trying to uncover abuses in Potosí. AGI, Lima, 309, Pedro de Villagómez to crown, Arequipa, April 11, 1636. For an account of Carvajal y Sandi's visita of Potosí, see AGI, Charcas, 113.

33. AGI, Lima, 309, Pedro de Villagómez to crown, Lima, April 30, 1635.

34. Ibid.; AGI, Lima, 309, Pedro de Villagómez to crown, Lima, May 2, 1634.

35. AGI, Lima, 309, Pedro de Villagómez to crown, Lima, January 19, 1636.

36. AGI, Indiferente general, 2690, Cédula, Madrid, April 9, 1627.

37. Ibid.

38. A recent study of Spanish military policy provides a revisionist interpretation of the union of arms, viewing it not as a policy aimed at centralizing the state, but as "establishing a framework for the mutual co-operation of more clearly differentiated regional forces." I. A. A. Thompson, *War and Government in Habsburg Spain, 1580–1620* (London, 1976), p. 275.

39. Góngora, *Studies in Colonial History,* p. 80.

40. Ibid.

41. AGI, Indiferente general, 2690, Cédula, Madrid, April 9, 1627.

42. AGI, Indiferente general, 2690, Crown to Marqués de Guadalcázar, Madrid, March 27, 1627.

43. Fred Bronner, "La unión de armas en el Perú: Aspectos político-legales," *Anuario de Estudios Americanos,* 24 (1967), 5–6.

44. Ibid., p. 6.

45. Ibid., pp. 6–7; AGI, Indiferente general, 2690, conde de Chinchón to Rodrigo de Aguiar, Lima, March 14, 1633.
46. Bronner, "Unión de armas," pp. 6–7.
47. Ibid., p. 9.
48. Ibid., p. 10.
49. AGI, Indiferente general, 2690, Arbitrios of Council of the Indies, Madrid, December 23, 1629; Arbitrios of "personas particulares," Madrid, December 23, 1629; Pedro Ugarte de la Hermosa to crown, Lima, April 28, 1622; Arbitrios of Juan de Solórzano y Pereya, Madrid, no date.
50. Bronner, "Unión de armas," pp. 40–41.
51. Ibid.
52. AGI, Indiferente general, 429, Cédula, Madrid, 1631.
53. Mendiburu, *Diccionario biográfico,* 3:172.
54. Bronner, "Peruvian Arbitristas," p. 51.
55. Ibid.
56. Suardo, *Diario de Lima,* 1:212.
57. Ibid.
58. Ibid., pp. 217, 224, 231, 234, 240.
59. AGI, Indiferente general, 2690, Hernando de Valencia to conde de Chinchón, Lima, August 8, 1633.
60. AGI, Indiferente general, 2690, Hernando de Valencia to crown, Lima, March 31, 1634.
61. Bronner, "Unión de armas," pp. 37–38.
62. Suardo, *Diario de Lima,* 1:25, 72, 147, 151, 166, 177; *Títulos de Indias,* p. 400; AGS, DGT, Títulos de Indias, 1–6, 147–48.
63. AGI, Indiferente general, 2690, conde de Chinchón to crown, March 31, 1634; AGI, Lima, 43, conde de Chinchón to crown, May 9, 1633.
64. AGI, Indiferente general, 2690, conde de Chinchón to crown, May 1, 1634; AGI, Lima, 162, conde de Chinchón to crown, Lima, June 16, 1633.
65. Suardo, *Diario de Lima,* 1:281; AGI, Lima, 162, Hernando de Valencia to crown, Lima, July 30, 1633.
66. AGI, Lima, 162, Hernando de Valencia to crown, Lima, July 30 1633.
67. Suardo, *Diario de Lima,* 1:286; 2:28; AGI, Lima, 162, Hernando de Valencia to crown, Lima, July 30, 1633; July 5, 1633.
68. Valencia denied the charges leveled against him by the viceroy and contended that the conde de Chinchón had established excessively close ties with the Lima merchant community and with the

aldermen of the cabildo. The consulado collected the union of arms levies in the city of Lima and the cabildo held the asiento for the levy on pulperías; Valencia charged that this gave both bodies the opportunity to defraud the crown. AGI, Lima, 162, Hernando de Valencia to crown, Lima, 1634.

69. Mendiburu, *Diccionario biográfico,* 1:335; Suardo, *Diario de Lima,* 1:264, 265, 271.

70. Mendiburu, *Diccionario biográfico,* 1:48; Suardo, *Diario de Lima,* 1:270, 297, 299; 2:5, 120, 128, 184; AGI, Indiferente general, 427, libro 37, folios 24–27; AGI, Lima, 162, Diego de Ayala to crown, Lima, May 4, 1634.

71. Suardo, *Diario de Lima,* 2:5, 28, 31.

72. Ibid., pp. 128, 237, 270, 271.

73. AGI, Lima, 163, Diego de Ayala to crown, Lima, May 28, 1637.

74. Israel, *Race, Class, and Politics,* pp. 135–60; Bronner, "Unión de armas," p. 30.

75. Bronner, "Unión de armas," p. 23.

76. Ibid.

77. AGI, Indiferente general, 2690, Cédula, Madrid, March 26, 1636; and Consulta, Madrid, April 3, 1635.

78. AGI, Indiferente general, 2690, Acuerdo de hacienda, Lima, June 8, 1638.

79. Ibid.

80. Ibid.

81. AGI, Lima, 47, conde de Chinchón to crown, Lima, February 4, 1636; AGI, Indiferente general, 2690, Consulta, Madrid, March 23, 1637.

82. AGI, Indiferente general, 2690, Cabildo of Lima to crown, Lima, no date.

83. BM, Libros de cabildo, 1639–1644. The opposition of the cabildo continued each time the crown renewed the union of arms plan. AGI, Lima, 109, Cabildo of Lima to crown, Lima, October 26, 1648; July 20, 1657.

84. *Annales del Cuzco, 1600–1750* (Lima, 1905), p. 77.

85. Bronner, "Unión de armas," p. 44.

86. Domínguez Ortiz, "Los caudales de Indias," p. 6.

87. Ibid.

88. Elliott, *Imperial Spain,* p. 337; Andrien, "Sale of Juros," p. 11.

89. AGI, Lima, 1171, Cédula, Madrid, September 17, 1639; July 4, 1640.

90. AGI, Lima, 1171, Cédula, Madrid, July 4, 1640.

91. Andrien, "Sale of Juros," pp. 12–13.
92. Ibid., pp. 13–19.
93. Ibid., pp. 15, n. 46.
94. Ibid., pp. 18–19. For a complete discussion of Peruvian *censos* see Brian R. Hamnett, "Church Wealth in Peru," pp. 113–32.
95. Andrien, "Sale of Juros," pp. 14–16.
96. Ibid.
97. AGI, Indiferente general, 429, Cédula, Madrid, May 27, 1631; AGI, Lima, 573, Cédula, May 27, 1631; Escalona Agüero, *Gazofilacio,* libro II, parte II, capítulo XX, números 1–5.
98. Ibid.
99. Altoaguirre, *Memorías,* p. 157.
100. AGI, Lima, 573, Cédula, Madrid, October 13, 1660.
101. Sebastián Lorente, ed., *Relaciones de los virreyes y audiencias,* 2 (Madrid, 1871), p. 169.
102. AGI, Lima, 278, Lázaro Juloguamán to crown, Cajamarca, 1650.
103. AGI, Lima 278, Juan de Meneses to crown, Lima, September 15, 1651.
104. AGI, Contaduría, 1780A, conde de Santisteban to crown, Lima, November 10, 1661.
105. See graph, chapter 3.
106. AGI, Contaduría, 1742, Cuentas de la caja de Lima, Lima, 1653–54; AGI, Contaduría, 1744, Cuentas de la caja de Lima, Lima, 1656–57.
107. AGI, Contaduría, 1780A, "Razón general del estado en que está la real hacienda según los instrumentos que la comprueban como se refiere en los puntos que contiene que corresponde desde el número 1–27 en el índice general desde el número 16 hasta el número 40 los quales se refieren en la carta de hacienda número 75." Parte 1, "Relación del estado en que se halla la real hacienda al tiempo que entré a governar estos reynos." conde de Santisteban to crown, Lima, February 12, 1662.
108. Ibid.
109. Ibid.; AGI, Lima, 66, conde de Santisteban to crown, Lima, November 20, 1664.
110. Ibid.
111. AGI, Contaduría, 1780B, Juan de Quesada y Sotomayor to crown, Lima, November 22, 1661.
112. AGI, Contaduría, 1780B, conde de Alba de Liste to crown, Lima, February 22, 1662.

113. Ibid.
114. Ibid.

Chapter 7

1. J. I. Israel indicates that Olivares was primarily responsible for launching a campaign of "non-doctrinal puritanism" to eliminate corruption and waste in the colonial bureaucracy in New Spain. In Peru his policies stressed taxation rather than efforts to eliminate corruption and inefficiency. This phase of the reform movement in Peru began over two decades after the fall of Olivares, with the establishment of the visita general. See J. I. Israel, "Mexico and the General Crisis," pp. 33–57.
2. AGI, Lima, 280, "Avisos tocantes a los grandes fraudes que hay en el reyno del Perú contra la real hacienda y otras cosas que deven remediar," Lima, November 12, 1660.
3. According to Guillermo Lohmann Villena, the detail and general accuracy of the memorial indicates that the author was very familiar with the operation of the viceregal treasury; he was probably a member of the tribunal of accounts in Lima. See Lohmann Villena, *Conde de Lemos,* p. 72.
4. The contador of the caja of Huancavelica, Alonso Fineo de Solís, wrote the crown in July 1660 about corruption in the district. This report was confirmed in another letter sent on July 24, 1660, by the fiscal of the Lima Audiencia, Tomás Berjón de Caviedes, who uncovered 115,000 pesos in findings against miners and treasury officials. AGI, Lima, 280, Crown to Juan de Cornejo, Madrid, March 16, 1663.
5. Lohmann Villena, *Conde de Lemos,* p. 72.
6. AGI, Lima, 280, Cédula, Madrid, October 7, 1662; Cédula, Madrid, October 13, 1662.
7. Lohmann Villena, *Conde de Lemos,* p. 72.
8. AGI, Lima, 9, Consulta, Madrid, April 11, 1658; Lohmann Villena, *Conde de Lemos,* p. 72.
9. AGI, Lima, 280, Autos de la visita general, Madrid, February 19, 1663.
10. Officials in Madrid were particularly concerned about reports of over 500,000 pesos withheld by the Audiencia of Panama from the Armada of 1656, and a further 180,000 pesos retained by order of the audiencia in 1659. In addition the crown urged the investigators to study the request of the comptroller of the Lima treasury, Bartolomé

Astete de Ulloa, for a position in one of the knightly orders and a future appointment to the Lima office for his son, Nicolás. See AGI, Lima, 280, Autos de la visita general, Madrid, February 19, 1663.

11. Lohmann Villena, *Conde de Lemos,* p. 73.

12. Hanke and Rodríguez, *Los virreyes,* 4:155; Manzolo's son also married a daughter of Bravo de Lagunas by a previous marriage. See Lohmann Villena, *Conde de Lemos,* p. 73.

13. Mugaburu and Mugaburu, *Chronicle,* p. 88.

14. AGI, Lima, 280, Francisco Antonio de Manzolo to crown, Lima, November 20, 1665.

15. Ibid.

16. Mendiburu, *Diccionario biográfico,* 2:413–28; Lohmann Villena, *Conde de Lemos,* p. 66.

17. Hanke and Rodríguez, *Los virreyes,* 4:155.

18. AGI, Lima, 67, Audiencia of Lima to crown, Lima, November 20, 1666.

19. Lohmann Villena, *Conde de Lemos,* p. 385, n. 24. In this same passage Lohmann Villena refers to Francisco de Colmenares as: "uno de aquellos hombres que existen en la tierra para el castigo de ella, y ejercicio de la paciencia de los buenos."

20. Hanke and Rodríguez, *Los virreyes,* 4:266; AGI, Lima, 115, Consulta, Madrid, September 16, 1665; Mugaburu and Mugaburu, *Chronicle,* p. 88.

21. AGI, Lima, 280, Juan de Cornejo to crown, Lima, June 15, 1666.

22. Ibid.

23. As oidor decano Mendoza would become president of the Lima Audiencia on the viceroy's death. Since the Audiencia of Lima ruled on an ad interim basis upon the death of the viceroy, Mendoza, as its president, would have been the most powerful political leader in the viceroyalty. Cornejo had no desire for his chief rival to attain this position, which explains his desire to be rid of Mendoza before he could assume the presidency of the audiencia.

24. Mugaburu and Mugaburu, *Chronicle,* pp. 88, 102.

25. AGI, Lima, 280, Juan de Cornejo to crown, Lima, June 15, 1666.

26. Ibid.

27. Ibid. Diego de Leon Pinelo had studied at Chuquisaca, Salamanca, and San Marcos universities. His elder brother, Antonio de Leon Pinelo, had a distinguished political and academic career in Spain, serving on the Council of the Indies and authoring numerous tracts, including his famous scholarly commentary on the *Recopilación.*

See Jorge Basadre, *El Conde de Lemos, y su tiempo* (Lima, 1945), pp. 228–32.

28. AGI, Lima, 280, Juan de Cornejo to crown, Lima, June 15, 1666. Of those justices favored by Cornejo, the most famous was Juan de Padilla, the author of a famous memorial in the 1650s, condemning Spanish treatment of the Amerindians. See Basadre, *El Conde de Lemos,* pp. 112–13.

29. One of the tasks before Manzolo was an inspection of Huancavelica. He found that the former treasurer of the district, Alonso Fineo de Solís, who had originally uncovered the 115,000 peso shortfall, had been unjustly imprisoned by his enemies. The money had never been retrieved. AGI, Lima, 280, Francisco Antonio de Manzolo to crown, Lima, 1664.

30. AGI, Lima, 280, Nicolas Polánco de Santillán to crown, Lima, July 31, 1663. The visitadores demanded a number of changes to remedy the situation, including closer supervision of the tribute collection process, more up-to-date census materials, and more reasonable tribute rates (tasas). AGI, Lima, 280, Francisco Antonio de Manzolo to crown, Lima, March 22, 1669.

31. See chapter 4.

32. Mugaburu and Mugaburu, *Chronicle,* pp. 54–55.

33. AGI, Lima, 67, Audiencia of Lima to crown, Lima, July 4, 1666; Hanke and Rodríguez, *Los virreyes,* 4:257–58.

34. Hanke and Rodríguez, *Los virreyes,* 4:259; Mendiburu, *Diccionario biográfico,* 4:3.

35. According to the conde de Lemos, Viceroy of Peru from 1666 until 1672, Bartolomé de Salazar was also responsible for these promotions. Hanke and Rodríguez, *Los virreyes,* 4:258.

36. Ibid.

37. Ibid., p. 259; Mugaburu and Mugaburu, *Chronicle,* p. 109. Navarrete lost the use of one hand as a result of the injuries he suffered.

38. Lohmann Villena, *Conde de Lemos,* p. 78.

39. Ibid.

40. Ibid., pp. 68–70.

41. Ibid.; Eugene H. Korth, *Spanish Policy in Colonial Chile* (Stanford, 1968), pp. 190–91.

42. The first major uprising in the 1660s in Upper Peru occurred at La Paz, in 1661, when a group of mestizos went on a rampage, killing the corregidor and looting the city. Although a well-financed force led by the governors of Laicocota and Chucuito defeated the mestizo force, it dispersed across the region and later formed the

nucleus for the armies of the warring factions in Laicocota. Excellent summaries of these uprisings may be found in Hanke and Rodríguez, *Los virreyes,* 4:90–100, 188–91; Basadre, *El Conde de Lemos,* pp. 81–111; and Lohmann Villena, *Conde de Lemos,* pp. 151–229. A more recent, revisionist account of the rebellion in Laicocota is Meredith Dodge, "The Impact of Racial Fears on Viceregal Policy-Making in Peru, 1661–1665," (Unpublished paper delivered at the American Historical Association Meeting, 1979). According to Dodge, the viceregal government's perception of the rebellion as a continuation of the mestizo revolt at La Paz, in 1661, led to indecisiveness, as policy makers feared causing further racial unrest.

43. Basadre, *El Conde de Lemos,* pp. 90, 94.

44. Ibid., p. 94.

45. Lohmann Villena, *Conde de Lemos,* p. 180.

46. Ibid., p. 186.

47. Ibid., pp. 193–96. Hanke and Rodríguez, *Los virreyes,* 4:260.

48. AGI, Lima, 67, Audiencia of Lima to crown, Lima, November 29, 1665; November 15, 1666; and December 3, 1666.

49. Mugaburu and Mugaburu, *Chronicle,* p. 107.

50. Basadre, *El Conde de Lemos,* p. 26.

51. Ibid.

52. Ibid.

53. Hanke and Rodríguez, *Los virreyes,* 4:240–51.

54. Juan Pérez de Guzmán was well connected in Madrid. As the conde de Peñaranda told the conde de Lemos: "Of the president of Panama, I have a good opinion, and I see that all of the council also has." Nevertheless the conde de Lemos found the president guilty of a number of improprieties, including the illegal use of royal funds, extorting 25,000 pesos to allow a silver shipment to cross the isthmus of Panama, setting rates for commercial taxes at unfair levels, sanctioning fraud in the collection of the sales tax in 1665, nepotism, and illegally selling government offices. With the support of the audiencia and the royal treasury office, the viceroy compiled a circumstantial case against Guzmán and suspended him from office, fined him 12,000 pesos, confiscated his wealth, and took him to Lima as a captive. See Hanke and Rodríguez, *Los virreyes,* 4:249; Lohmann Villena, *Conde de Lemos,* p. 38; and Basadre, *El Conde de Lemos,* p. 49.

55. Lohmann Villena, *Conde de Lemos,* pp. 38–39, 46–48; Mugaburu and Mugaburu, *Chronicle,* pp. 111, 120, 138.

56. After arriving in Lima itself, on November 21, 1667, the conde de Lemos issued a flurry of proclamations dealing with a series of

municipal problems. To ease street crime, he restricted the use and purchase of firearms and swords. He also forbade black and mulatto women from improperly dressing above their station in life, such as wearing silks or other fine clothes. He demanded that local authorities arrest and sentence the many vagabonds and criminals in the city. Lohmann Villena, *Conde de Lemos,* p. 98; Mugaburu and Mugaburu, *Chronicle,* pp. 123–26.

57. Mendiburu, *Diccionario biográfico,* 5:130–33; and Korth, *Spanish Policy,* p. 191.

58. Mugaburu and Mugaburu, *Chronicle,* pp. 131–32.

59. *Ibid.*, p. 136; Basadre, *El Conde de Lemos,* p. 102.

60. Basadre, *El Conde de Lemos,* p. 101.

61. Mugaburu and Mugaburu, *Chronicle,* p. 102.

62. Mendiburu, *Diccionario biográfico,* 5:168.

63. Hanke and Rodríguez, *Los virreyes,* 4:265–66.

64. AGI,, Lima, Cargos de la visita general, Lima, August 22, 1668.

65. Hanke and Rodríguez, *Los virreyes,* 4:266.

66. Ibid.

67. Ibid.

68. For a more detailed discussion of the factions supporting and opposing the conde de Lemos in Lima, see Lohmann Villena, *Conde de Lemos,* pp. 81–85; and Basadre, *El Conde de Lemos,* pp. 224–28.

69. Basadre, *El Conde de Lemos,* pp. 236–43; and Lohmann Villena, *Conde de Lemos,* pp. 133–49.

70. Basadre, *El Conde de Lemos,* pp. 228–36; and Lohmann Villena, *Conde de Lemos,* pp. 127–33.

71. Basadre, *El Conde de Lemos,* pp. 135.

72. Ibid., pp. 228, 236.

73. Lohmann Villena, *Conde de Lemos,* pp. 84, 130–31.

74. AGI, Lima, 280, Francisco Antonio de Manzolo to crown, Lima, March 22, 1669.

75. Ibid.

76. Mugaburu and Mugaburu, *Chronicle,* pp. 146–47.

77. Lohmann Villena, *Conde de Lemos,* p. 143.

78. Ibid.; Basadre, *El Conde de Lemos,* pp. 243–44.

79. Basadre, *El Conde de Lemos,* pp. 245–46

80. Lilly Library, Indiana University, Manuscript Division, conde de Lemos to royal officials of Huancavelica, Lima, January 31, 1668; Hanke and Rodríguez, *Los virreyes,* 4:255.

81. Cole, *The Potosí Mita,* pp. 317–18.

82. Ibid., pp. 325–28.

83. Mugaburu and Mugaburu, *Chronicle,* p. 196.
84. Lohmann Villena, *Conde de Lemos,* pp. 147, 380–81.
85. Ibid.
86. Ibid.
87. Ibid., p. 379.
88. Ibid., pp. 383–84.
89. Ibid., p. 386; Hanke and Rodríguez, *Los virreyes,* 4:266.
90. Mugaburu and Mugaburu, *Chronicle,* p. 152.
91. Hanke and Rodríguez, *Los virreyes,* 4:292, 297–98.
92. Lohmann Villena, *Conde de Lemos,* pp. 44, 223.
93. Mendiburu, *Diccionario biográfico,* 4:302.
94. Mugaburu and Mugaburu, *Chronicle,* p. 224.
95. Mendiburu, *Diccionario biográfico,* 4:304.
96. Ibid., pp. 304–7.
97. AGI, Lima, 73, conde de Castellar to crown, Lima, April 12, 1675.
98. Mendiburu, *Diccionario biográfico,* 4:304; Hanke and Rodríguez, *Los virreyes,* 5:90.
99. Mendiburu, *Diccionario biográfico,* 4:308; Hanke and Rodríguez, *Los virreyes,* 5:75.
100. Mendiburu, *Diccionario biográfico,* 4:310; Hanke and Rodríguez, *Los virreyes,* 5:78.
101. Mendiburu, *Diccionario biográfico,* 4:307–9; Céspedes del Castillo and Moreyra y Paz Soldán, *Virreinato peruano,* 2:23–25.
102. Mendiburu, *Diccionario biográfico,* 4:309; Hanke and Rodríguez, *Los virreyes,* 5:43, 76.
103. Mendiburu, *Diccionario biográfico,* 4:309; Mugaburu and Mugaburu, *Chronicle,* p. 225.
104. Mendiburu, *Diccionario biográfico,* 4:309; Hanke and Rodríguez, *Los virreyes,* 5:76.
105. Mendiburu, *Diccionario biográfico,* 4:324.
106. Ibid.
107. AGI, Lima, 81, Melchor de Liñan y Cisneros to crown, Lima, 1681; Hanke and Rodríguez, *Los virreyes,* 5: 187–232; AGI, Lima, 288, Treasury officials to crown, Lima, September 20, 1681.
108. AGI, Lima, 81, Melchor de Liñan y Cisneros to crown, Lima, 1681; Hanke and Rodríguez, *Los virreyes,* 5:187–232; AGI, Lima, 780, Títulos de la Audiencia de Lima, Madrid, October 11, 1680; AGI, Lima, 1123, Títulos del tribunal de cuentas de Lima, Madrid, April 2, 1652.
109. Hanke and Rodríguez, *Los virreyes,* 4:266; 5:72.
110. Mendiburu, *Diccionario biográfico,* 7:23.

111. AGI, Lima, 288, Cristóbal de Llanos Jaraba and Francisco de Colmenares to crown, Lima, no date.

112. Ibid.

113. AGI, Lima, 288, Sebastián de Navarrete to crown, Lima, no date; AGI, Lima, 288, Sebastián de Navarrete to crown, Mexico City, August 15, 1684.

114. AGI, Lima, 288, Cristóbal de Llanos Jaraba and Francisco de Colmenares to crown, Lima, no date.

115. Mugaburu and Mugaburu, *Chronicle,* pp. 161, 273; AGI, Lima, 288, Juan de Peñalosa to crown, Lima, February 16, 1683; April 12, 1683; November 4, 1683.

116. Mugaburu and Mugaburu, *Chronicle,* p. 261; Mendiburu, *Diccionario biográfico,* 8:61; Margaret Crahan, "The Administration of Don Melchor de Navarra y Rocaful, Duque de la Palata, 1681–1689", *The Americas,* 27 (April 1971), 389–90.

117. AGI, Lima, 288, Duque de la Palata to crown, Lima, December 20, 1682.

118. AGI, Lima, 288, Juan de Peñalosa to duque de la Palata, Lima, February 16, 1683; Juan de Peñalosa to crown, Lima, November 4, 1683.

119. AGI, Lima, 288, Duque de la Palata to Juan de Peñalosa, Lima, February 18, 1683; Duque de la Palata to crown, Lima, April 12, 1683.

120. AGI, Lima, 288, Informe of tribunal of accounts, Lima, December 17, 1681; Duque de la Palata to tribunal of accounts, Lima, December 17, 1681.

121. AGI, Lima, 288, "Relación que el tribunal de Lima dió al señor Juan de Peñalosa en virtud de cédula de su magd. del estado de cuentas de las cajas de este reyno y los alcances y resultas que procedieron de los fenecimientos," Lima, November 3, 1683.

122. AGI, Lima, 288, Duque de la Palata to crown, Lima, June 1687.

123. AGI, Lima, 288, Juan de Saiceta y Cucho to crown, Lima, November 14, 1684.

124. AGI, Lima, 288, Juan de Saiceta y Cucho to crown, Lima, June 10, 1684; December 12, 1682; November 14, 1683.

125. AGI, Lima, 288, Juan de Saiceta y Cucho to crown, Lima, Decmeber 12, 1682; November 14, 1683.

126. Ibid.

127. AGI, Lima, 288, Treasury officials to crown, Lima, December 9, 1682.

128. AGI, Lima, 288, Treasury officials to crown, Lima, November 22, 1683.

129. AGI, Lima, 288, Treasury officials to crown, Lima, no date.
130. Ibid.
131. AGI, Lima, 288, Treasury officials to crown, Lima, December 9, 1682; November 22, 1683.
132. Mendiburu, *Diccionario biográfico,* 8:73; Crahan, "The Administration of Don Melchor de Navarra," p. 395.
133. Mendiburu, *Diccionario biográfico,* 8:73; Crahan, "The Administration of Don Melchor de Navarra," pp. 396–97.
134. Crahan, "The Administration of Don Melchor de Navarra," p. 397; Cole, *The Potosí Mita,* pp. 394–403.
135. Crahan, "The Administration of Don Melchor de Navarra, pp. 403–4; Mendiburu, *Diccionario biográfico,* 8:73; Hanke and Rodríguez, *Los virreyes,* 7:134.
136. Crahan, "The Administration of Don Melchor de Navarra, pp. 403–4; Mendiburu, *Diccionario biográfico,* 8:73; Hanke and Rodríguez, *Los virreyes,* 7:134.
137. Céspedes del Castillo and Mereyra y Paz Soldán, *Virreinato peruano,* 2:138–41, 162.
138. AGI, Lima, 288, Juan de Peñalosa to crown, Lima, September 15, 1696.

Conclusion

1. For an excellent summary of the revolts in Spain's European Kingdoms see J.H. Elliott, "Revolts in the Spanish Monarchy," in Robert Forster and Jack P. Greene, eds., *Preconditions of Revolution in Early Modern Europe* (Baltimore, 1970) pp. 109–30.
2. Israel, "Mexico and the General Crisis," p. 54.
3. TePaske and Klein, "Seventeenth-Century Crisis in New Spain," p.128.
4. Ibid., p. 120.
5. Israel, "Mexico and the General Crisis," p. 44.
6. Elliott, "Revolts in the Spanish Monarchy," pp. 113–21.
7. Even in Mexico new levies on agricultural and commercial sectors failed to raise large sums. During the century income from these taxes fluctuated only slightly between 14 and 18 percent. See TePaske and Klein, "Seventeenth-Century Crisis," p.129.
8. Elliott, "Revolts in the Spanish Monarchy," p. 118.
9. Ibid., pp. 111–12.

Glossary

administración por mayor: chief policy-making officials or agencies for the viceregal treasury—viceroy, audiencia, tribunal of accounts, and junta de hacienda

administración por menor: officials or agencies entrusted with enforcing treasury policies—royal officials, tax farmers, and individuals or agencies collecting specific tax levies

ají: hot peppers

alcalde del crimen: criminal judge serving in an audiencia

alcances de cuentas: collected debts or back taxes

arbitrio: means or expedient designed to reform or improve an existing procedure

arbitristas: group of reformers in Spain and the Indies, espousing a wide range of changes in the empire

armada del mar del sur: the Pacific fleet

ascenso: recognized ladder of career advancement in the bureaucracy

asiento: contract between the crown and an individual, organization, or group to collect taxes in the Indies

aviador: moneylender, usually a merchant who advanced capital to miners

azatea: attendant to a member of the royal family

azoguero: owner of an amalgamation mill and silver mines

bando: edict issued by the viceroy and audiencia

cabildo: municipal council in the Indies

caja de comunidad: community chest in Amerindian villages for money, valuables, and documents

caja fuerte: strongbox

caja matríz, or *principal:* treasury office serving as a clearing house for funds from subordinate offices

caja real: royal treasury office or the strongbox in that office

caja subordinada: subtreasury that remitted its surplus income to a caja principal

carnero de la tierra: grazing animals indigenous to Peru—llama, alpaca, and vicuña

carta de pago: receipt

cédula: royal edict

censo: long-term mortgage, usually advanced by clerical organizations to rural landowners

chacra, or fundo: small estate, usually supplying profitable and stable regional markets

consulado: merchant guild and commercial court

contador: comptroller of a treasury office

contador de resultas: subordinate accountant on the tribunal of accounts who worked on the backlog of unfinished past accounts

contador entretenido: ad interim accountant serving on the tribunal of accounts, usually at partial pay

contador mayor: chief accountant serving on the tribunal of accounts

contador ordenador: subordinate accountant serving on the tribunal of accounts

converso: Jew who converted to Roman Catholicism

corregidor de indios: rural magistrate in the Amerindian communities who collected the tribute tax

correo mayor: the mail system

criado: retainer of the viceroy or a nobleman

cuenta: account

desmonte: unrefined ore that had been mined and thrown into slag piles

donativo, or *servicio gracioso:* forced donation

ducado: ducat, unit of money valued at ten or eleven reales

encomienda: protectorate over a number of Amerindian villages, first given to the original conquerors, which carried the right to receive a portion of the tribute paid in the region

ensayador: official entrusted with smelting silver into royal coinage

escribano: scribe

estancia de pan llevar: large, wheat-producing estate in central Peru

factor: business manager in a treasury office

fianza: security bond

fiscal: crown attorney to an audiencia

forastero: Amerindian immigrant no longer living with his clan group

futura: promise of an appointment or succession to a goverment post at some date in the future

gremio: guild

hacendado: estate owner

hacienda: large farm or estate
hacienda real: royal treasury
indio de faltriquera: Amerindian who sent sufficient funds to hire a wage laborer to fulfill his forced labor obligations at the mines
juez de residencia: justice who conducted a judicial review of a crown official at the end of his term of office
juez executor: justice sent to enforce a ruling from a higher court
junta de hacienda: council of finance composed of the viceroy or governor, members of the nearby audiencia, the tribunal of accounts, and the local treasury officials, that set financial policies for a region
junta particular: an ad hoc meeting to deal with a pressing problem
juro: annuity sold by the crown
juzgado de bienes de difuntos: intestate goods held in escrow,usually from the estate of peninsular Spaniards
kuraka: Andean clan leader
libro común: workbook kept in common by treasury officials
libro manual: daily workbook kept by each treasury official, recording every transaction in the office
limeño: native of Lima
lloma: desert land receiving sufficient seasonal moisture to support vegetation
minga: wage laborer at the mines
mitayo: forced laborer at the mines
obraje: textile mill
obrajero: owner of a textile mill
oficial real: royal official, usually a royal treasury officer
oidor: civil justice serving on an audiencia
ordenanza: ordinance
paño azul: blue cloth, usually from the obrajes of Quito
perulero: Peruvian merchant who traded directly with markets in Europe, the Indies, and the Far East
peso de ocho: peso of eight reales
peso ensayado: peso of 12½ reales
pesquisa: government investigation of a specific problem
porteño: resident of Buenos Aires
privado: chief advisor or minister
procurador: legal representative
protector de indios, or naturales: audiencia justice or attorney entrusted with bringing cases regarding the Amerindians before the tribunal
radicado: crown official strongly rooted to local interests by social and economic ties
ramo: separate income or expenditure entry in the treasury accounts
repartimiento: encomienda district or royal jurisdiction inhabited by Amerindians
repartimiento de comercio, or *mercancías:* European goods

legally distributed by the corregidor de indios

residencia: judicial review held when a crown official left office

sala: chamber

sínodo: portion of the tribute tax going to the local parish priest

sisa: excise tax, usually on foodstuffs

situado: subsidy

solimán: a corrosive sublimate (biochloride of mercury) used as an antiseptic and in certain cosmetics

supernumerario: official temporarily occupying a crown post, usually at half pay, until a full-time opening developed

título: royal letter of appointment to a bureaucratic post

tribunal de la santa cruzada: tribunal administering the sale of papal indulgences

tribunal mayor de cuentas: tribunal of accounts

válido: chief advisor or minister of the crown, with patronage as well as political power

vara: unit of measurement, 838 meters

veedor: inspector in a treasury office

visitador: head of an inspection tour

visita general: inspection tour

yanacona: Amerindian serf

yerba mate: Paraguayan tea

Bibliography

Archival Sources:

Archivo General de Indias, Seville
Contaduría. Legajos 1693–1759B, 1778–1781, 1791, 1815, 1820, 1827, 1845.
Escribanía de Cámara. Legajos 515A, 533A, 568A, 1189, 1190.
Indiferente general. Legajos 429, 430, 618, 754, 757, 820, 1692, 1767, 1848, 2690, 2865.
Lima. Legajos 3–10, 13, 36, 37, 39, 41, 42, 43, 44, 45, 46, 47, 48, 53–55, 57, 58, 66, 67, 73, 81, 91, 106, 109, 114, 115, 162–65, 276–78, 280, 281, 288–95, 309–11, 425, 427, 429, 464, 473, 572, 573, 609, 633, 635, 789, 790, 1066, 1070, 1077, 1122, 1123, 1171, 1181, 1271, 1273, 1274.
Archivo General de Simancas, Simancas
Sección XXII, Dirección General de Tesoro.
Inventario 1. Legajos 1–28.
Inventario 24. Legajos 167–70, 173, 177, 316, 326, 530.
Biblioteca del Palacio Real, Madrid.
Manuscritos, Legajos 1278, 1634.
Archivo General de la Nación, Lima
ex-Archivo Histórico del Ministerio de Hacienda y Comercio. Legajo 3, Cuaderno 106, Manuscritos 58, 81, 91, 93, 100, 109, 122, 131, 156, 157, 160, 162, 164, 172, 201, 240, 243, 672.
Derecho Indígena. Legajo 5, Cuadernos 87, 90, 91, 92, Legajo 39, Cuaderno 799, 803.
Real Hacienda. Caja of Cuzco 1629, Caja of Lima 1629–1680, Caja of Pasco, 1631–1679, Caja of Potosí 1642.
Superior Gobierno. Legajo 3, Cuadernos 50, 53, 54, 55, Legajo 4, Cuadernos 62, 63, 67, 68, Legajo 5, Cuaderno 74, Legajo 29, Cuaderno 83, Legajo 30, Cuaderno 85, Legajo 32, Cuadernos 91, 92.

Protocolos. Ante Francisco Sánchez Becerra, 1699, folio 338.

Biblioteca National, Lima

Manuscritos, B249, B1107, B1438, B1465, B1489, F472, F508, F768, Z220.

Biblioteca Municipal, Lima

Libros de Cabildo de Lima, 1628–1690.

Printed Primary Sources

Alcedo, Antonio de. *Diccionario geográfico histórico de las Indias occidentales o America*. Vols. 205–8 of *Biblioteca de autores españoles*. Madrid: Ediciones Átlas, 1967.

Altoaguirre, Angel. *Colección de las memorias o relaciones que escribieron los virreyes del Perú acerca del estado en que dejaban las cosas generales del reino*. Madrid: Imprenta Mujeres Españoles, 1930.

Annales del Cuzco, 1600–1750. Lima: Imprenta del Estado, 1905.

Ballesteros, Tomás de, ed. *Tomo primero de las ordenanzas del Perú*. Lima: Joseph de Contreras, 1685.

Bravo de Lagunas y Castilla, Pedro. *Voto consultivo que ofrece al excelentísimo señor, Joseph Antonio Manso de Velasco, Conde de Superunda, cavallero del orden de Santiago, gentilhombre de la cámara de su magestad, teniente general de sus reales ejércitos, virrey, gobernador, y capitán general de los reynos del Perú*. Lima: Oficina de Huérfanos, 1761.

Bromley, Juan, ed. *Libros de Cabildo de Lima*. 20 vols. Lima: Impresores Torres Aguirre, 1937.

Burkholder, Mark A., and Chandler, D. S. *Biographical Dictionary of Audiencia Ministers in the Americas, 1687–1821*. Westport: Greenwood Press, 1982.

Cobo, Bernabé. "Historia del nuevo mundo," *Obras del Padre Bernabé Cobo*. Vol. 91 of *Biblioteca de autores españoles*. Madrid: Ediciones Átlas, 1956.

———. "Libro primero de la fundación de Lima," *Obras del Padre Bernabé Cobo*. Vol. 92 of *Biblioteca de autores españoles*. Madrid: Ediciones Átlas, 1956.

Cook, Noble David, ed. *Tasa de la visita general de Francisco de Toledo*. Lima: Universidad Nacional de San Marcos, 1975.

Elliott, John H., and de la Pena, José F., eds. *Memoriales y cartas del Conde Duque de Olivares. Política interior, 1621 a 1627*. Madrid: Ediciones Alfaguara, 1978.

Escalona y Agüero, Gaspar de. *Gazofilacio real del Perú*. Vol. 2, series 2 of *Biblioteca boliviana*. La Paz: Editorial del Estado, 1941.

García Carraffa, Alberto, and García Carraffa, Arturo, eds. *Enciclopedia heráldica y genealógica hispano-americana* 88 vols. Madrid, 1952–63.

Hanke, Lewis, and Rodríguez, Celso. *Los virreyes Españoles en América durante el gobierno de la casa de Austria.* Vols. 280–86 of *Biblioteca de autores españoles.* Madrid: Ediciones Átlas, 1978–80.

Jiménez de la Espada, Marcos. *Relaciones geográficas de Indias—Perú.* Vols. 183–85 of *Biblioteca de autores españoles.* Madrid: Ediciones Átlas, 1965.

Juan, Jorge, and Ulloa, Antonio de. *Discourse and Political Reflections on the Kingdom of Peru.* Ed. and trans. by John J. TePaske and Besse A. Clement. Norman: University of Oklahoma Press, 1978.

Levillier, Roberto, ed. *Gobernantes del Perú, cartas y papeles del siglo XVI.* Vol. 8. Madrid: Imprenta de Juan Penyo, 1925.

Lizarraga, Fray Reginaldo. *Descripción breve de toda la tierra del Perú, Tucumán, Río de la Plata, y Chile.* Vol. 216 of *Biblioteca de autores españoles.* Madrid: Ediciones Átlas, 1968.

Lorente, Sebastián, ed. *Relaciones de los virreyes y audiencias.* 2 vols. Madrid: Imprenta M. Rivadeneyra, 1871.

Magdaleno, Ricardo, ed. *Catálogo XX, Archivo General de Simancas. Títulos de Indias.* Valladolid: Casa Martín, 1954.

Mendiburu, Manuel de. *Diccionario histórico biográfico del Perú.* 15 vols. Lima: Imprenta Enrique Palacios, 1931–38.

Moreyra y Paz Soldán, Manuel, and Céspedes del Castillo, Guillermo. *Virreinato peruano: Documentos para su historia. Colección de cartas de Virreyes, Conde de Monclova, 1689–1705.* 3 vols. Lima: Instituto histórico del Perú, 1954.

Mugaburu, Joseph, and Mugaburu, Francisco. *Chronicle of Colonial Lima, 1640–1697.* Trans. by Robert R. Miller. Norman: University of Oklahoma Press, 1975.

Recopilación de leyes de los reynos de las Indias. 4 vols. Madrid: Ediciones Cultura Hispánica, 1973.

Salinas y Córdoba, Fray Buenaventura de. *Memorial de las historias del nuevo mundo, Pirú.* Lima: Universidad Nacional de San Marcos, 1973.

Sánchez Albornoz, Nicolas, ed. *El indio en el Alto Perú a fines del siglo XVII.* Lima: Seminario de historia rural andina, 1973.

Solórzano y Pereyra, Juan de. *Política indiana.* Vols. 252–56 of *Biblioteca de autores españoles.* Madrid: Ediciones Átlas, 1972.

Suardo, Juan Antonio de. *Diario de Lima.* 2 vols. Ed. by Rubén Vargas Ugarte. Lima: Biblioteca Histórica Peruana, 1936.

TePaske, John J. *La real hacienda de Nueva España: La real caja de*

México, 1576–1818. México: Instituto Nacional de Anthropología e Historia, 1976.

TePaske, John J., and Klein, Herbert S. *The Royal Treasuries of the Spanish Empire in America*. 3 vols. Durham: Duke University Press, 1982.

Secondary Works: Books

Aston, Trevor. *Crisis in Europe, 1560–1660: Essays from Past and Present*. London: Routledge and Kegan Paul, 1965.

Bakewell, P. J. *Silver Mining and Society in Colonial Mexico: Zacatecas, 1546–1700*. Cambridge, Eng.: Cambridge University Press, 1971.

Bargalló, Modesto. *La minería y la metalurgía en la América española durante la época colonial*. México: Fonde de Cultura Económica, 1955.

Basadre, Jorge. *El Conde de Lemos y su tiempo*. Lima: Editorial Huascarán, 1945.

Bayle, Constantino. *El protector de indios*. Sevilla: Escuela de Estudios Hispano-Americanos, 1945.

Borah, Woodrow. *Early Colonial Trade and Navigation Between Mexico and Peru*. Berkeley: University of California Press, 1954.

———. *New Spain's Century of Despression*. Vol. 35 of *Ibero-Americana*. Berkeley: University of California Press, 1951.

Bowser, Frederick P. *The African Slave in Colonial Peru, 1524–1650*. Stanford: Stanford University Press, 1974.

Bromley, Juan. *Evolución urbana de Lima*. Lima: Editorial Lumen, 1945.

———. *La fundación de la ciudad de los reyes*. Lima: Imprenta Editorial Excelsior, 1935.

———. *Virreyes, cabildantes, y oidores*. Lima: P. Barrantes, 1944.

Brown, Jonathan C. *A Socioeconomic History of Argentina*. Cambridge,Eng.: Cambridge University Press, 1979.

Burkholder, Mark A. and Chandler D. S. *From Impotence to Authority: The Spanish Crown and the American Audiencias, 1687–1808*. Columbia: University of Missouri Press, 1977.

Carrande, Ramón. *Carlos V y sus banqueros*. 2 vols. Madrid: Sociedad de Estudios y Publicaciones, 1967.

Chaunu, Pierre. *Les Philippines et le Pacifique des Ibériques (XVIe, XVIIe, XVIIIe siècles): Introduction Méthodologique et Indices d'activité*. Paris: S.E.V.P.E.N., 1960.

Chaunu, Pierre, and Chaunu, Huguette. *Séville et l'Atlantique*. 8 vols. in 13 parts. Paris: Colin, 1955–59.

Chevalier, Francois. *Land and Society in Colonial Mexico: The Great Ha-*

cienda. Trans. by Alvin Eustis. Berkeley: University of California Press, 1963.

Clayton, Lawrence A. *Caulkers and Carpenters in a New World: The Shipyards of Colonial Guayaquil.* Athens: Ohio University Press, 1980.

Cook, Noble David. *Demographic Collapse: Indian Peru, 1520–1620.* Cambridge, Eng.: Cambridge University Press, 1981.

Cooper, J. P., ed. *The Decline of Spain and the Thirty Years War.* Vol. 4 of *The New Cambridge Modern History.* Cambridge, Eng.: Cambridge University Press, 1970.

Cushner, Nicholas P. *Farm and Factory: The Jesuits and the Development of Agrarian Capitalism in Colonial Quito, 1600–1767.* Albany: State Universty of New York Press, 1982.

————. *Lords of the Land: Sugar, Wine, and Jesuit Estates of Colonial Peru, 1600–1767.* Albany: State University of New York Press, 1980.

DeVries, Jan. *The Economy of Europe in an Age of Crisis, 1600–1750.* Cambridge, Eng.: Cambridge University Press, 1976.

Dobyns, Henry, and Vásquez, Mario. *Migración e integracion en el Perú.* Lima: Editorial Estudios Andinos, 1963.

Domínquez Ortiz, Antonio. *Política y hacienda de Felipe IV.* Madrid: Editorial del Derecho Financiero, 1960.

Eisenstadt, S. N. *The Political Systems of Empires.* New York: Free Press of Glencoe, 1963.

Elliott, J. H. *Imperial Spain, 1469–1716.* New York: New American Library, 1977.

Encarnación Rodríguez Vicente, María. *El tribunal del consulado de Lima en la primera mitad del siglo XVII.* Madrid: Ediciones Cultura Hispánica, 1960.

Escobedo, Ronald. *El tributo indígena en el Perú (siglos XVI–XVII).* Pamplona: Universidad de Navarra, 1979.

Frank, Andre Gunder. *Latin America: Underdevelopment or Revolution.* London and New York: Monthly Review Press, 1969.

Girard, Albert. *Le commerce français a Séville et Cadiz au temps des Habsbourg.* Paris: E. De Boccard, 1932.

Góngora, Mario. *Studies in the Colonial History of Spanish America.* Trans. by Richard Southern. Cambridge, Eng.: Cambridge University Press, 1975.

Grice-Hutchinson, Marjorie. *Early Economic Thought in Spain, 1177–1740.* London: George Allen and Unwin, 1978.

Hamerly, Michael T. *El comercio de cacao de Guayaquil durante el periodo colonial: Un estudio cuantitativo.* Quito: Comandancia General de Marina, 1976.

Haring, Clarence. *The Spanish Empire in America.* New York: Harcourt, Brace, and World, 1947.

Israel, J. I. *Race, Class, and Politics in Colonial Mexico, 1610–1670.* Oxford: Oxford University Press, 1975.

Kamen, Henry. *Spain in the Later Seventeenth Century, 1665–1700.* London and New York: Longman, 1980.

Keith, Robert G. *Conquest and Agrarian Change: The Emergence of the Hacienda System on the Peruvian Coast.* Cambridge, Mass.: Harvard University Press, 1976.

Keith, Robert G., ed. *Haciendas and Plantations in Latin American History.* New York and London: Holmes and Meier Publications, 1977.

Korth, Eugene. *Spanish Policy in Colonial Chile.* Stanford: Stanford University Press, 1968.

Leonard, Irving A. *Baroque Times in Old Mexico.* Ann Arbor: University of Michigan Press, 1966.

Lockhart, James. *Spanish Peru, 1532–1560: A Colonial Society.* Madison: University of Wisconsin Press, 1966.

Lohmann Villena, Guillermo. *Los americanos en las ordenes nobiliarias, 1529–1900.* Madrid: Consejo Superior de Investigaciones Científicas, 1947.

————. *El Conde de Lemos, Virrey del Perú.* Madrid: Escuela de Estudios Hispano-Americanos, 1946.

————. *El corregidor de indios en el Perú bajo los Austrias.* Madrid: Ediciones Cultura Hispánica, 1957.

————. *Las defensas militares de Lima y Callao.* Sevilla: Escuela de Estudios Hispano-Americanos, 1964.

————. *Las minas de Huancavelica en los siglos XVI y XVII.* Sevilla: Escuela de Estudios Hispano-Americanos, 1949.

————. *Los ministros de la Audiencia de Lima.* Sevilla: Escuela de Estudios Hispano-Americanos, 1974.

————. *Los relaciones de los virreyes del Perú.* Sevilla: Escuela de Estudios Hispano-Americanos, 1959.

Lynch, John. *Spain under the Habsburgs, 1598–1700.* Vol. 2. Oxford: Basil Blackwell, 1969, 1982.

MacLeod, Murdo J. *Spanish Central America: A Socioeconomic History, 1520–1720.* Berkeley: University of California Press, 1973.

Marzahl, Peter. *Town in the Empire: Government, Politics and Society in Seventeenth-Century Popayán.* Austin: University of Texas Press, 1978.

Mathias, Peter. *The First Industrial Nation: An Economic History of Britain, 1700–1914.* London: Methuen and Co., 1969.

Moreyra y Paz Soldán, Manuel. *Biografías de oidores del siglo XVII y otros estudios.* Lima: Imprenta Lumen, 1957.

———. *El tráfico marítimo en la época colonial.* Lima: Imprenta Gil, 1944.

Múzquiz de Miguel, José Luis. *El Conde de Chinchón, virrey del Perú.* Madrid: Escuela de Estudios Hispano-Americanos, 1945.

Parker, Geoffrey, and Smith, Leslie, eds. *The General Crisis of the Seventeenth Century.* London: Routledge and Kegan Paul, 1978.

Parry, J. H. *The Sale of Public Office in the Spanish Indies Under the Habsburgs.* Vol. 37 of *Ibero-Americana.* Berkeley: University of California Press, 1953.

Phelan, John L. *The Kingdom of Quito in the Seventeenth Century: Bureaucratic Politics in the Spanish Empire.* Madison: University of Wisconsin Press, 1968.

Ramos Pérez, Demetrio. *Minería y comercio interprovincial en hispanoamérica (siglos XVI, XVII, XVIII).* Valladolid: Universidad de Valladolid, 1970.

———. *Trigo chileno, navieros del Callao, y hacendados limeños entre la crisis agrícola del siglo XVII y la comercial de la primera mitad del XVIII.* Madrid: Consejo Superior de Investigaciones Científicas, 1967.

Roel, Virgilio. *Historia social y económica de la colonia.* Lima: Editorial Gráfica Labor, 1970.

Romero, Emilio. *Historia económica y financiera del Perú.* Lima: Imprenta Torres Aguirre, 1937.

Rosenblat, Ángel. *La población indígena y el mestizaje en América, 1492–1950.* 2 vols. Buenos Aires: Editorial Nova, 1954.

Sánchez Bella, Ismael. *La organización financiera de las Indias (siglo XVI).* Sevilla: Escuela de Estudios Hispano-Americanos, 1968.

Sarfatti, Magali. *Spanish Bureaucratic Patrimonialism in America.* Berkeley: Institute of International Studies, 1966.

Schafer, Ernesto. *El consejo real y supremo de las Indias.* 2 vols. Sevilla: Escuela de Estudios Hispano-Americanos, 1935–47.

Schurz, William Lytle. *The Manila Galleon.* New York: E. P. Dutton and Co., 1939.

Schwartz, Stuart B. *Sovereignty and Society in Colonial Brazil: The High Court of Bahia and Its Judges, 1609–1751.* Berkeley: University of California Press, 1973.

Silva Santisteban, Fernando. *Los obrajes en el virreinato del Perú.* Lima: Publicaciones del Museo Nacional de Historia, 1964.

Spalding, Karen. *De indio a Campesino: Cambios en la estructura social del Perú colonial.* Lima: Instituto de Estudios Peruanos, 1974.

Stern, Steve J. *Peru's Indian Peoples and the Challenge of Spanish Conquest: Huamanga to 1640*. Madison: University of Wisconsin Press, 1982.

Stradling, R. A. *Europe and the Decline of Spain*. London: George Allen and Unwin, 1981.

Taylor, William B. *Landlord and Peasant in Colonial Oaxaca*. Stanford: Stanford University Press, 1972.

Thompson, I. A. A. *War and Government in Habsburg Spain, 1580–1620*. London: Athlone Press, 1976.

Ugarte, César Antonio. *Bosquejo de la historia económica del Perú*. Lima: Imprenta Cabieses, 1926.

Ulloa, Modesto. *La hacienda real de Castilla en el reinado de Felipe IV*. Roma: Libreria Sforzini, 1963.

Varallaros, José. *Historia de Huánuco*. Buenos Aires: Imprenta López, 1959.

Varela y Orbegoso, Luis. *Apuntes para la historia de la sociedad colonial*. 2 vols. Lima: Imprenta Liberal, 1905.

Vargas Ugarte, Rubén. *Historia del Perú, virreinato (siglo XVII)*. Buenos Aires: Librería Studium, 1955.

———. *Títulos nobiliarios en el Perú*. Lima: Compañía de Impresiones y Publicidad, 1948.

Vicens Vives, Jaime, ed. *Historia social y económica de España y América*. Vols. 2, 3, 4. Barcelona: Editorial Vicens Vives, 1961.

Vidaurre, Pedro. *Relación cronológica de los alcaldes que han presidido del Ayuntamiento de Lima*. Lima: J. Francisco Solís, 1889.

Walker, Geoffrey. *Spanish Politics and Imperial Trade, 1700–1789*. Bloomington: Indiana University Press, 1979.

Wallerstein, Immanuel. *The Modern World System: Capitalist Agriculture and the Origins of the European World-Economy in the Sixteenth Century*. New York: Academic Press, 1974.

———. *The Modern World System II: Mercantilism and the Consolidation of the European-World Economy, 1603–1750*. New York: Academic Press, 1980.

Weber, Max. *Economy and Society*. Trans. by Guenther Roth and Claus Wittich. Vol. 3. New York: Bedminster Press, 1968.

———. *The Theory of Social and Economic Organization*. Trans. by A. M. Henderson and Talcott Parsons. New York: MacMillan Publishing Company, 1947.

Whitaker, Arthur P. *The Huancavelica Mercury Mine*. Cambridge, Mass.: Harvard University Press, 1941.

Wortman, Miles L. *Government and Society in Central America, 1680–1840*. New York: Columbia University Press, 1982.

Secondary Works: Articles

Aguilar, Miguel. "Control de la real hacienda en el Virreinato del Perú." *Anales del III Congreso Nacional del Perú*. Lima: Centro de Estudios Histórica-Militares del Perú, 1965.

Andrien, Kenneth J. "Bureaucratic Responses to the Fiscal Crisis of Seventeenth-Century Peru," Unpublished paper delivered at the American Historical Association Meeting, 1980.

———. "The Sale of Fiscal Offices and the Decline of Royal Authority in the Viceroyalty of Peru, 1633–1700." *Hispanic American Historial Review*, 62 (February 1982), 49–71.

———. "The Sale of Juros and the Politics of Reform in the Viceroyalty of Peru, 1608–1695." *Journal of Latin American Studies*, 13 (May 1981), 1–19.

Armas, Fernando de. "Los oficiales de la real hacienda en las Indias." *Revista de Historia*, 16 (1963), 11–34.

Assadourián, Carlos Sempat. "Sobre un elemento de la economía colonial: Producción y circulación de mercancías en el interior de un conjunto regional." *EURE*, 8 (1973), 135–181.

Bakewell, Peter J. "Registered Silver Production in the Potosí District, 1550–1735." *Jahrbuch für Geschichte von Staat, Wirtschaft, und Gesellschaft Lateinamerikas*, 12 (1975), 67–103.

Bancora Cañero, Carmen. "Las remesas de metales preciosos desde el Callao a España en la primera mitad del siglo XVII." *Revista de Indias*, 75 (1959), 35–88.

Boxer, C. R. "Plata es sangre: Sidelights on the Drain of Spanish-American Silver to the Far East, 1550–1700." *Journal of Philippine Studies*, 18 (1970), 457–78.

Boyer, Richard. "Mexico in the Seventeenth Century: Transition of a Colonial Society." *Hispanic American Historical Review*, 57 (August 1977), 455–78.

Bradley, Peter T. "Maritime Defence of the Viceroyalty of Peru (1600–1700)." *The Americas*, 36 (October 1979), 155–75.

Bronner, Fred. "Peruvian Arbitristas under Viceroy Chinchón, 1629–1639." *Scripta Hierosolymitana*, 26 (1974), 34–77.

———. "The Population of Lima, 1593–1647: In Quest of a Statistical Bench Mark." *Ibero-Amerikanisches Archiv*, 2 (1979), 107–19.

———. "La unión de armas en el Perú. Aspectos político-legales." *Anuario de Estudios Americanos*, 24 (1967), 1133–1176.

Céspedes del Castillo, Guillermo. "Lima y Buenos Aires: Repercusiones económicas y políticas de la creación del virreinato de la Río de la Plata." *Anuario de Estudios Americanos,* 31 (1946), 677–874.

———. "Reorganización de la hacienda virreinal peruana en el siglo XVIII." *Anuario de Historia del Derecho Español,* 23 (1953), 329–69.

Clayton, Lawrence A. "Local Initiative and Finance in Defense of the Viceroyalty of Peru: The Development of Self-Reliance." *Hispanic American Historical Review,* 54 (May 1974), 284–304.

———. "Trade and Navigation in the Seventeenth-Century Viceroyalty of Peru." *Journal of Latin American Studies,* 7 (May 1975), 1–21.

Cobb, Gwendolin. "Supply and Transport for the Potosí Mines, 1545–1640." *Hispanic American Historical Reivew,* 29 (February 1949), 24–45.

Cook, Noble David. "La población indígena en el Perú colonial." *Anuario del Instituto de Investigaciones Históricas,* 8 (1965), 73–110.

Crahan, Margaret. "The Administration of Don Melchor de Navarra y Rocaful, Duque de la Palata, 1681–1689." *The Americas,* 27 (April 1971), 389–412.

Dobyns, H. F. "Estimating Aboriginal American Population: An Appraisal of Techniques with a New Hemispheric Estimate." *Current Anthropology,* 7 (1966), 395–449.

Dodge, Meredith. "The Impact of Racial Fears on Viceregal Policy-Making in Peru, 1661–1665." Unpublished paper delivered at the American Historical Association Meeting, 1979.

Domínguez Ortiz, Antonio. "Los caudales de Indias y la política exterior de Felipe IV." *Anuario de Estudios Americanos,* 12 (1956), 311–83.

———. "Un virreinato en venta." *Mercurio Peruano,* 49 (enero-febrero 1965), 46–51.

Elliott, J. H. "The Statecraft of Olivares." *The Diversity of History: Essays in Honor of Sir Herbert Butterfield.* Ed. by J. H. Elliott and H. G. Koenigsberger. New York: Cornell University Press, 1970, 119–47.

———. "Revolts in the Spanish Monarchy." *Preconditions of Revolution in Early Modern Europe.* Ed. by Robert Forster and Jack P. Greene. Baltimore: John Hopkins Press, 1970, 109–30.

Encarnación Rodríguez Vicente, María. "Los caudales remitidos desde el Perú a España por cuenta de la real hacienda: Series estadísticas (1651–1739)." *Anuario de Estudios Americanos,* 21 (1964), 1–24.

———. "Una quiebra bancaria en el Perú del siglo XVII." *Anuario de Historia del Derecho Español,* 26 (1956), 707–39.

Favre, Henri. "Evolución y situación de la hacienda tradicional de la region de Huancavelica." *Hacienda, comunidad, y campesinado en el Perú*. Ed. by José Matos Mar. Lima: Instituto de Estudios Peruanos, 1976, 105–38.

Hamnett, Brian R. "Church Wealth in Peru: Estates and Loans in the Archdiocese of Lima in the Seventeenth Century." *Jahrbuch für Geschichte von Staat, Wirtschaft, und Gesellschaft Lateinamerikas*, 10 (1973), 113–32.

Hanke, Lewis. "An Unpublished Document on the Junta de Hacienda de Indias." *Revista de Indias*, 80 (1960), 135–41.

Haring, C. H. "Early Spanish Colonial Exchequer." *American Historical Review*, 23 (July 1918), 779–96.

———. "Los libros mayores de los tesoros reales de Hispanoamerica en el siglo XVI." *Hispanic American Historical Review*, 2 (May 1919), 173–87.

Helmer, Marie. "Le Callao (1615–1618)." *Jahrbuch für Geschichte von Staat, Wirtschaft, und Gesellschaft Lateinamerikas*, 2 (1965), 145–95.

Hoberman, Louisa S. "Elites and the Commercial Crisis in Seventeenth-Century New Spain." Unpublished paper delivered at the American Historical Association Meeting, 1980.

———. "Merchants in Seventeenth-Century Mexico City: A Preliminary Portrait." *Hispanic American Historical Review*, 57 (August 1977), 479–503.

Israel, J. I. "Mexico and the General Crisis of the Seventeenth Century." *Past and Present*, 63 (May 1974), 33–57.

Mellafe, Rolando. "The Importance of Migration in the Viceroyalty of Peru." *Population and Economics: Proceedings of Section V of the International Economic History Association*. Ed. by Paul DePrez. Winnipeg: Universty of Manitoba Press, 1970, 303–13.

Moreno, Frank Jay. "The Spanish Colonial System: A Functional Approach." *Western Political Quarterly*, 20 (June 1967), 308–20.

Moreyra y Paz Soldán, Manuel. "Valor histórico de los libros de contabilidad hacendaria colonial." *Revista Histórica*, 22 (1955–56), 311–35.

Ots Capdequi, José María. "El tributo en la época colonial." *El Trimestre Económico*, 7 (1940–41), 586–615.

Phelan, John L. "Authority and Flexibility in the Spanish Imperial Bureaucracy." *Administrative Sciences Quarterly*, 5 (June 1960), 47–65.

Rodríguez Crespo, Pedro. "Sobre parentescos de los oidores con los grupos superiores de la sociedad limeña (a comienzos del siglo XVII)." *Mercurio Peruano*, 45 (julio-septiembre 1964), 49–63.

Sánchez Bella, Ismael. "La jurisdicción de hacienda en las Indias." *Anuario de Historia del Derecho Español*, 29 (1959), 176–227.

Sluitor, Engel. "Francisco López de Caravantes: Historical Sketch of Fiscal Administration in Colonial Peru, 1538–1618." *Hispanic American Historical Review*, 25 (May 1945), 225–56.

Smith, Clifford Thorpe. "Depopulation of the Central Andes in the Sixteenth Century." *Current Anthropology*, 11 (1970), 453–64.

Spalding, Karen. "Kurakas and Commerce: A Chapter in the Evolution of Andean Society." *Hispanic American Historical Review*, 53 (November 1973), 581–99.

TePaske, John J. "New World Silver, Castile and the Far East (1590–1750)," *Precious Metals in the Later Medieval and Early Modern World*, Ed. by John Richards. Durham: Carolina Academic Press, 1982.

TePaske, John J., and Klein, Herbert S. "The Seventeenth-Century Crisis in New Spain: Myth or Reality." *Past and Present*, 90 (February 1981), 116–35.

Tord Nicolini, Javier. "El corregidor de indios del Perú: Comercio y tributos." *Historia y Cultura*, 8 (1974) 173–214.

Wittman, Tibor. "La crisis Europea del siglo XVII e Hispano-América." *Anuario de Estudios Americanos*, 28 (1971) 25–44.

Wortman, Miles L. "Elites and Habsburg Administration: Adaptations to Economic Fluctuations in Seventeenth-Century Central America." Unpublished paper delivered at the American Historical Association Meeting, 1980.

———. "Government Revenue and Economic Trends in Central America, 1787–1819." *Hispanic American Historical Review*, 55 (May 1975), 251–86.

Yalí Román, Alberto. "Sobre alcaldías mayores y corregimientos en Indias." *Jahrbuch für Geschichte von Staat, Wirtschaft, und Gesellschaft Lateinamerikas*, 9 (1974), 1–39.

Secondary Works: Dissertations

Brown, Kendall W. "The Economic and Fiscal Structure of Eighteenth-Century Arequipa." Ph.D. dissertation, Duke University, 1978.

Cole, Jeffrey Austin. "The Potosí Mita under Habsburg Administration: The Seventeenth Century." Ph.D. dissertation, University of Massachusetts, 1981.

Cook, Noble David. "The Indian Population of Peru, 1570–1620." Ph.D. dissertation, University of Texas at Austin, 1973.

Davies, Keith Arfon. "The Rural Domain of the City of Arequipa, 1540–1665." Ph.D. dissertation, University of Connecticut, 1974.

Evans, M. G. D. "The Landed Aristocracy of Peru, 1600–1680." Ph.D. dissertation, University of London, 1972.

Ramirez Horton, Susan E. "Land Tenure and the Economics of Power in Colonial Peru." Ph.D. dissertation, University of Wisconsin at Madison, 1977.

Super, John C. "Querétaro: Society and Economy in Early Provincial Mexico, 1590–1630." Ph.D. dissertation, University of California at Los Angeles, 1973.

Tyrer, Robson Brines. "The Demographic and Economic History of the Audiencia of Quito: Indian Population and the Textile Industry, 1600–1800." Ph.D. dissertation, University of California at Berkeley, 1976.

Index